HOAXES AND DECEPTIONS

HOAXES AND DECEPTIONS

By the Editors of Time-Life Books

TIME-LIFE BOOKS, ALEXANDRIA, VIRGINIA

CONTENTS

THE ART OF DECEPTION

Like an odd echo in the song of civilization, fakes have attended every great artistic achievement: the marble masterpieces of Greek sculptors, the epic literature of the Celts, the shimmering beauty of rococo music, the bold visions of twentieth-century painters. From Phidias to Picasso, Cicero to Shakespeare, no work of genius has been immune from counterfeiting. Such is the craving to own a rare work of art that forgeries have found their way into most of the world's museums and trimmed the wallets of countless knowledgeable, but not infallible, collectors.

Nor have forgers confined themselves to the arts. In their cunning appeal to the collecting instinct, they have dangled bait ranging from a concocted copy of America's Declaration of Independence to a set of startling diaries that Hitler never wrote. Money is often the motive of the perpetrators—but not always. Many fakes are fielded to advance careers, embarrass critics, or merely play pranks. And sometimes, like the art it imitates, a hoax may be worth doing for its own sake.

1

Etruscans Alfredo

Much excitement attended the discovery of the trio of Etruscan treasures acquired by New York's Metropolitan Museum of Art early in the twentieth century. The first of the three, a six-foot terra-cotta warrior, was bought from a Rome dealer in 1915 by John Marshall, a museum purchasing agent. A year later, Marshall snared a massive helmeted terra-cotta head, and in 1921, he sent another large warrior, this one eight feet tall *(below)*. Dated to about 500 BC, the three works magnificently embodied the mysterious, largely vanished culture of Etruria that preceded Roman rule in central Italy.

The fragmented acquisitions were carefully restored, put on display, and admired by millions of museumgoers. Some scholars expressed doubts about the figures' authenticity, but they retained their pride of place until 1960. Then, Bostonian Harold Woodbury Parsons, a seventy-eight-year-old art expert and cultural detective living in retirement in Rome, began hearing rumors about an old artisan and his fake Etruscan art. Parsons looked up Alfredo Fioravanti, also seventy-eight, who repaired antiques and jewelry. The elderly craftsman had a story to tell. As a young man, Fioravanti had worked for a time as a tailor, then joined two brothers named Riccardi in a firm that specialized in mending antique pottery. Their skills soon found expression in more creative endeavors—the manufacture of Etruscanesque vases and small statues. This was so profitable that the partners decided to scale up their operations. Guided by a catalog illustration, they modeled their first warrior in clay, mixing in manganese dioxide to simulate the type of glaze called Greek black. Since their kiln was too small to accommodate the life-size figure, they broke the hardened clay into pieces and fired them separately. A suitably noninquisitive dealer had sold this and the other two large figures to John Marshall. Then one of the Riccardi brothers died, and Alfredo Fioravanti drifted away.

Parsons's letter informing the Metropolitan Museum of this tale proposed a simple proof: Someone should come to Italy with a plaster cast of the larger warrior's left hand, which was missing its thumb. The curator of the museum's classics collection at once flew to Rome, was introduced to the old sculptor, and looked on sadly as Signor Fioravanti produced the perfectly fitting thumb he had snapped off the statue more than forty years before. The warrior was a fake—and the son of a fake, as well. The Etruscan figure was modeled on a figure that Fioravanti and the Riccardis had seen in a British Museum photograph of an Etruscan sarcophagus, an artifact that itself turned out to be bogus. Any remaining doubts were dispelled by chemical tests, which found that the black glaze contained manganese, not used until the early nineteenth century. □

Leonardo's Cat

With a restless and powerful intellect that quested in a thousand directions, Leonardo da Vinci found time to produce only a handful of paintings. Art historians were thus electrified in 1938 when an Italian nobleman walked into a Milan exhibition of Leonardo's work with a painting that appeared to be by the Renaissance master. It had "been in the family forever," the nobleman explained.

Rendered in oil on wood, the image showed a Madonna with a child and a cat. Leonardo had drawn several pen-and-ink studies for the scene, but no painting had been discovered. Newspapers and magazines worldwide rejoiced at the find, and a spate of scholarly treatises honored this further proof of Leonardo's genius. Then the painting disappeared, presumably snapped up by some publicity-shy, but well-heeled, collector.

In fact, for the next fifty-two years it adorned the bedroom wall of Cesare Tubino, an artist in Turin who was well known for turning out reproductions of old masters, complete with a convincingly crackled surface achieved by cooling and then baking the paintings. He had exhibited his imitations. And, as only he and his family had known for more than half a century, Tubino had painted the famous *Madonna with the Cat (left)*.

Evidently, he had intended the false Leonardo as a joke or test of his skills, enlisted a nobleman friend for its public debut, then taken it back for his personal enjoyment. When Tubino's death at the age of ninety-one brought the painting to light once more, any linkage to Leonardo was formally severed by the artist's final message: "I painted it myself." To his survivors, he wrote, "If you should ever sell it, you must do so only under my name." □

Why Not the Best?

In Renaissance Italy, the sculpture of ancient Greece and Rome was held in such high esteem that classical statuary commanded a better price than the work of contemporary artists. Thus, when a twenty-one-year-old Florentine named Buonarroti carved a marble figure of a sleeping Cupid, he was advised that it would bring a handsome fee as an antique. Taking the hint, he aged his sculpture by burying it for a time. It was then sold in 1496 for a sizable sum to Cardinal San Georgio of Rome. When the cardinal discovered that the Cupid was a recent work, however, he did not rant about being cheated. Instead, he sent an emissary to Florence to offer his patronage to the sculptor, best known by his given name: Michelangelo. □

Tintoretto's painting of Venus and Vulcan modeled the Cupid in the background on Michelangelo's "antique" statue.

This playable boudoir guitar by Franciolini has an elaborately inlaid lyre-shaped body, with a mirrored center that opens (*below*) into a jewel case.

Instruments of Deception

Many of the world's great collections of old musical instruments were assembled around the turn of the twentieth century, creating a boom in the antiques market. For prospectors in this specialized field, the mother lode was the Florence shop of Leopoldo Franciolini. There, a buyer could choose from the Italian antiquarian's huge array of spinets, clavichords, harpsichords, violins, drums, lutes, cellos, and other relics of the musical past. Some of the instruments were genuine, but Franciolini did not hesitate to amplify his revenues by fabrication.

His strategy was not to copy old instruments, but to modify them. Sometimes he increased their value by adding decorative embellishments. Sometimes he pumped up the price with a false inscription of an early date or a famous maker. Often he would take instruments apart and recombine them in new, more salable forms—a process that led him to create some wholly imaginary, and dysfunctional, devices, which he described as "rare instruments." Because scholarship in the field was embryonic, he was able to conduct a highly profitable trade in forgeries from 1890 until 1910, when the law caught up with him.

After the collapse of a proposed sale of forty-six bogus musical instruments to a Professor Giuseppe Passerini—who was also, it seems, embarked on a swindle—Franciolini was hauled into court and convicted of cheating his fellow Florentine. The sixty-five-year-old fraud's four-month sentence was suspended in favor of a 1,000-lire fine because of his age. Free, the old faker put out a precautionary rumor of his death, then forged on unrepentantly until he died in February 1920.

So extensive was his fakery that museum curators and musical historians are still trying to undo the damage. But they are aided by a peculiar clue. Although Franciolini's instrument makers were excellent craftsmen, they had what one historian has called "a truly amazing inability to copy even the simplest Latin phrase correctly." Thus, the impressive inscriptions added to the fakes are invariably wrong and sometimes pure gibberish—a sure sign that Franciolini had a hand in their composition. □

Bad Strads

Among the instruments of classical music, the most popular by far is the violin, mass-produced by the tens of thousands each year. At the same time, violins can be rare and precious almost beyond measure, particularly those made three centuries ago by Antonio Stradivari in Cremona, Italy. Between the 1660s and his death in 1737, he and his two sons created scores of violins using the finest materials and a distinctive deep orange-red varnish that has never been equaled. His most famous instruments are each named. Their tone, it is said, has yet to be matched. On the distinctive label that Stradivari placed inside each instrument, he used the Latinized version of his name that has come to epitomize priceless violins: Stradivarius.

But Stradivari also established the model for violins, both fine and ordinary. Replicas of his de-

Alexander Galiani fecit Neapoli 17

Antonius Amati Cremonensis Fecit Anno Domini nostri 16

Joannes Baptista Guadagnini Cremonensis fecit Taurini aluminus Antoni Stradivari 17 GBG T

Andreas Guarnerius fecit Cremonæ sub titulo Sanctæ Teresiæ 16

J. B. VUILLAUME N 170 Rue Croix-des Petits Paris an 1829 JBV

Joseph Gagliano Filius Nicolai fecit Neap. 17

Antonius Stradivarius Cremonensis Faciebat Anno 17

Joseph Guarnerius fecit Cremonæ anno 17 IHS

...io Paolo Maggini in Brescia 16

sign began to appear in large numbers in the mid-nineteenth century, produced in scores of workshops in Germany and France. They were not intended as forgeries. Exact copies of Stradivarius labels (and labels of other legendary makers such as Amati, Rugieri, and Guarneri) were applied simply to indicate that the instruments were faithful to a certain design.

Although buyers of that era understood that the instruments were reproductions, the violins themselves may deceive their owners' heirs. Today, collectors, museums, and musicians are regularly offered signed Stradivari discovered, like lost treasure, in attics or cellars. Expert appraisers have no great difficulty in determining the truth. Still, the news generally comes as a wrenching disappointment for the discoverer: The difference in value between a good nineteenth-century Stradivarius look-alike and the genuine article from Cremona is about $250,000. □

The Marvelous Boy

Nature lavished gifts on the eighteenth-century English poet Thomas Chatterton that were largely wasted during his short and troubled life. Still, the genius of his faked masterpieces has been enough for posterity to honor him, not for what he was, but for what he might have been.

Born in Bristol in 1752, Chatterton was raised by his widowed mother in bleak surroundings and had to leave school at fourteen to earn his living in an attorney's office. A scholarly hobby provided an escape of sorts: He was fascinated by medieval documents and studied them in every free moment. In 1768, he impressed local antiquarians by publishing an excerpt from a journal supposedly written by a former mayor of Bristol. He followed with poems by an imaginary fifteenth-century priest named Thomas Rowley; Chatterton said he had found the material in a chest in a church where his uncle was sexton. Soon Bristol medievalists

were treated to more discoveries—proclamations, deeds, and pedigrees whose diction and style of lettering appeared authentic.

Looking beyond the confines of his seaside town, Chatterton in 1769 sought the patronage of Horace Walpole, earl of Orford and well-known author. His choice of a backer was perhaps prompted by knowledge that Walpole had gained his early reputation with *The Castle of Otranto,* a concocted tale of the Crusader era, saying he came across it "in the library of an ancient Catholic family in the ◊

north of England." Walpole asserted that the story had been printed in Naples in 1529, its style "the purest Italian." *Otranto* was the prototype Gothic romance in English.

At first, Walpole was convinced by the works Chatterton sent him—a trove of writings by the fictitious Rowley that ranged from a treatise on painting to some polished poems on themes from Bristol history. But the sheer mass of the submissions stirred skepticism. When Walpole's poet friends pronounced the works not medieval but modern, he advised Chatterton to focus on a law career.

Instead, Chatterton went to London, where he had enjoyed some sales of his own work, under his own name, to small periodicals. Arriving there in April 1770, he quickly became a writer of all disciplines, penning everything from political letters to satires, in prose and poetry, writing in a variety of styles. But such small payment as he received from publishers was always too little, too late. In June 1770, resuming his romance with the Middle Ages, the seventeen-year-old bard fabricated his last Rowley poem, which a magazine rejected. On August 24, 1770, penniless and in despair, Chatterton penned a final poem that ended: "Have mercy, Heaven!

when here I cease to live/ And this last act of wretchedness forgive." Then he took arsenic and died.

Several years later, the Rowley poems were published by an admirer. Their quality was so high that Chatterton was hailed as a literary giant. "I do not believe," wrote a contrite Horace Walpole in 1778, "there ever existed so masterly a genius." To the romantic poets of the next century, Chatterton would be seen as a tragic hero, mournfully described by one of them, William Wordsworth, as "the marvellous Boy/ The sleepless Soul that perished in his pride." □

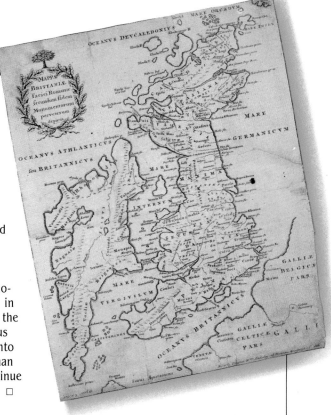

Roman Conquest

In 1747, a twenty-four-year-old Englishman named Charles Bertram, then working in Copenhagen as a teacher, wrote a prominent countryman, antiquarian William Stukeley, about a discovery he had made. While visiting a friend's house, Bertram said, he had seen a "curious manuscript history," a medieval work relating to the Roman period of British history—from AD 43 into the fifth century. Stukeley asked Bertram to copy a small portion of the document and send it for inspection. The excerpt was dispatched, passed expert scrutiny, and so intrigued the antiquarian that he begged his young correspondent to replicate the whole thing. Bit by bit, Bertram obliged, and the treatise was published in its entirety in 1757.

It was Stukeley's carefully considered opinion that the document's original author was one Richard of Cirencester, a monk who had lived at Westminster in the fourteenth century. This learned cleric plainly belonged in the pantheon of British chroniclers: His manuscript and accompanying map referred to more than 100 places and people mentioned in no other source, and presented a multitude of previously unknown details about the early Christian martyrs in England. The discovery was nothing short of a historical bonanza, and its wealth of new information was swiftly incorporated into books on Roman Britain.

Unfortunately, none of the fresh facts was true. But it was more than 100 years before two sharp-eyed Victorian scholars proved that the text was actually a clever mosaic of borrowings from Julius Caesar, Tacitus, and other classical sources, all liberally enriched with Bertram inventions. No one knows why Bertram embarked on this elaborate deception or why he chose Stukeley as his dupe. Whatever the motive, his creation has, in a perverse way, stood the test of time. His bogus facts were so woven into later histories of Roman Britain that they continue to appear to this day. □

MacFraud

When a young Scottish schoolmaster named James Macpherson startled the literary world in 1760 with what he said were translations of long-lost Celtic poetry, he was—perhaps only half consciously—performing an act of national healing. His fellow Scots had recently suffered a series of defeats at the hands of the English, and their pride was sorely wounded. These poems—splendid legends that Macpherson claimed to have collected in the Highlands—suggested that martial greatness flowed in Scottish veins.

Readers were thrilled, and some of Macpherson's fans gave him money to go find more evidence of Highland glory. Two years later, he obliged his backers with a full-length epic titled *Fingal;* he said it had been composed in the third century by a Gaelic bard named Ossian, son of Fingal. The following year, Macpherson brought forth *Temora,* another supposed treasure authored by the prolific Ossian. Like Macpherson's previous translations, it portrayed a Celtic past vibrant with passion and valor.

The tales of Ossian were rapidly issued in languages other than English and found a large audience on the Continent. "To judge by their recently discovered poems and songs," effused one German critic, "there has never been a race possessed of such powerful and at the same time such tender emotions, who, individually, were so heroic, and yet at the same time, so supremely human, as the ancient Scots."

Still, discerning readers found odd notes in all this clamorous ◊

music from the past: Ossian's warriors fought the Romans; engaged in adventures that, according to other Celtic legends, had occurred centuries apart; and gave such soppy speeches as: "Thou hast heard the music of departed bards in the dreams of thy rest, when sleep fell on thine eyes, at the murmur of Moruth."

England's greatest man of letters, Samuel Johnson, stated in no uncertain terms that the translations were fraudulent. Macpherson promised to produce the originals but—now a prosperous literary figure and member of Parliament—he continued to fend off the doubters for more than thirty years, until his death in 1796. Although scholars exposed the truth about Macpherson's inventions a few years later, Ossian emanated a convincing Celtic afterglow for decades. No less a warrior than Napoleon had scenes from the epics painted on the ceiling of his study, and a book of Ossian's poetry accompanied him on his military campaigns. □

Bardlet's Quotations

For sheer nerve, no literary counterfeiter ever surpassed William Henry Ireland, a well-to-do young Englishman who chose the cultural colossus William Shakespeare as the target for a yearlong binge of forgery.

Ireland's spree began in 1794, when he was seventeen years old. Although he was not particularly well-educated, he knew Shakespeare almost as a family intimate: His bibliophile father worshiped the memory of the great playwright and often said that he would give all his books to possess a single scrap of Bardic handwriting. While almost nothing in Shakespeare's own hand survived from Elizabethan times, young William Ireland felt that a discovery could be arranged.

After obtaining ink that would look suitably aged, he studied Shakespeare's signature, then produced a sixteenth-century land deed and signed the Bard's name to it. When he presented the docu-

ment to his father, he explained that he had found it while rummaging through some old papers belonging to an acquaintance—a man who was fiercely averse to publicity and had insisted he must never be identified. The elder Ireland believed his son completely and immediately asked him if perhaps the stash of old papers might not hold some more Shakespeare relics.

It was a challenge the youth could not resist. He bought some blank sheets of antique paper from a bookseller, practiced writing in the hand of the Elizabethan period, and concocted a sensational document called Profession of Faith—proof, by Shakespeare's own testimony, it seemed, that he was Protestant rather than Roman Catholic, as was sometimes claimed. The elder Ireland, wild with joy, showed this to his many literary friends. A few suspected forgery, but even some Shakespeare experts were taken in. They joined the father in crying for more.

William raised his aim. He produced an extraordinary treasure, an original manuscript of *King Lear*, one of his favorite plays, but in need of slight stylistic repairs, he felt. These he did not hesitate to make. To reinforce the manuscript's claim to authenticity, he created playhouse receipts and other minor documents Shakespeare might have had and tied up the whole bundle in string unraveled from an old tapestry. This find, followed by portions of the original manuscript for *Hamlet*, deepened suspicions of counterfeiting. But William was unstoppable. His next step, spectacularly daring, was to amaze the world with a lost play by the Bard.

In the space of a few weeks, he composed more than 2,000 Shakespearean lines dramatizing an obscure legend from early English history: Vortigern and Rowena. When he announced that the ever-bountiful cache of old papers had yielded up an unknown tragedy by the Bard, a prominent figure in the theater world, William Sheridan, bought it and arranged for a production. Sheridan was nervous about the work, commenting that "one would be led to think that Shakespeare must have been very young when he wrote the play." During the first (and last) performance, the audience reacted with greater certainty, groaning at leaden speeches and giving way to ten minutes of uproar when an actor intoned the line: "I would this solemn mockery were over."

Now critics and scholars were closing in. William composed another lost play, entitled *Henry II*, but the counterfeiter's father—who continued to insist that everything was genuine—had come under vigorous attack. The lad finally confessed all.

After these adventures, he went on to a modestly successful career as a novelist. But he felt that his greatest work had been nipped in the bud. He had intended to produce "lost" plays covering English history up to the time of Elizabeth I—a project that would have doubled Shakespeare's output. □

Tiarafied

During the nineteenth century, an archaeological gold strike focused the world's attention on the northern coast of the Black Sea. There, about 2,500 years earlier, nomadic warriors called the Scythians had come into contact with Greek colonies. The mingled vigor of the two cultures had produced dazzling works of gold—cups, helmets, necklaces, funeral masks, and other splendors of the smith's art. A few of the treasures were discovered in the 1830s. Then, as the interest of antiquarians and museums grew, a veritable freshet of gold objects sprang from the Crimean soil.

What appeared to be the ultimate prize was a tiara that came on the market in 1895.

Elaborately decorated with reliefs that included scenes from the *Iliad*, the headpiece bore an inscription indicating that it had been offered to the Scythian king Sa-

itapharnes by grateful subjects. The current owner of the tiara was a Russian corn merchant named Schapshelle Hochman, who was prepared to part with it for a large sum of money. His first stop was Vienna. He was rebuffed there by skeptical archaeologists and then was turned down by the British Museum. Finally, working through agents, in 1896 he sold the object to the Louvre in Paris for a staggering 200,000 francs. But some archaeologists continued to question the tiara's authenticity. They noted, for example, that some of the scenes rendered in relief seemed to have been copied from other objects and that certain decorative motifs were of the wrong period. The Louvre shrugged off all at- ◊

Supposedly from ancient Scythia, the gold tiara of Saitapharnes was the work of a Russian goldsmith.

tacks until 1903, when a French artist said he had created the piece. He had not, but his claim prompted a Parisian goldsmith to declare that he knew the true maker, fellow goldsmith Israel Rouchomovsky, who lived in Odessa.

With the press now in full cry and huge crowds pouring through the Louvre to view the controversial object, Rouchomovsky was brought from Russia to Paris to settle the matter. He cheerfully explained how, with Hochman's help, he had spent eight months making the tiara, using books on antiquities as his guide. Still, he did not consider it his best Scythian creation. "The tiara is no work of art," said Rouchomovsky, "it is crude work. You should see my sarcophagus."

An American showman offered to buy the tiara from the Louvre and take it on tour in the United States as a demonstration of what one archaeologist called "the hypnotic effect of gold on man." But museum officials, not eager to be seen as victims of hypnosis, respectfully declined. And Schapshelle Hochman, who had initiated the fraud, managed somehow to disappear from the public eye forever. □

Super Dupe

Denis Vrain-Lucas taught himself the arts of forgery while working as a low-level employee in a Paris firm that specialized in heraldry, a field that involves extensive use of old documents. But his career as a counterfeiter relied less on his considerable skills than on his acquisition of a spectacularly gullible French client: Michel Chasles, commander of the Legion of Honor, holder of England's prestigious Coplan Medal, and the most illustrious geometrician of his day.

Their relationship began in 1861, when Vrain-Lucas told Chasles that he had inherited a collection of letters from immigrant forebears and offered the scholar some items supposedly written by Molière, François Rabelais, and Jean Racine. Chasles hap-

pily bought these mementos of French literary greatness.

Seeing the bait so easily swallowed, the forger brought out some rarer items—letters he said were written by Charlemagne. Again, Chasles was only too happy to take them. Vrain-Lucas then moved on to a letter in which Alexander the Great gave Aristotle permission to visit Gaul and study druidic wisdom. Chasles was pleased at this Gallic theme and untroubled that Alexander the Great had on this occasion expressed himself in Old French.

More trophies from Vrain-Lucas's collection suggested that the language and a concern for the welfare of what would one day become France had been widespread in the ancient world. For example, Vrain-Lucas produced a letter from Lazarus to St. Peter that spoke of the end of human sacrifices in Gaul under Roman rule.

Things went on in this vein for years, with Chasles purchasing an immense range of epistolary cre-

If imitation is a compliment, nineteenth-century landscapist Jean-Baptiste-Camille Corot was the most-honored artist in France. Known for his saint-like generosity, Corot would willingly retouch and sign his name to the work of struggling young colleagues. He also loaned sketches to artists who copied them. His kindness created thousands of bogus Corots and inadvertently made him France's most-forged painter. After his death in 1875, he was said to have produced some 2,460 paintings, 100 prints, and 761 drawings—5,000 of which, according to art-minded wags, were in private collections. □

ations, including letters ancient Frenchmen had written to Jesus and a letter in which Shakespeare paid a respectful bow to the splendors of French literature. No absurdity seemed beyond his acceptance. Knowing that Chasles believed the laws of gravity had first been formulated by the French mathematician Blaise Pascal—not Britain's Sir Isaac Newton—Vrain-Lucas sold his dupe an exchange of letters between Newton and Pascal that indicated the French scientist was the true discoverer. When Chasles announced this startling news to the French Academy of Sciences, however, it was pointed out that Newton would have been only eleven at the time of the supposed correspondence.

Incredibly, Chasles continued to believe in the authenticity of documents obtained from Vrain-Lucas, who ultimately placed more than 27,000 forgeries with the savant and earned some 200,000 francs in the process. But in 1870, the forger failed to produce another 3,000 documents after taking an advance payment, and Chasles sued.

In the trial, Vrain-Lucas's defense attorney turned on Chasles. Who, he asked the court, had bought the letters for an unimaginable price? Who had insisted on publicizing them and declared their authenticity? Pointing his finger at the plaintiff, he declared that Chasles, not Vrain-Lucas, had been the real provocateur of the deception. But the drama went for naught. A confessed forger, Vrain-Lucas received a 500-franc fine and two years in prison. After his release, he took his products elsewhere and continued to earn a good living by reworking history for the gullible. □

Fiddled Strings

Fritz Kreisler's gifts as a violinist were evident as soon as he began to study the instrument in 1879, when he was four years old. He entered the Vienna Conservatory at seven, won its highest award when he was ten, and was touring America by the age of fourteen.

But for all this youthful success, Kreisler felt blocked as he embarked on an adult career. The problem—familiar to any young violinist of the day—was a paucity of music to make up a concert. At that time, the accepted violin repertory of unaccompanied pieces was limited, and a fledgling performer had difficulty enlisting accompanists for pieces that required a piano or orchestra. Kreisler's solution to the dilemma was to compose his own repertory.

Convinced that audiences and critics would condemn a self-created program as arrogant, he attributed his violin compositions mostly to obscure figures in musical history—Gaetano Pugnani, Padre Martini, and the like—although occasionally he borrowed the illustrious name of Antonio Vivaldi, Italy's great baroque master. When asked how he had acquired the works, Kreisler said he had copied dusty old manuscripts in libraries and monasteries.

This explanation seemed to satisfy questioners, and the pieces themselves more than satisfied audiences: They were so well-received that fellow performers asked if they could have copies of their own. Bowing to pressure, Kreisler had them published in 1912. In time, the compositions—"little masterpieces," as critics called them—became a part of the standard violin repertory. ◊

The renowned violinist Fritz Kreisler embarks for Brussels, bound for a 1938 command performance before the court of Elizabeth, queen mother of the Belgians.

Their origin remained a well-kept secret until 1935, when, on his sixtieth birthday, Kreisler answered a question from the *New York Times* about the compositions. He freely admitted they were his—obviously so. "I made no effort whatever to stick closely to the style of the period to which they were alleged to date," he wired the *Times* from Vienna. "Had I been bent upon assuming an impenetrable mask, you may rest assured that I might have given my pieces a form quite irreproachable, so that even clever connoisseurs would have been deceived."

Mainly, Kreisler was baffled that musical experts had not spotted the deception immediately. Since their first publication in 1912, the compositions had carried a cryptic but telltale warning in English, French, and German. "This concerto is freely treated from old manuscripts and constitutes an original work," read the inscription on a bogus Vivaldi score. "When the concerto is played in public, Fritz Kreisler's name must be mentioned in the program." □

False Li

For William F. Mannix, a footloose, hard-drinking American newspaperman in the nineteenth century, life was a protracted excursion in the borderlands between fact and fiction. He first displayed his dubious talents as a youthful reporter in upstate New York. His work, low-paid and uninspiring, included keeping metropolitan newspapers informed of prominent guests staying at Adirondack resorts. Never one for unnecessary legwork, he sometimes placed the same guests simultaneously at several different hotels, a tactic that finally cost him his job.

Journalism was in his blood, however, and Mannix made his way to Cuba—from 1895 to 1898 the scene of a revolt against Spanish rule—and set himself up as a war correspondent. Soon his reports from the front were appearing in the *New York Times*, the *Philadelphia Press*, and other major papers. Unlike competing correspondents, he seemed able to bypass Spanish censorship, and his accounts were full of colorful details about combat and atrocities, much of it reported from the side of shadowy Cuban insurgents. He also wrote up interviews with high officials and served as a conduit for messages from the Republic of Cuba to the American people. Every word was invented. Carrying his dislike of legwork to an extreme, he had manufactured this flood of war reportage in the bar of the Hotel Mascotte in Havana.

Before losing the cachet of war correspondent, the immensely likable Mannix, who despite his lack of scruples was a gifted writer, managed to land a job on a Philadelphia paper. One night, he was told to look into a rumor that a bank official had gone into default. In his usual fashion, he sought the answer in a series of saloons. The story printed the next day named the right man but the wrong institution, causing a run on the bank and a million-dollar lawsuit against the newspaper, which quickly dropped Mannix.

Stigmatized as a reporter whose efforts produced large libel suits, he confined his compositional efforts to the writing of rubber checks. In 1901—the year that the eminent Chinese statesman Li Hongzhang *(left)* died in Peking— Mannix joined the army and was sent to China to help protect foreign legations following the Boxer Rebellion. A decade later, after further boozy wanderings, this experience would supply atmospheric detail for his magnum opus.

The year 1912 found Mannix jailed in Honolulu for forging an employer's name to a check. With plenty of time on his hands, he began reading extensively on the Far East, the material being supplied by the loyal friends he invariably attracted. Using paper furnished by a kindly jailer and a spare typewriter loaned him by the governor of Hawaii, Mannix began to put his Oriental studies to work. He wrote a series of articles on the late Li Hongzhang, an internationally famous viceroy of Imperial China during the final quarter of the nineteenth century. Mannix's imagination was too powerful, however, to settle for a mere portrait of Li. He sold his articles to newspapers as excerpts from Li Hongzhang's own diary, "translated from the original manuscripts at Canton China" and edited by one William F. Mannix.

Emerging from jail after eight months, he expanded the supposed diary excerpts into a full book and peddled it to publishers in the United States and Britain. He corresponded with them on stationery whose letterhead indicated he was the president of the Pacific Associated Press, a sprawling (but totally fictitious) organization with imaginary offices scattered from Honolulu to Shanghai.

The book was a significant publishing event, and it fooled virtually all readers with its skillful mimicry and artful inflation of spare historical facts. But some flaws were spotted. In one long passage, Li Hongzhang recounted his feelings as he left San Francisco for China at the end of an international tour. He had, in fact, departed from Vancouver on that occasion.

Asked for an explanation, Mannix did not respond to critics directly. Instead, he spoke through the persona of a nonexistent agent named William Leonard, who placed the blame for errors on careless translators, on the fact that the memoirs had been culled from "the equivalent of some 1.6 million English words," and on Li's sloppiness as a diarist. This agent offered to go to China to clear up the discrepancies if someone would send him the travel money. In this way, Mannix braved his way through rising criticism for almost a decade but lost the war: The work, its publishers finally realized, was an inspired fraud. Finally, in 1923, the embarrassed bookmen reissued the spurious memoir with an explanation that it was "not fact, but fiction, woven from whole cloth with a skill so extraordinary as to have deceived the very elect."

By then, Mannix had dropped from view, concluding his career of deception with another, seedier Oriental scam. As president of the Pacific Associated Press, he wrote to American manufacturers of vacuum cleaners describing an interesting discovery. During the course of his travels, he said, he had gained entry to the Forbidden City, the imperial sanctuary in Peking. There, he had seen a vacuum cleaner made by ——— (here he inserted the appropriate company name). For a suitable fee, this evidence of imperial approval might form the basis of a magazine article. His scheme came to nothing when the manufacturers learned that their competitors had received identical queries. A similar swindle of varnish makers likewise failed.

But Mannix, perhaps unable to surpass his Li Hongzhang hoax, seems to have abandoned both dissipation and deception after that. He died the staid business manager of a West Coast daily newspaper. □

Little Sprite Lie

On a Sunday afternoon in 1917 in the Yorkshire village of Cottingley, fifteen-year-old Elsie Wright and her nine-year-old cousin Frances Griffiths arrived home late for tea. The reason, they said, was that they had been playing with fairies. This explanation met the predictable response, but the girls said that they could prove it. Elsie, who had worked briefly for a photographer, borrowed a box camera from her father and used it to take a photograph of Frances in the woods with three of the little people. Then Frances snapped a picture of Elsie playing with a gnome.

The girls' parents were more ◊

annoyed than impressed by the prank, and there the matter might have ended. But word of the fairy pictures spread, and what had begun as a minor domestic event quickly became a celebrated supernatural story in the British press.

Accounts of the Cottingley fairy pictures soon reached members of Britain's thriving Spiritualist movement. Prominent in these circles was Sir Arthur Conan Doyle, creator of the supremely rational detective Sherlock Holmes but himself ready to accept almost any claim of paranormal doings. He wrote up the case in a breathless article in a national magazine, then published a second article when the cousins supplied three more pixie shots.

Not only did Sir Arthur consider the photographs genuine, he speculated at length on how certain people could tune in on "a race of beings which were constructed in material which threw out shorter or longer vibrations."

His articles brought the cousins enduring celebrity, nurtured by their coy evasion of questions about their woodland picture taking. Not until 1982 was a serious analysis of the pictures done, by British photo expert Geoffrey Crawley. His inferences came so close to the mark that in 1983 the cousins came clean—sixty-six years after the fact. They had,

they said, simply created cutouts of fairies and held them in place with hatpins. The status of photography in 1917 had aided in the illusion—and it appeared some retouching by unknown hands along the way had also helped keep alive belief in the girls' spurious teatime adventure. □

In this first Cottingley fairy photograph, Frances Griffiths seems to sit among a flock of sprites—actually paper cutouts that were cleverly devised by her older cousin Elsie Wright.

Rhymes with Cheating

Tom Keating felt that it was all society's fault. Over a twenty-five-year period that ended in his exposure in 1976, the feisty Briton produced some 2,000 fakes—Sexton Blakes, he called them in cockney rhyming slang. More than 100 different artists were represented in this flood of fraud, ranging from Rembrandt to Renoir. The motive: "It was not for gain (I hope I am no materialist), but simply as a protest against merchants who make capital out of those I am proud to call my brother artists, both living and dead."

Keating arrived at this mission by a roundabout route. He was born in 1917, one of seven children of a cockney house painter. "I came from what was euphemistically termed the working class—in other words, the slums: twenty-four people sharing the same lavatory, that kind of thing; fascist landlords; poverty." He left school at fourteen and worked in the building trades. After service in the navy during World War II, he received a grant to study art at a London college. Twice he failed to get his diploma. Thereafter, he restored paintings for a living, an occupation that provided an excellent education in art styles and techniques—soon applied to forgery.

Keating used a variety of self-taught tricks; the ink for Rembrandt drawings, for example, was made from the brown juice of simmered apples plus a little instant coffee. At the same time, he often left clues that a painting or drawing was not what it seemed to be. When he started work on a canvas, he would sometimes write an expletive or the word *fake* in white-lead paint—which would be visible in an x-ray—then cover it with other pigments. He labeled his forged drawings as fakes by using paper from the wrong century.

His days of fakery ended when a reporter got wind of his activities and persuaded him to make a full confession. Keating was arrested, but the charges were subsequently dropped because of his poor health. By now a popular hero, he proceeded to star in a series of television programs about how great artists achieved their effects. He died on February 12, 1984, thumbing his nose at the arts establishment to the last. □

South Seas Send-Up

As Cubism and other schools of painting hoisted their banners over the battlefield of modern art in the early decades of the twentieth century, no one felt less like saluting than Paul Jordan Smith, a novelist living in Los Angeles. He thought the new schools poppycock, not least because the works of his artist wife were dismissed by critics as "distinctly of the old school."

One day in 1924, on a whim, he borrowed her oil paints and brushes and dashed off a painting of his own, his first. The image showed a crudely outlined South Seas woman holding a banana aloft, with a skull in the background. That, he told his family, summed up aesthetic standards of the day. He titled it *Yes, We Have No Bananas* and used the canvas as a fire screen. Not long afterward, a young art critic visiting the house pronounced it extremely interesting—not unlike the Tahitian works of France's Paul Gauguin, in fact. That casual word of praise sent Smith on his one-man campaign against the arbiters of modern art.

Adopting the exotic name Pavel Jerdanowitch, he grew a suitably rough beard and retitled his painting *Exaltation,* then entered it in a New York exhibition of independent artists. A Paris journal, scenting a new talent, asked "Jerdanowitch" for biographical details and a personal interpretation of the work. The creator of *Exaltation* obliged, and soon his wildly romantic fictive history appeared in the pages of the art journal. Readers learned that Pavel Jerdanowitch was born in Moscow, immigrated to America, became tubercular, and traveled for his health to the South

Seas, where he developed the bold style of painting known as the Disumbrationist School.

"Pavel Jerdanowitch is not content to follow ordinary paths," said the journal. "He prefers to explore the heights and even, if necessary, to peer into the abysses. His spirit delights in intoxication, and he is a prey to the aesthetic agonies which are not experienced without suffering." As for the meaning of *Exaltation,* it was simple, said the artist: The painting represents the breaking of the shackles of womanhood because women are forbidden to eat bananas on that island; as a further expression of her personal freedom, the woman has killed a missionary, represented by the skull in the background.

With his credentials now established, the founder of Disumbrationism exhibited a second work, *Aspiration,* in Chicago in 1926, and two more—*Adoration* and *Illumination*—in New York the following year. Art publications continued to mention him, and he was inundated with letters asking about the Disumbrationist canon. By then, however, Smith had tired of the game. He told the full story of the hoax to the *Los Angeles Times,* in effect declaring victory over the modern art establishment.

But his confession was not the end of Disumbrationism. A Boston gallery owner felt that the deception simply made the school of painting that much more interesting. Acting on this expansive view of art, the gallery owner put the four Jerdanowitch works on show in 1928 and accompanied the exhibit with a catalog predicting that "these soul-revealing creations will be sources of ecstatic, moronic rapture." □

Founding Forger

Joseph Cosey, nemesis of twentieth-century American document collectors, found his true calling late. A petty criminal for much of his life, he dabbled in check forging, then—more or less by accident—discovered that he could become a Founding Father with a stroke of a pen.

Born Martin Coneely in upstate New York in 1887, he adopted many aliases in his early years, but his all-time favorite was Joseph Cosey. Hot-tempered and restless, he left school early, held a succession of menial jobs, joined the army and received a dishonorable discharge for assault, became a small-time thief, and spent about ten years in prison for various misdeeds by the time he was forty. Then, at forty-two, his life turned.

One day in 1929, he visited the Library of Congress and pilfered a small piece of American history—a pay warrant signed by Benjamin Franklin in 1786. "It wasn't stealing, really," he later said, "because the Library of Congress belongs to the people and I'm one of the people." He tried to sell this document to an autograph dealer and was told it was a fake. This so annoyed Cosey that he decided to come back with a forged historical signature the dealer would accept as genuine. He devoted himself to studying old texts and practicing the autographs of famous Americans. Some months later, the dealer bought a faked Lincoln autograph from him for ten dollars—and Cosey had a new career.

Lincoln was always one of his best signatures, but over the next two decades, he successfully signed letters, notes, and concocted documents with the names of Patrick Henry, Ben Franklin, Thomas Jefferson, George Washington, Alexander Hamilton, and a range of later political and literary figures. One of his most ambitious fakes was a complete draft of the Declaration of Independence in the hand of Jefferson; he sold it to a history professor. Occasionally, he rewrote his own history. To soothe an old hurt, he forged himself an honorable discharge from the army.

A proud man, Cosey never sold his creations to amateur collectors. "I take pleasure in fooling the professionals," he explained. Occasionally, he used paper of the wrong period or sealed a letter incorrectly or erred in the style of salutations. But these mistakes were few. His most notable error came in copying a document that Ben Franklin had written in 1757; his error was to change the date to 1787, when Franklin was eighty-one and—as experts knew—wrote in a notably shaky hand.

Cosey slipped from view in the 1950s. But by then his reputation had reached such heights that his creations were collected in their own right as masterpieces of the forger's art. □

Near Vermeer

Collectors of Northern Renaissance art should have been troubled by the number of previously unknown masterpieces that appeared in the Netherlands between 1937 and 1943—among them, six works by the great seventeenth-century Dutch artist Johannes (Jan) Vermeer and two by his contemporary Pieter de Hooch. But the turbulence of the war-plagued times may have lowered their guard, and, besides, the paintings were pronounced genuine by leading scholars. In fact, the works were fakes—the spawn of critic-hating, drug-addicted artist Hans van Meegeren.

Born in Holland in 1889, van Meegeren studied drawing and architecture in Delft—the birthplace of Vermeer—and sought to make a name for himself as a painter. He showed talent as a draftsman, and his works sold fairly well; but critics considered him a mediocrity, unimaginative and excessively dramatic. They were fools, van Meegeren felt, and he would expose their lack of judgment.

He may have launched his career as a forger in the early 1920s, while working with a restorer of old masters. But the idea for what would become his masterpieces came from his seeing a 1936 book that described Vermeer's relatively few early paintings with religious themes. The content and style of these pictures appealed to van Meegeren, and he began to paint a Vermeer of his own.

No expense was spared in carrying out the deception. He purchased a minor seventeenth-century painting and used it as his canvas. He invested large sums in the kind of pigments used by Vermeer—white lead, an ultramarine made of lapis lazuli, a crimson derived from crushed insect shells. After much experimentation, he hit upon a highly effective aging technique, mixing his colors with a dissolved resin of phenol-formaldehyde and baking the picture at 220 degrees Fahrenheit for two hours. Seven months were devoted to crafting the illusion, which he called *Christ at Emmaus.*

In 1937, an Amsterdam lawyer—van Meegeren's intermediary—"discovered" the canvas in the Paris apartment of a recently deceased Dutch businessman. The attorney took the painting to Monte Carlo, where it could be examined by a venerable expert, Abraham Bredius, then in his eighties. Bredius decreed it a Vermeer "of the highest art, the highest beauty." A prestigious British art review weighed in with the opinion that it was "*the* masterpiece of Johannes Vermeer of Delft." A Dutch museum bought it for the equivalent of $270,000, completing van Meegeren's revenge on what he called the high priesthood of the art world.

Over the next few years, the forger continued his lucrative game, bringing dealers additional masterworks he said came from the collection of an ancient Italian family that did not wish to be identified. Some of the paintings were purchased by private collectors; one was bought for Amsterdam's renowned Rijksmuseum by the government; and one—to van Meegeren's ruination—found its way into the collection of the rapacious Nazi art thief, Reich Marshal Hermann Göring.

After the liberation of the Netherlands in 1945, Göring's Vermeer was found stashed in a cavern in Germany. Investigators traced it to the dealer and from there to van Meegeren, whose own art had been popular with the Nazi occupation forces. His protestations that the Vermeers had come from an Italian family sounded suspicious to Dutch authorities, and they arrested him for conveying a national treasure to the enemy.

In custody, deprived of his drugs and desperate to regain his freedom, the fifty-seven-year-old forger said that the Göring Vermeer was not a national treasure, but a fake—one of many that he had created. He named the others. When the police refused to believe him, van Meegeren said he would prove it by demonstrating his technique. This proposal was accepted. In two months, with the police observing him every minute, he confected another seventeenth-century masterwork. Charges of collaborating with the enemy were dropped—and van Meegeren was charged with forgery.

The subsequent trial was a prolonged mortification for the curators, dealers, and critics whom van Meegeren loathed. On the stand, one of them admitted, "It is unbelievable that it fooled me. A psychologist could explain it better than I can." Convicted as charged, van Meegeren was sentenced to a year in prison on November 12, 1947. But the bitter little man who had fooled the experts was by then a folk hero, and his attorney sought a pardon from the queen. Before she reached a decision, however, van Meegeren suffered a fatal heart attack. He died in Amsterdam on December 29, his faith in his great, neglected talent unshaken to the end. □

Duped by Dossena

In 1952, the art museum of St. Louis made a purchase that its director considered a coup. The museum paid a Los Angeles art dealer $56,000 for a four-foot-tall terra-cotta figure of Diana the Huntress—a ravishing sculpture of the goddess striding forward with a fawn frisking at her side. The Etruscan statue, said the director, "is one of the most important revelations of the art of antiquity made in the twentieth century."

It was not. Publicity about the museum's prize caught the attention of an art expert and amateur sleuth named Harold Woodbury Parsons *(page 8)*. He informed the St. Louis museum—as he had the Cleveland Museum of Art some two decades before—that their priceless statue was a fake. "You have bought a work by Alceo Dossena," he wrote, and subsequent investigation proved him right.

Although it was small consolation, the museum had plenty of company. For many years, curators and collectors around the world had been falling victim to Dossena's masterful imitations of antique statuary—not just Etruscan creations, but Greek, Roman, Gothic, and Italian Renaissance look-alikes as well. Millions of dollars went to dealers who provided this miraculous flood of sculpture, but little of it reached Dossena. In his own way, the compact, powerfully built sculptor seems also to have been something of a victim.

Alceo Dossena spent most of his life in obscurity. He was born in 1878 in the northern Italian town of Cremona, home to a family of violinmakers named Stradivari and a veritable hive of art restoration—and imitation. He served as an apprentice to a stonemason, worked for a time as a restorer of marble, and in 1916 embarked on a new career when he carved a Madonna from wood and sold it to a Roman art dealer for food money. The dealer at first thought it was a genuine Renaissance work, then realized that it was of recent vintage. Clearly, a man who could create such convincing imitations would be a money spinner.

Soon Dossena was turning out a stream of brand-new antiquities in his small studio in Rome. That was not especially unusual. The city's artisans had been manufacturing fakes in volume ever since the demand for Greek sculpture outstripped supply during the heyday of the Roman Empire. But Dossena was a genius, supremely gifted at catching the look and feel of ancient sculpture and also highly skilled at techniques of simulating aging. Soon numerous dealers were marketing his wares.

Collectors did not become alert to the danger until Dossena himself revealed what was going on. When a Roman dealer sold one of Dossena's creations for the equivalent of $150,000 and gave him only $7,500, Dossena went to a magistrate, announced he was the creator of the classic statues pouring onto the market, and produced pictures to prove it. He had never claimed the sculptures were genuine, he insisted; he made them simply as pieces for decoration.

Newspapers proclaimed him a modern-day Michelangelo, albeit a somewhat misguided one. Art experts came to watch him work. Wrote one: "When he inquired ◊

what he should make, I asked him for a Greek goddess. Half an hour later we were looking at an Attic goddess, some two feet tall, modeled in clay, with the captivating beauty that springs from the only slightly relieved rigidity that we admire in the best genuine pieces." Then, "the head took shape with equal fluency, and quite suddenly a smile dawned on the face of a woman to whom the Greeks had prayed 2,500 years before."

Ironically, Dossena's talent lay more with the past than the present. None of his contemporary art, critics complained, had the fine sense they had detected in his archaic imitations. Said one German expert in 1930, "The faker Dossena is finished; but the artist Dossena does not appear." That presumably great artist never surfaced, and even his imitations began to fall out of favor. A huge Dossena sale in New York in 1933, for example, brought in only $9,125. Four years later, Dossena (*above*) was killed by a stroke, leaving a legacy of remarkable fakes to plague the world's museum keepers—and little else. □

Quiz Skids

Charles Van Doren seemed to know all. Appearing week after week on the television quiz show *Twenty One* in 1956 and 1957, the Columbia University English instructor rang up $129,000 in winnings, gave NBC a huge ratings lift, and was the talk of America. Said *Time* magazine, "Along with charm, he combines the universal erudition of a Renaissance man with the nerve and cunning of a riverboat gambler and the showmanship of a born actor." Little did they know.

There was no doubt that Van Doren was brainy. He could hardly have been anything else: His father, Mark Van Doren, was a Pulitzer Prize-winning poet and his mother was a novelist; his uncle, Carl Van Doren, was a leading biographer and also had won a Pulitzer. Off to a solid start in his academic career, Charles seemed to be following in their footsteps; moreover, he was tall, handsome, and, to at least some of the tens of millions of American viewers, a pleasantly clean-cut alternative to another ratings star, Elvis Presley.

For four months, at 9:00 p.m. eastern time each Monday, Van Doren entered an onstage glass-walled "isolation booth," donned headphones, and pitted his wits against a contestant in a second booth. The game was played like blackjack, with the object being to approach a score of twenty-one more closely than the competition. Fielding questions with point values from one to eleven, contestants could decide when to turn over their figurative cards. Winners earned points by answering questions correctly and were paid $500 for each point separating them from the loser's score. In the event of a tie, points acquired an additional $500 value.

Van Doren had mounted to the winner's booth in late 1956 by defeating another strong, but less sympathetic, player named Herbert Stempel, billed as a poor boy from Brooklyn with a 170 IQ. The young English teacher then leaped to celebrity after four consecutive ties raised the point value to $2,500, and he won, 21-0—a $52,500 pot, a fortune in 1957. Before finally losing to another contender, however, he would more than double that figure in the isolation booth.

A prodigious reader, Van Doren seemed to have accumulated deep knowledge in every intellectual field and could summon from the vault of memory the most obscure details of geography, history, chemistry, and art. The audience loved his suspenseful antics as he groped for facts that would defeat the opponent of the evening. He would furrow his brow, breathe heavily, talk to himself, and let the clock tick down to the last instant before blurting out a game-winning answer. When asked to identify the character in the opera *La Traviata* who sings a particular aria, for example, he treated the audience to delicious tension by whispering into the microphone, "She sings it right at the end of a party given by . . . What's her name! Soprano. Her name is like . . . Violetta. Violetta!"

But as Van Doren's fortunes rose, Stempel brooded about his loss, which had been no accident: The show's producers had

told him to take a dive and, as usual, had supplied Van Doren with all the answers he needed, plus a script on how to deliver them with maximum drama. Stempel chafed, then began to tell journalists the show was rigged. When the Manhattan district attorney announced an investigation, the producers of *Twenty One* desperately contacted contestants they had prepped and begged them to deny the charges. But the jig was up.

In the course of the grand jury hearings and a subsequent congressional investigation, it became clear that *Twenty One* was one of many rigged television quiz shows—including the other blockbuster, the *$64,000 Question*. Sponsors and network executives bobbed and weaved, attempting to deny knowledge of the producers'

methods, but without much success. Van Doren, by far the most celebrated of witnesses, initially claimed innocence, then issued a self-serving apology. ("I've learned a lot about life. I've learned a lot about good and evil.") He resigned from Columbia, lost his $50,000-a-year position with NBC, and retreated from the public eye. And giveaway quiz shows, universally pilloried as corrupt and immoral, went off the air—for a while. □

What's de Hory?

Elmyr de Hory's two-decade career as a painter of ersatz masterpieces began in 1946, when an Englishwoman visited his studio in Paris, fastened her gaze on a drawing he had done, and said in tones of certainty, "Elmyr, that's a Picasso, isn't it?" De Hory, who had fallen on hard times, granted that she had a keen eye. She wondered if he would sell it. He would. The price was forty pounds.

With that, he stepped into a new life as a modern master—as many masters, in fact: Manet, Vlaminck, Matisse, Toulouse-Lautrec, Gauguin, Modigliani, Picasso, Dufy, and others, enlisted to finance the lifestyle to which de Hory had long been accustomed. He had been born in 1906 into a wealthy Hungarian family and raised ◊

MR. VAN DOREN
ON THE AIR

Secretly briefed quiz whiz Charles Van Doren feigns puzzlement on U.S. television's *Twenty One*.

in luxury, with every wish granted, including the wish to be an artist. He studied in Budapest, Munich, and Paris in the 1920s and 1930s, getting to know many of the Lost Generation painters whom he would later profitably emulate. Dapper, frivolous, free-spending, the young expatriate did little more than have fun. But when the Germans confiscated his family's property at the beginning of World War II, de Hory found himself one of a legion of impoverished, Paris-bound Hungarian refugees.

The chance sale of his bogus Picasso put him on the road to

wealth, however. Provenance was always a vital issue in the art market; de Hory, with his aristocratic heritage, was able to make a credi-

ble claim that the splendid artworks in his possession had come from his family's collection. Over the next two decades, he traveled throughout Europe, to South America, and to the United States, selling to dealers and art galleries, changing his name—he became Baron de Hory—and moving on if customers in a particular area began to grow suspicious. During a long period spent in the United States, he developed a gift for mail-order marketing, ar-

ranging many transactions entirely by letter. Fearful of being arrested for mail fraud, he delivered the goods by railway express.

In the early 1960s, de Hory settled on the Spanish island of Ibiza in the western Mediterranean, a haven for expatriate artists and a playground of the idle rich. The sale of his fakes was turned over to assorted art dealers not burdened by an excess of scruple. But greed finally brought down de Hory and his accomplices. In 1968, two large canvases said to be by Henri Matisse, who had died in 1954, were offered before their oil paint had fully dried. The dealers went to prison in France, and Spanish authorities interned de Hory for two months as a vagrant. He was finished as a forger, but not as an artist. Since his death in 1979, his forged masterpieces, billed as being painted "in the manner of" the great, have become eminently collectible for their own sake. □

Hello, Dalis

In money terms, one of the largest art frauds in history was the worldwide traffic in supposedly original prints by Spanish surrealist Salvador Dali—images said to have been created under his supervision and signed by him. Estimates of the profit earned on bogus Dalis range as high as three billion dollars. Some of the dubious Dalis were sold from high-toned galleries, others from so-called boiler rooms where salespersons styling themselves as "assistant curators" worked the telephones, stressing

Capable of painting "in the manner of" almost anyone, Hungarian-born artist Elmyr de Hory produced many modern look-alikes, including this Matisse-like still life (above) and this pair of Gauguinesque women (left).

the investment value of such art, especially as the artist was old and frail.

Yet the question of fraud in the glut of Dalis is not clear. During the 1960s, the flamboyant abstractionist found that, rather than conceiving of an image as a lithograph or an etching and then overseeing its production in strictly limited quantities—the traditional criteria for a print to be called original—he could simply produce a watercolor, license it to a printmaker, and sign thousands of blank sheets of the paper on which the picture was to be printed.

And he went further. He sold reproduction rights to such "lithographic interpretations" and "authorized graphics" that belonged to collectors or museums, often finding more than one buyer. The result: hundreds of thousands of Dali prints, many peddled for $5,000 or more, but worth little more than the paper on which they appear. Having taken his profits up front, Dali seemed not to care. "If people want to produce poor reproductions of my work and other people want to buy them," Dali, eighty-three, said just before his 1989 death, "they deserve each other." □

Hughes Sorry Now?

Casting about for his next book project in the late 1960s, American expatriate Clifford Irving fastened upon a golden idea. Like many people, he was curious about the world's reigning mystery man, billionaire Howard Hughes. Once a pioneering aviator, moviemaker, and lover of Hollywood stars, Hughes became a recluse whose whereabouts were always uncertain and whose lifestyle was largely unknown. The true story of this strange man's life would be a literary blockbuster, but there was no real hope that the bashful billionaire would ever tell it. So Irving decided to do it for him. As the writer had never met Hughes, however, and had no hope of ever meeting him, it would be necessary to make the whole thing up.

Gambling that Hughes would not challenge the fabrication—after all, the tycoon had not been willing to appear in person even to protect his multimillion-dollar gambling licenses in Nevada—Irving embarked on his audacious hoax. Crafty and glib, he claimed the reclusive mogul had admired one of his earlier books—*Fake!*, a biography of art forger Elmyr de Hory *(pages 27-28)*—and had asked him to ghostwrite an autobiography. To lend credibility to this improbable claim, Irving studied published samples of Hughes's handwriting and proceeded to forge a series of letters about the arrangement, capped by a contract purportedly signed by Hughes. The publishing house of McGraw-Hill, dazzled by prospects of a runaway bestseller, agreed to pay Hughes $750,000, of which Irving would presumably get a fair share. ◊

In fact, he got it all. The contract stipulated that all fees were to be passed through him and that the checks were to be made payable to H. R. Hughes. As it happened, Irving's wife, equipped with false identity papers, had opened a Swiss bank account in Zurich under the name Helga R. Hughes.

Now Irving had to produce the book. He and a co-conspirator named Richard Suskind spent months reading everything about Hughes that they could get their hands on. Then, in a great stroke of luck, they learned that a business intimate of the billionaire, Noah Dietrich, was collaborating with a journalist to tell his story of the Hughes empire. Irving managed to borrow the manuscript and made a photocopy; it provided just the sort of authentic detail he needed to pull off the con.

As Irving delivered chapters of the autobiography from his home on the Spanish island of Ibiza, his editors grew certain that they had a publishing triumph on their hands. But in 1971, after issuing an official announcement of the forthcoming autobiography, they received a disconcerting jolt. Aides of Hughes declared that the project was fraudulent. Irving replied that this was merely another demonstration of Hughes's penchant for secrecy: Obviously, Irving said, the recluse had not told any of his corporate minions about it. *Life* magazine, which had bought reprint rights to the work, insisted that the Hughes-Irving correspondence be submitted to handwriting experts for verification. The experts delivered an unambiguous verdict: The letters were authentic; "careful study had failed to reveal any features which raise the slightest question" about Hughes's authorship. On the basis of that judgment and the mass of convincing details in the manuscript, the publishers prepared to go forward.

Then, from an utterly unexpected quarter, a key witness stepped forward. On January 7, 1972, Howard Hughes broke a fourteen-year silence to speak to a group of journalists by telephone from his longtime hideout in Nassau. He spoke for two hours, denouncing the autobiography as a confection. Follow-up investigations soon revealed the check-cashing ruse of Helga R. Hughes and identified the Noah Dietrich manuscript as the probable source of the "autobiography." Finally, the besieged Irving confessed all. He and his wife—but not Suskind, who was not charged as a co-conspirator—received short prison sentences. Irving was paroled in 1974, and his wife received a parole from her Swiss prison in 1975. Howard Hughes, whose penchant for seclusion had led Irving to undertake his brazen deception in the first place, died in 1976—his own story still untold. □

Hughes Tool's Dick Hanna (standing) connects seven reporters with his reclusive boss, billionaire Howard Hughes, who broke his accustomed silence in order to discredit writer Clifford Irving's bogus autobiography.

A Life Ajar

Illusion, even delusion, shaped the childhood of the French novelist Romain Gary *(below)*. Born into a Russian Jewish family in 1914, he was reared in Poland by his mother, a former actress who earned a meager living with a clothing business that specialized in forged Parisian labels. She doted on her son and wove for him a richly fantasized future: He would be an ambassador of France and also a great artist of some kind—a violinist, perhaps, or a writer. In 1927, she and her son moved to Nice, where she made ends meet by selling trinkets that she said were family jewels smuggled from revolutionary Russia.

True to her hopes, her son was destined for fame. During World War II, he fought with the Free French Air Force and returned home a hero. Only then did he discover that his mother had died several years earlier—after setting up one final illusion. Throughout the war, he had been receiving letters from her, all written shortly before her death and mailed afterward to Gary at intervals by an obliging friend. Sadly, she missed the literary success she had imagined for her son.

By war's end, Gary had already turned his experiences into a bestseller. In 1945, he joined the French diplomatic service and devoted his sur-plus energies to writing more books. In 1958, his *Les Racines du Ciel* (The Roots of Heaven) won the Prix Goncourt, France's greatest literary prize, which an author is allowed to win only once.

Even as he maintained a steady output under his own name, Gary secretly produced four other books under the pseudonym Émile Ajar. Knowing a real author would be sought by the press, he arranged to have his second cousin, Paul Pavlowitch, take the credit. But when one of the Ajar books won the 1975 Prix Goncourt, Gary instructed his cousin to refuse it.

Despite wild speculation as to Ajar's real identity, the truth did not come out until the author confessed. "I was tired of being nothing but myself," Gary explained in *Life and Death of Émile Ajar*, written in March 1979. "To renew myself, to relive, to be someone else, was always the great temptation of my existence." On November 30, 1980, he drafted a note that said the revelation about his alter ego was to be released at the discretion of his publishers and his son. Two days later, having arranged the demise of the imaginary Ajar, Romain Gary destroyed himself. He died in Paris on December 2 of a self-inflicted gunshot wound. □

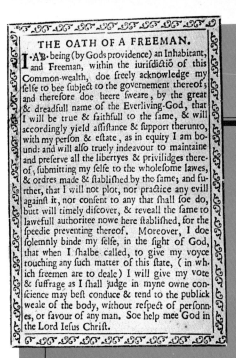

THE OATH OF A FREEMAN.

I.A.B. being (by Gods providence) an Inhabitant, and Freeman, within the iurifdictiō of this Common-wealth, doe freely acknowledge my felfe to bee fubject to the governement thereof; and therefore doe heere fweare, by the great & dreadfull name of the Everliving-God, that I will be true & faithfull to the fame, & will accordingly yield affiftance & fupport therunto, with my perfon & eftate, as in equity I am bound: and will alfo truely indeavour to maintaine and preferve all the libertyes & privilidges thereof, fubmitting my felfe to the wholefome lawes, & ordres made & ftablifhed by the fame; and further, that I will not plot, nor practice any evill againft it, nor confent to any that fhall foe do, butt will timely difcover, & reveall the fame to lawefull authoritee nowe here ftablifhed, for the fpeedie preventing thereof. Moreover, I doe folemnly binde my felfe, in the fight of God, that when I fhalbe called, to give my voyce touching any fuch matter of this ftate, (in which freemen are to deale) I will give my vote & fuffrage as I fhall judge in myne owne confcience may beft conduce & tend to the publick weale of the body, without refpect of perfonnes, or favour of any man. Soe help mee God in the Lord Iefus Chrift.

A master forger of documents, Mormon murderer Mark Hofmann claimed this bogus 350-year-old broadside called "Oath of a Freeman" as his crowning achievement, cleverly simulating colonial typography and chemistry.

The Salamander's Sting

Like the many historical documents he forged over a period of six years, Mark Hofmann was a masterpiece of deception. Shy, soft-spoken, hesitant in manner, every inch the hardworking scholar, he gulled the Mormon Church, the Library of Congress, and numerous collectors; then in October 1985, as his schemes threatened to come unraveled, he murdered two people and prepared to kill a third—himself, or so he said.

A sixth-generation Mormon, the young dissembler used his knowledge of the Church of Jesus Christ of Latter-day Saints as the launching platform for his activities. Setting himself up as a dealer in rare documents by the age of twenty-five, he sold Mormon officials a variety of texts relating to the early days of the church. Most were uncontroversial, but some cast the foundation of the church in a disturbing new light, hinting at folk magic. The most alarming, a letter supposedly written by a convert in 1830, offered an account of how founding father Joseph Smith had discovered the sacred golden plates that he translated into the *Book of Mormon*.

Conventional Mormon doctrine held that Smith had been led to the tablets by an angel of God named Moroni. The letter, however, said that Smith received the revelations from a "white salamander"—implying the occult. Another Hofmann offering was a "blessing" by Joseph Smith that promised his son, not Brigham Young, the right of succession. And there was talk of other documents, including the 116 missing pages said to open the *Book of Mormon*. As Hofmann came forward with more such material—all of it convincing in its style of writing and historical detail—church leaders bought it and pondered its effect on their institutions.

Meanwhile, Hofmann was expanding his list of victims, selling collectors and dealers forged documents by at least eighty-three American and European historical figures—among them, John Milton, Myles Standish, George Washington, Daniel Boone, and Abraham Lincoln. His work was superb. Highly intelligent, he not only had the ability to re-create another era, but knew every trick of the faker's trade: where to get old paper, how to mix antique inks, how to age documents. When he claimed to have recovered a long-lost seventeenth-century broadside known as the "Oath of a Freeman"—the first document printed in the New World—his fabrication fooled the appraisers of the Library of Congress; only his $1.5 million asking price prevented the purchase from going through.

But even with his remarkable talent as a forger, Hofmann could never put his own financial house in order. By 1985, he had become seriously overextended, unable to deliver documents he had already sold, his deceptions teetering on the brink of exposure. His back to the wall, Hofmann turned to murder. He had sold the so-called salamander letter to two church bishops, Steven Christensen and J. Gary Sheets, for $40,000 and apparently feared they would expose his forgery. On Tuesday morning, October 22, 1985, Christensen was killed by a pipe bomb outside his office. Three hours later, Kathleen Sheets was blown up outside her Salt Lake City home by a bomb almost certainly intended for her husband. A day later, a third bomb exploded—this one in Hofmann's car—and it nearly cost him his life. According to Hofmann, he had decided to kill himself. But police believe the third bomb had been intended for another Mormon official who stood in Hofmann's way, and it had detonated accidentally.

Still, much about Hofmann and his motives remains enigmatic. He was the most persuasive of dissemblers, capable of passing a lie-detector test with ease. Nor was his story aired in a trial; he pleaded guilty to two counts of second-degree murder, drawing a sentence of five years to life. Most believe he forged church documents for money, but some find a broader, more sinister design: By producing documents such as the salamander letter, he could actually skew the history and doctrine of the church, discrediting the fold he had privately abandoned years before.

Whatever his motives, Hofmann

is said to have shown no regret for the murders he committed. In 1986, the Utah Board of Pardons, finding him uncontrite, told Hofmann they would recommend he spend the rest of his life in prison with no hope of parole. Later, fellow prison inmates said Hofmann offered them thousands of dollars from a hidden cash hoard to arrange the killing of three board members. According to the convicts' account, he preferred that the job be done with bombs. □

Führer Furor

"The journalistic scoop of the post-World War period" was how the West German weekly magazine *Der Stern* described the discovery. That seemed an understatement. What *Der Stern* had in its possession, it claimed, were sixty-two volumes of the personal diaries of Adolf Hitler, covering the period from 1932 to 1945. The diaries had been acquired over a period of two years, it was later divulged, for a reported payment of four million dollars to one of the magazine's reporters, Gerd Heidemann.

Until the fifty-one-year-old journalist offered them to his employer in April 1983, no one suspected that Hitler had kept a diary. After all, the Führer had a known aversion to writing—even the rambling, rabid manifesto *Mein Kampf* had been dictated.

How had Heidemann come by this sensational material? That story began, he said, in the final days of the Third Reich. As Hitler huddled in his Berlin bunker in April of 1945, two Junkers transport planes carrying his staff and records left the besieged city, heading for the Führer's Alpine retreat at Berchtesgaden. One was shot down near Börnersdorf, outside Dresden. A Wehrmacht officer retrieved the records from the wreckage and kept them safe in an East German hayloft for more than three decades. Heidemann, a flamboyant reporter with a reputation for favoring long-shot stories, claimed he had found this man and his priceless trove after years of investigation. *Der Stern*'s efforts to authenticate the find were less than careful. Handwriting experts were allowed to give the diaries a quick look, and selected historians got a glimpse. Much influenced by the magazine's insistence that the airplane story had checked out, these examiners pronounced the volumes authentic.

Der Stern began selling serialization rights around the world—an easy job, since the diaries were hugely newsworthy. Although they contained much tedious complaining by the Führer about his digestion and insomnia, they also seemed to indicate—contrary to general belief—that Hitler had admired British Prime Minister Neville Chamberlain as a wily statesman, had allowed British forces to escape from Dunkirk in hopes of inducing a settlement, and had authorized his unstable deputy Rudolf Hess to fly alone to Britain in search of a peace deal.

No sooner had *Der Stern* rushed out the first installment of the Führer's scrawled thoughts and observations than scholars pounced. They noted a number of chronological inconsistencies and suggested that the diaries were largely plagiarized from a ◊

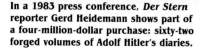

In a 1983 press conference, *Der Stern* reporter Gerd Heidemann shows part of a four-million-dollar purchase: sixty-two forged volumes of Adolf Hitler's diaries.

collection of Hitler's speeches published by a Nazi archivist in 1962. It was pointed out that one entry seemed to have been written without difficulty on the day an assassination attempt injured Hitler, leaving his forearms badly swollen and wrapped in bandages. Then a forensic laboratory subjected the diaries to chemical tests, determining that the paper and binding contained substances that did not come into use until after the war.

Inquiries about Gerd Heidemann revealed that he had a deep fascination with Nazi paraphernalia; he had even sold his house to buy a yacht that once belonged to Reich Marshal Hermann Göring and used it to entertain former Nazi officials. Arrested for fraud and pressed to name the source of the diaries, Heidemann fingered a Stuttgart relics dealer named Konrad Kujau. *Der Stern*, having belatedly sacked several high-ranking editors, attacked Kujau as an anti-Semite who enjoyed strutting around in an SS uniform. Under the onslaught, Kujau admitted that he had forged the diaries, taking a mere one million dollars as his fee. The vaunted scoop was in ruins—and, if the alleged price was right, three million dollars remained unaccounted for. □

Art à la Modi

Amadeo Modigliani had no great love for his hometown of Livorno, Italy, and the feeling was reciprocated. In 1906, at the age of twenty-one, he decamped for Paris to paint and sculpt. He came back three years later and labored in his studio for a time, but the town was so unsympathetic to his efforts— and to his fondness for alcohol and drugs—that "Dedo," as he was nicknamed, returned to Paris in a funk. According to Livorno legend, he dumped all of his scorned sculptures in a local canal as a parting gesture.

His works, especially his elongated nudes, have come to be ranked among the glories of the century's art, and in 1984, Livorno decided to make belated amends by staging an exhibition of his work on the 100th anniversary of his birth. The city council

Students Michele Ghelarducci, Pietro Luridiana, and Francesco Ferucci *(from left)* faked Modi 2 *(above)*, one of three bogus Modigliani sculptures found in 1984. Modis 1 and 3 are shown on the opposite page.

voted to spend $35,000 to dredge the canal for the supposedly jettisoned statuary—a modest investment, considering the market value of Modiglianis.

Dredging yielded rusty guns, bicycles, bathroom fixtures, a rocking horse, then a trove of three heads sculpted in granite and sandstone. The director of Rome's National Gallery of Modern Art had "no doubts at all" that they were Modiglianis. A prominent critic saw in these early works "a presage, a presence." They were labeled Modi 1, Modi 2, and Modi 3, and added to the exhibition.

But some six weeks later, three university students came forward as Modi 2's creators. Guided by pictures in a Livorno museum catalog, they had carved the stone with such makeshift tools as a screwdriver and an electric drill, photographing and videotaping the sculpting sessions as proof of authorship. At first, Livorno's art establishment was angry, suggesting that they were victims of a Mafia plot of some obscure kind. Besides, they noted, they still had Modis 1 and 3.

But only for a little while. Soon after the exposure of Modi 2, a twenty-nine-year-old dockworker identified himself as the creator of the two remaining heads. The only bright spot in the scandal, for the experts of Livorno, was that the resulting publicity brought huge crowds to the exhibition, re-covering nearly twice the dredging costs. Beyond that, the prank had a notable downside. The museum curator in Livorno resigned her post, and her brother, the director of Rome's National Gallery of Modern Art, was fired for authenticating the false Modis. "We love Modigliani too much," explained one duped critic. "This led us to betray ourselves." □

A Syncing Sensation

Pop-music fans loved them. Their videos and concerts were hugely successful. The National Academy of Recording Arts and Sciences awarded them a Grammy as the Best New Artist of 1989. Robert Pilatus and Fabrice Morvan, the two young men from Munich collectively known as Milli Vanilli, were on top of the world. Sales of their first album, *Girl You Know It's True*, had enriched them to the tune of about two million dollars. Now they ◊

Grammy-winning Milli Vanilli's Rob Pilatus (left) and Fab Morvan energetically pretend to sing a rock hit recorded by others.

The voices behind Milli Vanilli's winner were Brad Harell *(left)*, Gina Mohammed, and John Davis.

were ready to do their second album—but this time, for a change, they wanted to sing it themselves.

Unbeknown to the public, Milli Vanilli was a hall-of-mirrors concoction devised by the album's German producer, Frank Farian. The singing had been done by a trio of studio musicians. Pilatus, a German, and Morvan, who is French, were recruited in Munich to supply the flamboyant visuals, appearing in braided hair and sequined costumes on the album and lip-syncing their way through videos and "live" concerts.

When the decorative duo demanded that they be allowed to prove their vocal worth, Farian fired them and withdrew the Milli Vanilli name, which was in his legal control. As to the question of impropriety, he was unrepentant, calling the ruse an "art form." In fact, lip-syncing is a time-honored custom in certain areas of the recording industry—live performances, for instance. Sham singers mouth words for the audience while a recording is played offstage.

For their part, Pilatus and Morvan effused regret: "We're really, really sorry about our fans," they told reporters. "We love our fans. We just hope that they understand we were young and we wanted to live life the American way." They then announced that they would try to give the Grammy back, write a book about their experience, and go ahead with a new album on their own. The new name of their act: Rob and Fab. □

FALSE COLORS

Everyone dreams of something better, but some dreamers take a curious further step: They wrap themselves in the false colors of an invented identity and walk unblinkingly through life as someone, or something, they are not. Few of them are deluded souls who think themselves Napoleon or Joan of Arc. Rather, most are incomparable actors in roles they have composed, on stages they have chosen.

Some dedicate their new lives to perfecting a single creation—one false identity polished to perfection. Others don and discard personalities like hats. Women have posed as men to live more freely in what has been largely a man's world, a transformation that was sometimes simpler than it sounds. Back when clothes made the man, a woman became unrecognizable even to her father and siblings as soon as she put on trousers. Some impostors are clearly in it for money, fame, or glory, but the motives of many remain obscure.

No one knows, for example, what persuades a layperson to practice medicine or commoners to risk terrible punishment by putting on the shoes of the missing rich and royal. Perhaps, at bottom, such gambits realize a latent universal wish to be another, more interesting person, living a more richly textured life.

An engraving from the 1785 edition of a seventeenth-century polemic, *A Present for a Papist,* shows the fictive Pope Joan delivered of a child.

Papal Bull

Some impostures are so bizarre, so daring—so impossible, in fact—as to gain an unbreakable grip on the public imagination. None, however, has combined improbability with persistence to greater effect than the legend of Pope John Anglicus—familiarly, Pope Joan.

The idea that one of the Roman Catholic popes was female was re-current, surfacing occasionally between the ninth and the seventeenth centuries. Though never named—Joan apparently came into common parlance as a female corollary of John—the papal female supposedly ruled the Church for several years, between Leo IV and Benedict III. (Here, timing alone calls the legend into question. Official histories show Leo's rule ending in 855 and Benedict reigning from 855 to 858.) Nonetheless, according to the account of Marcus Polonus, a thirteenth-century Dominican friar, the German-born female pope was taken to Athens and dressed as a man by a lover. "There she became proficient in a diversity of branches of knowledge, until she had no equal," Polonus said, "and afterwards in Rome, she taught the liberal arts and had great masters among her students and audience. A high opinion of her life and learning arose in the city, and she was the choice of all for pope."

But one day, two or three years later, as the papal procession wound from St. Peter's to the Lateran, the pope's church, John's career came to a sudden, surprising end. In a narrow lane near the Colosseum, the legend goes, the pope gave birth to a child. Some writers said she died in the attempt and was buried on the spot. Others reported that she was tied to a horse's heels and dragged to her death as a mob pelted her with stones. Still others have her sentenced to a remote convent, to repent her sinful imposture and finally to die in the Church's good graces—buried, according to one suspect manuscript, by her illegitimate son, who had grown up to become bishop of Ostia.

For several centuries, almost everyone believed that there had once been a Pope Joan, and there was even a kind of evidence for her existence. In the fifteenth century, for example, marginal addenda in documents spoke of a statue called *The Woman Pope with Her Child,* a monument to the presumed birth of a papal child near the Lateran. There was also talk of two marble chairs used in papal consecrations.

Each chair had a hole in the seat, said to be for an official check of each pope's gender; but the chairs have never been found.

No one now believes that there ever was a Pope Joan. Nevertheless, by the time evidence against her existence overwhelmed the myths supporting it, she had become a leading lady in popular culture, featured as demon, whore, teacher, philosopher, reformer, bandit, witch. In the seventeenth century, she was trotted out by Protestant polemists to flagellate the Church and, in the 1960s, by feminists as an example of man's inhumanity to woman. But her most enduring performance began some 200 years after her story was first told, when Joan appeared as the High Priestess card in the Tarot deck—a symbol of hidden knowledge also known as the Female Pope. □

More than two years before the Battle of Bosworth Field, Richard's royal brother, Edward IV, had died, to be succeeded by the elder of his two sons, Edward, then twelve. Edward V was crowned in June 1483, with his uncle as Lord Protector. Then, as Richard had eliminated everyone else between him and the throne, he confined the young king and Edward's younger brother, also named Richard, in the Tower of London. There they were reportedly killed on the Lord Protector's orders, although

no bodies ever came to light. The uncle, called the Usurper by disillusioned subjects, seized power as Richard III. And the boys vanished into legend, not murdered, many believed, but somehow spirited away to safety.

Despite Richard's culling, there were, after Bosworth Field, twenty-nine people with better claims to the throne than Henry Tudor. The strongest was that of Edward, earl of Warwick and cousin to the missing princes. The ten-year-old peer was quickly incarcerated in the Tower of London, where years of harsh treatment made him simple-minded—and set the stage for an opening round of imposture.

The first pretender surfaced in Ireland in 1487. The boy, named Lambert Simnel, said he was the real Warwick, and contemporaries described him as ◊

New York, New York

One of the last battles of England's bitter Wars of the Roses—a struggle born of competing claims by the powerful Lancaster and York families—was fought on a field near Market Bosworth on August 22, 1485. There, Yorkist King Richard III was unhorsed and killed by the forces of Henry Tudor, who became King Henry VII. But Richard left a murky web of ambiguity spun before his death—one that seemed to offer the Yorkist claim to anybody rash enough to seize it.

In this fifteenth- or sixteenth-century rendering, Yorkist pretender Lambert Simnel does time as a royal turnspit in the kitchen of Henry VII, the Tudor king Simnel betrayed.

a "comely youth" with a strong family resemblance to his supposed York forebears. He had been coached by a priest, Richard Simons, and was vigorously backed by his "Aunt" Margaret, duchess of Burgundy, the sister of the two Yorkist kings Edward IV and Richard III. Simnel also found strong support from the Irish. Even when King Henry brought the authentic Warwick out of the Tower and displayed him in London, the Irish still said theirs was the real one and crowned him King Edward VI.

Soon afterward, a mixed army of supporters, German mercenaries, and "a great multitude of beggarly Irishmen" invaded England to unseat Henry VII. When the rebels lost the close-fought Battle of Stoke, however, Simnel realized the game was up and admitted he was only the son of an Oxford tradesman. He was duly convicted of treason, but the king, finding Simnel more useful alive than dead, put the impostor on kitchen duty in the palace, where he had the low, greasy job of turning the meat spit. When Irish lords came to dinner, Simnel was promoted to table server so that Henry could mock their choice of rulers: They would be crowning apes next, teased the king.

But, in 1491, Henry's attentions were captured by a second, and more dangerous, pretender to the Yorkist succession: Perkin Warbeck. This one claimed to be the younger of the missing princes, Richard, duke of York. Observers said he was "of visage beautiful" and looked very like King Edward IV. The duchess of Burgundy believed Warbeck, as did the king of France and the emperor of Germany. James IV of Scotland gave him an allowance and a beautiful royal cousin to marry. For reasons that often had nothing to do with Warbeck, all Europe, except Spain, recognized his claim.

Despite this wide acceptance, no effective rebel army coalesced around his cause. When Warbeck invaded England in 1495, proclaiming himself King Richard IV, the natives refused to help, and he was forced to withdraw. King Henry played his diplomatic cards so well that finally even Ireland gave up on the duke. In 1497—six years after his first appearance—Warbeck again tried to invade, to no effect. He took refuge in an abbey, from which he duly surrendered to the king. Henry found Warbeck less than royal material but promised him "honourable maintenance." For his part, Warbeck admitted that he was not Richard, but the son of a humble Flemish farmer, Jehan Werbecque.

Taken to London, Warbeck foolishly escaped—some said he was allowed to flee so that Henry could renege on his promise. The pretender was quickly recaptured, put in the stocks, and tortured on the rack to extract a more comprehensive confession. Then he was thrown into a windowless cell in the Tower, where the hapless earl of Warwick still languished.

Despite Warbeck's confession, Europe's rulers were not convinced; their skepticism sealed his fate. Henry decided to solve the problem in one bold stroke. Warbeck, he announced, had joined forces with the befuddled Warwick, plotting to seize the Tower and escape overseas, where one or the other would proclaim himself king of England. For this contrived treason, poor Warwick was beheaded. Warbeck fared worse: Dragged to the gallows, he was briefly hanged, then cut down and, still alive, disemboweled, castrated, and dismembered, his head finally displayed on a pole on London Bridge. Ironically, despite his extracted confessions, he died without ever being proved an impostor. The one person who could have exposed him—King Henry's wife, Elizabeth, eldest sister of the lost princes—apparently did not.

Stranger was the fate of Lambert Simnel, the first pretender. Removed from the palace, he entered service in an aristocratic household and died in 1525, aged fifty—extraordinary longevity for a man convicted of treason against a Tudor king. □

Nom de Guerre

Despite lusty celebrations in the French village of Artigat, the wedding night of fourteen-year-old Martin Guerre and his still-younger wife, Bertrande de Rols, did not go as it should have. Bertrande remained barren for years afterward, and Martin, from his marriage day in 1539 onward, suffered the gibes of his fellows and became increasingly testy. At Bertrande's insistence, the pair submitted to the ministrations of village wise women, and finally, after eight years and a regimen of masses and special foods, a son arrived—too late for the disgruntled Martin. Always at odds with his family, in 1548 he took some bags of grain that belonged to his father. Afraid of facing the consequences of his theft, he ran away to the wars that raged perennially in Spain and disappeared without a trace.

Eight years later, a stranger arrived in Artigat, a gentle, friendly man who seemed to remember everyone in the village and all the details of life there. He was, he told the amazed villagers, Martin Guerre, returned at last. Mellow now, he chatted amiably about boyhood escapades and was especially kind to Bertrande, who quickly verified that he was indeed her lost spouse. The rekindled marriage flourished, and the pair soon had two more children. After a few years, however, Martin decided to make up for his lost years. He asked Pierre, the uncle who led the extended Guerre family, to give him his share of their farm's profits for the years he had been absent. When the uncle refused, Martin filed a suit against him—and ignited a fatal fuse.

Infuriated, Pierre retaliated by calling Martin an impostor, for which Pierre had some anecdotal evidence. A soldier who had known Martin Guerre in Spain said, when passing through Artigat, that Martin had lost a leg in the war. Other travelers had identified the purported Guerre as one Arnaud du Tilh of the nearby village of Sajas. The uncle's charges split Artigat into two factions, one—including Martin's two sisters and Bertrande—giving him steadfast support, the other claiming fraud. ◊

Pierre pressured Bertrande to file suit for usurpation of identity and property. When she refused, he filed one in her name, warning her to cooperate or be ejected from his household. Gambling desperately that love would conquer all, Bertrande let the suit go forward against her beloved mate, hoping to lose the case.

But a dramatic trial, laced with the testimony of 150 witnesses, went against Martin, who was declared guilty and found to be the interloper du Tilh. In an appeal to a higher court, the defendant's credible testimony led to just the opposite verdict: Pierre was jailed for false accusation, along with the innocent Bertrande. The judge, who wrote a book about the case, had a difficult time finding the truth in an age when the only evidence was the testimony of others: There was no technology of identification, no fingerprints, identity cards, photographs, or, because literacy was rare, handwriting samples. On balance, the accused seemed more honest than his accusers and could recall the minutiae of his Artigat boyhood.

As the judge was about to pronounce Martin genuine, however, another player entered the courtroom, a dour man with a wooden leg. He, not the defendant, the stranger said, was the true Martin Guerre. One by one, the Guerre family acknowledged him to be their legitimate relative, some with evident regret. Even Bertrande finally admitted that he was her missing spouse. At first, the defendant refused to yield the point. He was the real Martin Guerre, he maintained stoutly, and this one-legged newcomer was a ringer sent forward by Pierre. But he was lost. Despite his confident defense, the judge found him guilty and sentenced him to die.

Only on his execution day did the impostor admit that he was Arnaud du Tilh and that he had intended only to impersonate Martin Guerre for a time—until he found himself so warmly welcomed by Bertrande. In 1560, asking forgiveness of God and the woman he loved, the false Martin was hanged. But poor Bertrande fared worse. Having watched her beloved man—whom she had evidently tutored in his role—go to the gallows, she was then compelled to spend her life with a sour, cruel substitute who may or may not have been the real Martin Guerre. □

All the King Men

King Sebastian of Portugal was adored by his subjects, who found the dashing blond warrior, though headstrong and ambitious, a man of reckless courage and deep religious feeling. Although he was slender and of middle height, the king was powerfully made, a renowned swordsman, and capable, it was said, of making a brave horse tremble and sweat by the mere pressure of his knees. Sebastian took the throne in 1557 at the age of three and was crowned at fourteen—"another Alexander," he was called, after the glorious young Alexander the Great of ancient Macedonia.

But Portugal could not contain a man of Sebastian's abilities, and he began looking for a worthy enterprise. In his willful fashion, he decided to renew the Crusades, against the advice of every counselor, and sailed off in 1578 to fight the Moors and claim Morocco for Portugal. At the Battle of Alcazarquivir, Sebastian threw his 18,000 soldiers against the 55,000 Moors of King Abd-el-Mulek, with predictable results: The Portuguese force was swiftly surrounded and destroyed.

Sebastian vanished at Alcazarquivir, although no one saw him killed. After a considerable amount of time had elapsed, the Moors sent back a corpse, but few Portuguese believed it was their king. From 1580, when Portugal came under the sway of powerful Spain, the lost king was a symbol of lost sovereignty. Sebastian, it was prophesied, was still alive and would return to throw off the Spanish yoke. Such belief was fertile ground for fraud.

The first impostor, known as the King of Penamacor, appeared in 1584 but was quickly exposed and sent to the galleys. He apparently escaped and ended in Paris as a bogus duke of Normandy. The second, a failed monk named Matheus Alvares, came forward in 1585 but was discovered and executed. The brazen third, a cook twenty years too old for the part, made his claim in 1594 and, like his predecessor, died trying.

The fourth and most convincing pretender surfaced in Venice in

1598. He told of marvelous adventures following the defeat at Alcazarquivir and said he had lived in a Georgian monastery until a dream urged him to resume his rightful role in the world. Asked to be interrogated by the governors of Venice, he acquitted himself well, except for one fatal deficiency: He spoke no Portuguese. At Spain's urging, the Venetians put him in prison—where he learned enough Portuguese to appeal his case.

Believers struggled to accept him. Time, they told themselves, can change anyone; it could explain Sebastian's Calabrian accent, his darkened hair, his swarthy skin. As he himself lamented, "What has become of my fairness?" Released from prison in 1600, he and his supporters carried his royal claims to Naples, where he was recognized as one Marco Tullio Catizzone and identified by his abandoned wife

and in-laws. Condemned to the galleys, Catizzone was not required to pull an oar—a hedge, perhaps, against his really being Sebastian—and continued to press his claim from a comfortable cell in Sanlúcar. But when he was caught wheedling money from the wife of the Andalusian governor, official patience ran out. He was dragged to the square of Sanlúcar, his right hand was cut off, and he was hanged.

The lost king did not go to the grave with the last impostor, however, but entered Portuguese myth. In 1807, seers held that Napoleon would be destroyed by Sebastian, returning after an inexplicable delay of more than two centuries. And in 1838, in Brazil, loyal Sebastianists peered out to sea for the sails that would bring back their promised "Hidden King," still brave and dashing—aged 284. □

Somebody Bet on the Bey

No one loves a good fraud like an old one, and P. T. Barnum, America's peerless humbug monger *(pages 68-69),* was no exception. His 1866 book, *Humbugs of the World,* amounted to a celebration of fakery, especially those shams carried off with dash, like the French visit of Riza Bey.

In 1667, Barnum recounted gleefully, Louis XIV was at the peak of his glory. France was rich and powerful, and Louis' splendid new palace of Versailles received the world's humble emissaries, all of them dazzled by the Sun King's opulent glare. Then came word of yet another embassy, this one from the only court to rival Louis' own: His Most Serene Excellency Riza Bey, envoy from the fabled shah of Persia, had landed with his entourage in Marseilles and would soon pay his respects at Versailles.

For four weeks, the exotic visitors blazed a well-publicized trail toward Paris, dressed, Barnum recounts, "in the most outrageous and outlandish attire." The Persian entourage traveled with monkeys and camels, and chattered in gibberish. When they arrived at the French court, Louis beamed with joy at Riza Bey, who wore huge gold rings on every finger and rich floor-length robes covered with paintings and shiny cutouts. The delighted monarch threw a grand ball and banquet for his guests, giving them rooms in the former royal residence.

Magnificent gifts from the shah were on their way, Bey declared, and he stayed at court for a month awaiting their arrival. King Louis ◊

lavished millions of francs in jewels and treasures upon the flamboyant envoy, which Bey duly packed up in chests. One by one his courtiers left on special missions, carrying chests, and His Most Serene Excellency went shopping in Paris, on credit.

Finally he sent word to the king that the shah's gifts had arrived. The Great Hall of Mirrors was thrown open, the king and courtiers waited—but neither the gifts nor Riza Bey appeared. Someone recalled that, at dawn, several humbly dressed men had slipped out of the palace carrying bundles, but nobody ever saw Riza Bey again. Barnum reported rumors that the bogus ambassador had been a notorious barber and bandit from the Italian city of Livorno who was known to be missing. But the only track Bey left was in the vernacular of France, in which "an embassy from Persia" became a synonym for fraud. □

Formosan Fantasy

The young man who called himself George Psalmanazar was in his early twenties when he arrived in London in 1703. He was introduced to the bishop of London by a clergyman named Innes, who said Psalmanazar was a heathen Formosan converted to Christianity. In eighteenth-century London, a Formosan was as great a sensation as a Martian would be today. The public's hunger for a closer knowledge of this strange race from the Far East brought Psalmanazar instant celebrity and led him within the year to publish his *Historical and Geographical Description of Formosa*.

The book was a sensational success. Even today, readers are riveted by its comprehensive descriptions of Formosan dress, art, architecture, geography, law, religion, diet, and language. Britons shuddered to learn that the Formosan deity required the annual burning of the hearts of 18,000 boys under the age of nine—a population-depleting practice offset by the sparing of eldest sons—and polygamy. Criminals had their tongues bored with a hot iron and their arms and legs cut off. Houses and clothing were liberally adorned with gold. Snakes and snakes' blood were delicacies: "In my humble opinion," wrote Psalmanazar, "the most wholesome breakfast a man can make." This practice, and eating meat raw, contributed to longevity: Formosans usually lived to at least 100. Cannibalism—many readers suspected the author may himself have tried it—was confined to the bodies of prisoners of war and executed criminals. Travel was by elephant-borne litters that carried fifty people. In the viceroy's palace, the royal apartments were two "bayks" in diameter, a bayk being a mile and a half. Wildlife included giraffes, lions, tigers, leopards, rhinoceroses, and tame seahorses.

Psalmanazar illustrated the book himself with detailed drawings of plain and fancy clothing, floating villages, complicated coins, the alphabet, altars, idols, boats, and buildings. Although he ran into trouble from time to time, as when Edmond Halley—of comet fame—stumped him on Formosan astronomy, the public preferred to believe the for-

eigner. And it made no difference that there were then other, duller accounts of Formosa written by missionaries who had been there. Psalmanazar was wined and dined in London, eating his meat raw and embroidering on his vast apparent knowledge of Formosa.

In fact, Psalmanazar had never set foot there, and everything, even the elaborate language, had been fabricated. Although his true origin is unknown, many believe he was born and reared near the French city of Avignon, and he appears to have posed as a persecuted Irishman before taking up the Psalmanazar identity. His immediate success in London led to what he later called ten years of "shameless idleness," after which he became clerk to a regiment, then worked as a translator for a printer. His hoaxing days were over, but a ◊

Phony Formosan George Psalmanazar, as portrayed in his 1765 memoirs, invented an entire civilization, right down to a curious imaginary alphabet.

The Formosan Alphabet
pag. 122.

Name	Power		Figure			Name
Am̃	A	a / ao	Ɪ	I	I	Il
Mem̃	M	m̃ / m	ɟ	ɟ	⅃	⅃
Neñ	N	ñ / n	u	ŭ	U	ʊc
Taph	T	th / t	ᴝ	Ƀ	O	xi O
Lamdo	L	ll / l	Γ	F	⅃	ILEE
Samdo	Š	ch / s	Ꮞ	Ꮚ	�	Ɔⅇ
Vomera	V	w / u	Δ	Δ	Δ	Ⅰℇ3Δ
Bagdo	B	b / b	/	/	/	ƆƆℾ
Hamno	H	kh / h	ᴷ	ᴷ	⅃	ƆuIℒ
Pedlo	P	pp / p	Ᵽ	ᴟ	Δ	℈ᴅℂΔ
Kaphi	K	k / x	Y	Y	V	oXI
Oda	O	o / ω	Ə	Ə	Ɛ	Ɩᴢᴅ
		y / i	O	□	ᴮ	ᴜℾ□
		/ x	Y	Ʒ	Ꮞ	Ɩℇꙥℒ
			Ɔ	Ɛ	⅃	⅃I
			ƀ	ƀ	凵	oXⅢ
			ᴄ	ᴄ	ᴄ	ℯᴅℾ
			X	x	X	℈uIX
			ꝑ	ꝑ	Ɋ	ΔI
			ᴎ	ᴎ	ᴾ	Ɩℯℯᴢ

T. Slater sculp.

painful moral hangover still await-
ed the reformed Psalmanazar.

In 1728, Psalmanazar suffered
a serious illness—and pangs of
guilt for his imposture. He began
to write his confessional *Memoirs,* which he completed by 1752;
the work was published in 1765,
two years after his death at
about eighty-four. In the meantime, he punished himself by publishing nothing under his own
name—or, rather, the name he
called himself. He became enormously pious and virtuous, and,
when eighty, befriended the great
lexicographer Samuel Johnson.
Johnson claimed that Psalmanazar
was "the best man I ever knew"
and wrote, "His piety, penitence,
and virtue exceeded almost what
we read as wonderful even in the
lives of the saints."

In his will, Psalmanazar begged
God's and the world's pardon for
his "forgery." He had spent half a
century regretting the sin of his
youth—a prank for which the
world, at least, had forgiven
him long before. □

Used Czar

The death of the Empress Elizabeth
propelled a thirty-three-year-old
prince, a German-born grandson of
Peter the Great, onto the throne of
Russia in January 1762—and
placed the vast empire in the unre-
liable hands of a destructive ado-
lescent: Peter III. Deceitful, lazy,
cruel, cowardly, and neurotic, he
played with toy soldiers, flaunted
his mistress openly, and alienat-
ed his own army by his passion for things Prussian.
Six months later, as Pe-
ter contrived a war
with Denmark, his

brilliant, ambitious wife, Catherine,
forced his abdication and declared
herself empress of all the Russias.
She ordered the defeated Peter to
an estate at Ropsha, near what is
now Leningrad, and he docilely
complied. "He allowed himself to
be deposed," quipped his great
hero, Prussia's Frederick the Great,
"like a child being sent to bed."
A week later, that child was dead,
apparently strangled or
suffocated by his
guards after a
drunken
quarrel of
which
there
was
no

clear
ac-
count.
Cather-
ine had
Peter's body
placed on public
view and built him
a splendid tomb, but she
could not forestall the legion of impostors that inevitably follows the ambiguous death of royalty.
Pretenders turned up in
droves, each of them, as one
historian put it, an improvement over the wretched original.
Most were quickly exposed. The two

Ten years after this 1752 engraving, Czar Peter III *(left)* took—
and lost—the Russian throne,
prompting the appearance of
such pretenders as Montenegrin
leader Stefan Mali *(above).*

who were most successful, however, prospered on their abilities, not their ability to deceive.

The first of these, a man named Stefan Mali (Stephen the Little), appeared in 1767, five years after Peter's death, in tiny, mountainous Montenegro. Now part of Yugoslavia, it was then an independent state, ruled by prince-bishops who acted as both spiritual and military leaders. Its people were famous for their dignity, their aversion to work, and their courage in endless battles against their neighbors; they alone of all the Balkan states were never conquered by the Turks. A remote but traditional ally of Russia's, it was a reasonable place for Stefan, claiming to be Peter III, to tell hair-raising stories of his escape from Ropsha and all the adventures since. In fact, he was a Montenegrin surgeon. Sensing opportunity in the murky circumstances of Peter's death, he had decided to try out the royal identity in Montenegro.

He was in luck. Sava, the current prince-bishop, preferred cloisters to battlefields and thought the newcomer might be just the kind of ruler the tough Montenegrins needed. Stefan "was of fine presence and well-proportioned form and of noble ways," wrote one observer. "He was so eloquent that he exercised with mere words power not only on the multitude but also on the higher classes." No one questioned his claimed identity. One man who had been to Russia thought that he remembered Stefan well from a glimpse of the deposed czar. Mainly, the Montenegrins were glad to have a strong hand, and if he really was Peter III, so much the better.

Sava went back to his prayers,

while Stefan reduced the prevailing blood feuds among Montenegrins, reformed the judicial system, improved communications, and generally put his tiny country on the map—where it began to catch the attention of other nations. Venice thought him a Russian agent and joined forces with Turkey against Stefan's feisty stronghold. In 1769, Empress Catherine II of Russia sent military aid and one of her best statesmen, Prince George Dolgoruky, to investigate, along with a letter saying Stefan was an impostor. Stefan confessed and went to prison. But when Sava came back from his cloister to resume command, Dolgoruky sensibly decided that the impostor was the better man to lead Montenegro, a Russian ally, against the Turks and restored Stefan to power.

Catherine was soon plagued by another, more dangerous reincarnation of her late husband: Yemelyan Ivanovich Pugachov. This stocky, tough-minded impostor surfaced in the Ural Mountains in 1772, claiming to be Peter III. He looked nothing like the dead czar, but he was mature, crafty, and courageous. Arrested, he quickly escaped and renewed his claims. A year after his first appearance, Pugachov had set up his own proclaimed nation in the Russian hinterland, replete with a mock court and coinage of his own design. Although it was generally known that he was Pugachov, not Peter, people nevertheless flocked to his populist reforms. At first, Catherine dismissively called him the Marquis Pugachov but became concerned as his armies set much of southern Russia in turmoil and killed nobility by the hundreds.

Coincidentally, 1774 saw the

undoing of both pretenders. Stefan Mali's throat was slashed by his trusted barber. Pugachov was finally run to earth by the Russian army and taken to Moscow in a cage, defiant all the way. His nerve failed as he heard his fate: He would be hanged, then drawn and quartered; his hands, feet, and head would be left as warnings to others. Fortunately for Pugachov, his executioners reversed the order of events— he had already lost his head when they carried out the rest of the sentence in January 1775. □

Sister Sarah

At sixteen, pretty Sarah Wilson, a girl of spirit and courage, left her home in the English midlands for London and adventure. There she met Caroline Vernon, lady-in-waiting to Queen Charlotte, who took Sarah on as her personal maid. The ambitious girl from rural Staffordshire went to live with Miss Vernon in the queen's house, which stood where Buckingham Palace does today.

Sarah loved the excitement surrounding the court of George III and vicariously shared the episodes of Georgian high life that her mistress recounted. But she also wanted to be closer to the centers of aristocratic action. One night she slipped into the queen's closet and stole a ring, a miniature portrait of Charlotte, and a fine dress that almost fit. Greedily, she came back the next night for more, but this time she was caught. Tried before Lord Talbot, Lord Steward of the royal household, Sarah was sentenced to death. Miss Vernon ◊

Accessories filched from Queen Charlotte, painted here by Allan Ramsay, aided the royal imposture of a colonial slave.

pleaded her case, however, and the sentence was softened to transportation to the American colonies.

Arriving in the New World in the fall of 1771, she was sold as a slave to William Devall of Bush Creek, Maryland, where she labored for some months. But Sarah Wilson had not come empty-handed: Somehow she had managed to keep some of the royal objects purloined from Queen Charlotte. Opting for freedom, she headed south with the stolen dress, portrait, and ring, with which she made a convincing Princess Susanna Carolina Matilda—the queen's younger sister. She had quarreled with her royal kin, she said, by way of explaining her presence in Virginia. Unaware that the queen had only an elder sister, Christina Sophia Albertina, the

southerners allowed themselves to be charmed by her poise, her cornflower blue eyes, and the wealth of court gossip she had at her fingertips. For a year and a half, she was a favorite houseguest in the southern colonies, and, to compensate their generosity, she promised appointments and privileges for her

benefactors, once she regained her influence in London.

In the meantime, Devall advertised for his missing property and sent his lawyer to track her down. She was finally caught and returned to him in 1773, but escaped again two years later, this time to the north, where her track was soon covered by the tumult of the Revolution. During the war, she met and married a British captain, who after the war went into the import-export business in New York. Sarah always kept the queen's portrait on the wall, as a souvenir of her daring impersonation. And she may have drawn ironic satisfaction from the fact that her husband, William Talbot, coincidentally gave her the surname of the Lord Steward who had sentenced her to die. □

Chain Link

Watching a battalion of the distinguished Legion of Paris wheel across the Place Vendôme on a fall day in 1817, a shabby stranger in the crowd asked the name of the lieutenant colonel in command. That, he was told, was Monsieur le Comte de Pontis de Sainte Hélène. But the stranger, who went by the name of Darius, believed he recognized the elegantly appointed, well-horsed count as a man he

knew as well as he knew himself: Pierre Coignard, the fellow convict to whom Darius had been chained for four long years.

Coignard, the son of a Langeais vinegar maker, was apprenticed at fifteen to a hatter. These were revolutionary times in France, and the young apprentice enlisted in a grenadier regiment in 1792; he supplemented his meager salary with petty larceny, then grander crimes. In 1801, he was convicted of theft and swindling and sen-

tenced to fourteen years' hard labor, tethered to another convict by a three-foot length of chain in the harsh prison at Toulon.

Ever willing to gamble for his own freedom, Coignard bided his time, waiting for a chance to escape—an act that, if unsuccessful, meant life in jail or even the guillotine. On July 27, 1805, when his guards momentarily relaxed their surveillance, Pierre Coignard severed his tie with Darius and escaped to Spain. In Barcelona,

Coignard had an extraordinary stroke of luck. By chance, he met a young woman named Rosa Marcen, who had been working for a dying, down-at-the-heel French émigré, the comte de Pontis de Sainte Hélène. Having no heirs, the old man left Marcen a box containing his papers, family history, an army commission—and a perfect covering identity for Coignard.

Pierre and Rosa married and became the comte and comtesse, with papers to prove it, and he joined the Spanish forces against Napoleon. He distinguished himself in combat, only to desert to the French, persuading them to give him the rank of major and send him against the Spanish. Captured by the Spanish, he was not recognized as a deserter and escaped with other prisoners of war to Algeria. Eventually, he made his way back to Paris, again risking everything: Recognized as Pierre Coignard, he would be returned to prison in Toulon; identified as a Frenchman who had fought for Spain, he would be shot as a traitor. But neither fate befell him. His wife's cache of documents protected Coignard's claim to nobility and his reputation as a gallant soldier. He was given the rank of lieutenant colonel, along with a battalion of the national guard.

In Paris, the Coignards lived opulently on what the colonel described as an inheritance. In fact, he had become the leader of a gang of thieves. His entrée into the fine homes and prestigious offices of the city permitted him to arrange many dazzling coups, including, according to some writers, the theft of the gold and silver stored in the War Office safe.

All went well for Coignard until the day in 1817 when Darius recognized his old chain mate. When Coignard, as the count, refused to see him, the spurned ex-convict went to the police. Coignard was seized but managed to escape. Sensational burglaries followed, until finally the police arrested Coignard's band of thieves, then trapped the erstwhile count himself when he tried to visit his wife. On June 22, 1819, the court acquitted Rosa, but locked her daring spouse away forever.

Having lost his freedom, however, he would not give up the congenial identity he had appropriated. To his fellow convicts, he remained the comte de Pontis de Sainte Hélène—indeed, he would not respond to any other name—until his death in a prison hospital, aged sixty, in 1834. □

In a sketch by Charles Rambert, Comte de Pontis de Sainte Hélène unexpectedly meets the convict to whom he had been chained for years.

Day of the Dauphin

On August 10, 1845, a death certificate was issued in the Dutch city of Delft for Charles Louis de Bourbon, duc de Normandie, born in Versailles on March 27, 1785. "Here lies Louis XVII," reads his gravestone, "Charles Louis, Duc de Normandie, Roi de France et de Navarre." And although no real royalty lies there, it is the only known grave identified as that of France's boy king, said to have died in a revolutionary prison in Paris half a century earlier, aged ten.

The sad story of Louis-Charles of France began in 1792, when French revolutionaries imprisoned King Louis XVI, Queen Marie-Antoinette, and their family, including the eight-year-old heir to the throne, or the dauphin (the name derives from the fourteenth-century agreement that brought Dauphiné under French rule). After his father was executed in January 1793, the dauphin was removed to another part of the Temple, as their castle-prison was called, to be raised rough and rebel-like by a cobbler named Antoine Simon and his wife. In October, the boy's mother was beheaded. His aunt, Madame Elisabeth, followed in May 1794. The dauphin's older sister, Marie-Thérèse, was released from prison in December 1795, the only member of her family known to have survived, and eventually became the duchesse d'Angoulême.

In the meantime, the dauphin's condition had gone steadily from bad to worse. The Simons resigned as his keepers in 1794, and he was placed in a small cell, no longer able to exercise or play, and with scant human companionship. Poor diet and the lack of fresh air and exercise took their toll. On the afternoon of June 8, 1795, he died of what an autopsy called scrofula—tuberculosis of the lymphatic system. He was buried in an unmarked grave at the Church of Saint Marguerite—and never seen again. His very private death, at a time when French streets were full of public ones, caused little stir, although there were whispers that he had been poisoned—even that he had been spirited away and another child left in his place. But because his grave was never found, his ambiguous death became the stuff of which impostures are made.

Over a period of sixty years, the world teemed with false dauphins—forty of them at least. Mark Twain's Huckleberry Finn ran into "the late Dauphin" on the Mississippi, and John James Audubon, the famous painter of American birds, was believed by some to be the lost prince. A half-Iroquois preacher named Eleazar Williams claimed that a blow to the head had suddenly revived his memories of being the dauphin.

In France, the first pretender, Jean Marie Hervagault, was a tailor's son who claimed to have been smuggled from the Temple in a laundry basket and replaced by the tailor's real son, a dull, scrofulous boy. Attractive and poised, Hervagault found enough believers to keep him going through four arrests, until the exasperated authorities locked him in an asylum, where he died in 1812. After an old soldier and then a bricklayer failed to win acceptance as the dauphin, shoemaker Mathurin Bruneau, a man without manners or education, drew enough followers to worry the government. He put up placards promising to reduce the price of bread when he was crowned and died in jail.

Henri Hébert, who called himself Baron de Richemont when he was not calling himself the lost heir to the French throne, wrote a wondrous memoir describing his Trojan Horse escape from the Temple. His allies, he wrote, brought him a toy horse in which they had concealed a deaf-mute child, whom they exchanged for the dauphin, smuggling the latter into Belgium inside a life-size wooden horse covered with real horsehide. In 1828, Hébert turned up in France as the duke of Normandy to make his claim so persistently that he was duly arrested and sentenced to twelve years' imprisonment for sedition. He escaped but kept up his appeals until he died in 1855.

In 1833, the year of Hébert's arrest, Karl Wilhelm Naundorff arrived in Paris to make his claim to the French monarchy. An unlikely candidate, he was said to be ten years older than the dauphin would have been, and was a Polish Jewish watchmaker with poor French besides. His career included arrests for arson and counterfeiting, a strong interest in designing explo-

sives, and a decided inclination toward mysticism. But he told a convincing story. As dauphin, he said, he had been moved to the Temple's attic, and a doll—later, a deaf-mute child—substituted for him. He had been taken from the attic in a coffin, bound for a royalist province in France and thence to exile in Italy, England, and Germany. Unable to obtain an audience with Marie-Thérèse, he tried

to sue the duchesse and was expelled from France. Pursued by debt, animosity, and bad luck, Naundorff continued to press his case from abroad. He moved to Holland in 1845, hoping to sell the government an explosive weapon he had designed. He died there on August 10, leaving two children, Louis and Marie-Antoinette, and the only gravestone for the lost boy king of France. □

Lady's Man

Dr. James Barry, British army surgeon, inspector general of hospitals, and pioneer in sanitary reforms, died in London in July 1865. The demise ended a career that had spanned nearly half a century, almost all of it spent in the distant reaches of the empire. Following a common practice of the day, Barry had entered Edinburgh University Medical School in 1809, when only about ten, and completed the grueling three-year course and a thesis written in Latin. Not yet fourteen, the youngster apprenticed to a London surgeon before taking up a medical career with the British army.

As a physician, the diminutive and acerbic Barry was precocious, outspoken, and, some believed, dangerously unconventional. But the doctor's legacy was impressive: smallpox vaccination in South Africa, twenty years

before it was introduced in England; a successful Cesarean delivery considered a near miracle for its day; a lifelong fight for better living conditions, diet, and hygiene for British troops and for such outcast groups as lepers, convicts, blacks, and the insane.

Insisting on cleanliness and ventilation, Barry pioneered concepts often attributed ◊

to Florence Nightingale—one of the doctor's many bitter enemies.

Except for occasional intervals of home leave, Barry spent the years serving in such outposts as Mauritius, Cape Town, Jamaica, and Canada, always the small, effeminate, eccentric figure, a tiny beardless doctor in a bright uniform, saber, and cocked hat, followed everywhere by a servant and one of a succession of poodles named Psyche. Far from keeping a low profile, the medic courted attention, picked quarrels, fought a duel, flirted outrageously with the ladies, and once horsewhipped a colonel in public. Adored by patients, but despised by colleagues, Barry was finally forced into early retirement in 1859.

Upon the inspector general's death six years later, staff surgeon Major D. R. McKinnon duly completed a death certificate explaining that his fellow officer had died of an attack of diarrhea. But Barry's charwoman had something to add: The general, she declared, was a woman and had once borne a child. At first glance, it appeared that Barry had been an extraordinary female who fooled the world from the time she first entered Edinburgh dressed in boy's clothes.

In fact, many people seem to have known her secret all along and simply—perhaps because of Barry's powerful patrons at home—declined to mention it. As early as 1816, for example, a ship's captain in Cape Town, referring to the doctor, wrote of the "prevailing opinion that he was a female," a theme that surfaced repeatedly as she posed as a man to follow her chosen profession. Ironically, 1865, the year of her death, was also the year that Elizabeth Garrett Anderson became the first woman graduated by a British medical school—well, almost the first. □

Wish-Borne Heir

Sailing from Rio de Janeiro in 1854, the ship *Bella* vanished with all hands, including the heir to a venerable British baronetcy. Sir Roger Charles Doughty Tichborne was presumed dead, and his title passed to a younger brother, Alfred. But Roger's mother, Henriette, the French-born wife of Sir James Francis Doughty Tichborne, never abandoned hope that her elder son was still alive. After her husband's death—and nine years after the loss of the *Bella*—Lady Tichborne placed advertisements in the *Times* of London and in South American and Australian newspapers, promising a reward for information about her lost son. Predictably, seamen came forward with further news—usually invented—of the ship, hoping for a piece of the reward. Then, in 1865, an Australian lawyer wrote that he knew her son, who lived in the New South Wales town of Wagga Wagga under the name of Thomas Castro—the man history remembers as the Tichborne Claimant.

The vanished baronet would have been a difficult man to imitate. He had been born in Paris in 1829 and reared there to age sixteen without learning a word of English. Then he was sent by his father to school in England and later became an officer in the Sixth Dragoons. As a young man, Roger Tichborne did not cut much of a figure, however. A frail, asthmatic, effeminate 120-pounder of middle height, he had a rapid, clumsy gait on thin legs and a long, sallow face framed in stringy black hair. Among his distinguishing features were earlobes attached to his cheeks and a heart-and-anchor tattoo on his left arm.

Although bashful, and often the butt of cruel jokes in the officer's mess, he appears to have been tender-hearted. At twenty-four he fell in love with his cousin Katherine, but her parents disapproved on the ground that, because they were first cousins, they could not marry in the Catholic church. Grieved, he sold his commission and sailed for South America, turning up in Rio in April 1854, whence he sailed for Jamaica on the ill-fated *Bella*.

Thomas Castro, the audacious man who claimed to be Sir Roger Tichborne, would have made several of the frail original: He weighed more than 300 pounds, worked as a butcher, and was barely literate. Instead of straight black hair, his was fair and curly, and his earlobes hung loose, unlike Roger's. He had no knowledge of French, which had been Sir Roger's true mother tongue, and no memory of home or school in England. He could not recall his mother's appearance or maiden name. Incredibly, after finding him devoid of any knowledge of Roger Tichborne's life, the Australians who tested Castro pronounced him genuine. Their endorsement enabled him to borrow tens of thousands of pounds sterling against his expectations. He had written Henriette, according to one historian, a letter "notable for its illiteracy and crudity," which she had nevertheless acknowledged as being from her long-lost son. In 1866, as his creditors began to stir restlessly, Castro decided he must go to England and stake his claim.

After stopping in London, he met his supposed mother, who had returned to France, in a room he had taken in Paris—a room kept in virtual darkness because of an illness he claimed to have contracted on the long voyage. Although nearly blind from cataracts, Lady Tichborne recognized him immediately. "He confuses everything as if in a dream," she said later, to explain why he remembered almost nothing of his past. She gave him a generous allowance.

Henriette never wavered in her belief that he was Roger, but no one else among the Tichbornes recognized Castro's claim. As the years passed and his creditors increased their clamor, however, the claimant was forced to pursue a suit of ejectment—an effort to have the court eject the late Alfred's infant son from the title and restore it to Sir Roger. Castro rounded up 100 favorable witnesses, including veterans of the Sixth Dragoons, and prepared for the fight. But he lost his most influential witness: In March 1868, Henriette died.

Once started, the trial dragged on for weeks. Castro himself was cross-examined for twenty-two days. "The colossal ignorance he displayed," reported one observer, "was only equalled by his boldness, dexterity and the bull-dog tenacity with which he faced the ordeal."

The ordeal ended on its 103d day, just as the question of Roger's tattoos was about to be raised (Castro had none). The foreman of the jury rose and said, "We have heard enough. We wish to find for the defendants." The suit settled, the judge swiftly remanded Castro for "wilful and corrupt perjury," initiating a second trial that lasted 188 days. The defense lawyer addressed the jury for 43 of them, but to no avail. Castro was convicted and sentenced to fourteen years in Dartmoor prison. He was released in 1884 and died in poverty and obscurity in 1898. Improbably, his coffin was inscribed "Sir Roger Charles Doughty Tichborne," by permission of the family whose ◊

title he had tried to claim.

The Tichborne Claimant was almost certainly not a transfigured Sir Roger, but Arthur Orton, one of twelve children of a butcher in Wapping, a poor district in London's east end. A sailor, Orton had gone out to Australia in 1852, using the names Arthur Orton and Joseph Orton on his seaman's papers. Working as a butcher in New South Wales, he had fallen in with horse thieves, and eventually fled to Wagga Wagga as Thomas Castro. When he learned of Lady Tichborne's advertisements, he did not come forward but skillfully planted hints that acquaintances could assemble.

But Orton must have had a fatally sentimental side. When he returned to England on Christmas Day, 1866, he made a secret visit before traveling on to Paris to meet his "mother"—a clandestine return to Wapping, where he learned that his real parents were dead. As one of the trial lawyers pointed out, Wapping was not Sir Roger's part of town. □

Peerless Performance

The stranger who arrived in Minneapolis in 1871 was impressively alien to the people of the frontier prairie town—a tall, slender man immaculately attired in fine clothing, with the slightly fatigued, unflappable mien of a contented, moneyed aristocrat. He brought letters of introduction from highly placed Britons and was soon identified as a great person in his own right—a Scottish nobleman related to Lord Byron and sporting a living of a million dollars a year: Lord Gordon-Gordon.

Depositing $40,000 in a local bank, the newcomer let it be known that he had come to Minnesota to buy up hundreds of thousands of acres on which to relocate his Scottish tenants. Seeing an influx of cash at hand, the director of the ailing Northern Pacific Railroad pampered and feted Gordon-Gordon as the newcomer chose—and even named the future communities of—his vast tracts of land. After several months of such treatment, Gordon-Gordon announced that he would go east to arrange for the transfer of funds to buy the property. He duly withdrew his $40,000 from the Minneapolis bank and, equipped with a fulsome letter of introduction to Horace Greeley, the powerful editor of the *New York Tribune*, made a leisurely trip to New York, where he took a suite in the elegant Metropolitan Hotel. Not coincidentally, he arrived at a propitious moment: A corporate war was raging for control of the Erie Railroad, as a rebel faction tried to unseat the notorious robber baron Jay Gould as chairman of the board.

Arranging to be called upon by Greeley, his lordship told the newspaperman that he and some friends had bought up enough Erie Railroad stock to control elections of the board of directors but that they wanted to clean up the railroad's image, much tarnished under Gould. "I've heard that he's an impossible rascal," said Gordon-Gordon, and he hinted that it would be best if Gould resigned. Greeley and the *Tribune* favored Gordon-Gordon's reforms and lost no time in spreading the word.

Gould, in a panic, begged an interview with the Scot and promised reforms if reelected to the board. Reluctantly, the aristocrat agreed—but he would need a pledge to hold in escrow, as a guarantee of Gould's reforms. With stocks and cash, this pledge came to over a million dollars, for which Gordon-Gordon disdainfully refused to give a receipt: A nobleman never gave more than his word. For good measure, Gould added his resignation for Gordon-Gordon to hold as a further warrant. Incredibly, although a confidence man of considerable abilities himself, Gould was utterly bamboozled by Gordon-Gordon's composed superiority—but not for long.

The Scot began at once to sell blocks of Gould's stock, and the tycoon was outraged. He demanded that his pledged capital be returned and sent Greeley as an emissary to retrieve it. Greeley brought it back—$150,000 short. Furious at being gulled, Gould took Gordon-Gordon to court. On the first day of the trial, the aristocrat, speaking with the relaxed air of a man incapable of doing wrong, made a strong case for his authenticity, supplying names of those in England who would verify all his claims. By the next day, however, Gould's minions had learned that there was no Lord Gordon-Gordon in Great Britain—or in New York: The defendant had taken the night train to Canada.

Gould offered a reward for his capture, and word of the daring crime spread far and wide. In

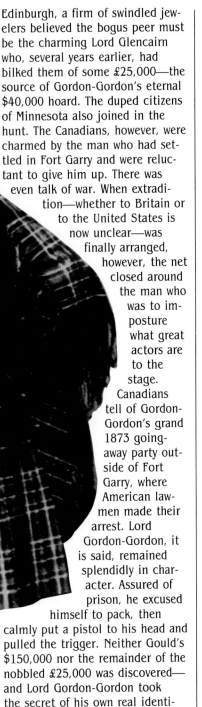

Edinburgh, a firm of swindled jewelers believed the bogus peer must be the charming Lord Glencairn who, several years earlier, had bilked them of some £25,000—the source of Gordon-Gordon's eternal $40,000 hoard. The duped citizens of Minnesota also joined in the hunt. The Canadians, however, were charmed by the man who had settled in Fort Garry and were reluctant to give him up. There was even talk of war. When extradition—whether to Britain or to the United States is now unclear—was finally arranged, however, the net closed around the man who was to imposture what great actors are to the stage. Canadians tell of Gordon-Gordon's grand 1873 going-away party outside of Fort Garry, where American lawmen made their arrest. Lord Gordon-Gordon, it is said, remained splendidly in character. Assured of prison, he excused himself to pack, then calmly put a pistol to his head and pulled the trigger. Neither Gould's $150,000 nor the remainder of the nobbled £25,000 was discovered—and Lord Gordon-Gordon took the secret of his own real identity to the grave. □

Love among the Cannibals

Louis de Rougemont first visited the offices of England's newest periodical of true adventure in the summer of 1898. He was a tall, ascetically slender man of aristocratic bearing, somewhere in his fifties, whose seamed, bearded face had been burned almost black by the sun. He had, he told editor William Fitzgerald, a remarkable story to reveal. After hearing only a little of it, the editor emphatically agreed. "We now commence," Fitzgerald exclaimed on the front page of *Wide World Magazine* in August, "what may truly be described as the most amazing story a man ever lived to tell." Monsieur de Rougemont had spent thirty years as a "cannibal chief in the wilds of unexplored Australia."

Born in Paris in 1844, de Rougemont recounted, he left France to avoid conscription and traveled in the Far East, where he joined the crew of a forty-ton schooner being readied for pearl fishing off northwestern Australia. A shipwreck put him ashore on a tiny barren island, alone except for Bruno, the lost captain's noble dog. Like Robinson Crusoe, de Rougemont adapted and even prospered there, learning to ride (and eat) giant sea turtles, growing corn in their empty shells, robbing seabirds of their catches. He built a house of oyster shells and, to ease the loneliness, preached scripture to Bruno. After two years on his own, he was joined by two shipwrecked Aborigines, whom he called Yamba and Mr. Yamba. Soon afterward, de Rougemont sailed with his companions on a boat ◊

The consummate con artist known only as Lord Gordon-Gordon poses in full regalia, wearing the borrowed tartan of the illustrious Scottish clan he adopted for his grand American scam.

he had built earlier to Australia, where a respectful chief gave him a maiden. He traded her to Mr. Yamba for Yamba.

Victorian England read avidly of how the bartered Aborigine became his devoted wife. Once, as de Rougemont burned and shivered with malaria, Yamba gave birth to a child. But, unable to nurse a sick husband and an infant at the same time—and following local custom regarding firstborn children—she ate the baby, then sentimentally stored its little bones in a bag around her neck. Still shivering with fever, de Rougemont nevertheless managed to kill a large bull, slice it open, and crawl into its carcass for warmth. In the morning, he had to be chopped out of the stiffened body, but he was quite cured.

His serialized account told how the natives had hunted flying wombats for their skins, dined on rats, kangaroos, snakes, grilled worms—and, after battles, the bodies of dead enemies. Trying to civilize his companions, he wrote, he had once rendered a large chalk drawing of a naked Queen Victoria with the bulging biceps and huge stomach that denoted physical strength and hunting prowess. Hearing of this, the queen reportedly said only, "We are not amused." But most readers were. They devoured accounts of explorations and rescues, duels and drownings, and nonstop derring-do.

After decades, however, the Australian adventure ended, de Rougemont recounted. Bruno died in his thirtieth year, followed by two chil-

dren who had escaped their mother's menu, and then Yamba herself. Grief-stricken, de Rougemont trekked through the desert to civilization, to England—and to the offices of *Wide World Magazine.*

Celebrated for his account of life in the Australian wilderness, de Rougemont was invited to speak before the British Association for the Advancement of Science and was widely quoted. But his fame was fleeting, for London's *Daily Chronicle* suspected fakery. The man posing as Louis de Rougemont, they reported on October 7, was a Swiss named Henri Louis Grien, who had gone east in 1874 as the butler of Western Australia's new governor. He had tried making his way as a boat captain, pearl fisherman, photographer, swindler, and cook, to little effect.

In 1882, Grien had married Elizabeth Jane Ravenscroft, of Sydney, who bore seven children; but, tired

of their straitened life, she left Grien in 1897, and he, at fifty, moved to New Zealand. In March 1898, Grien traveled to London and tried unsuccessfully to promote a diving apparatus once described as "a very fine death trap." Broke, he was saved from utter failure when a business acquaintance invited him home as a guest. There, having failed as Henri Grien, he became Louis de Rougemont.

In fact, his creation's spectacular life story had been shared by Grien, either at first hand or in the vivid tales told by the explorers and bushmen that he admired. Much of his account was true. His flying wombats were almost certainly the giant bats of Australia, and his knowledge of aboriginal life and the Kimberley district of northwest Australia has been shown to be accurate. He demonstrated, for instance, how one rode a large turtle. Moreover, Grien had been telling such stories for years. He had told them, his wife explained to reporters, to his beloved eldest son, who died young—Cecil de Rougemont Grien. And he may have told them also to his eldest and youngest daughters, Blanche and Gladys.

But the imposture ruined Grien, who stayed on in London as de Rougemont. After some business ventures that must have gone awry, he ended as he had begun, in poverty, making his way, some have said, by selling pencils on a London corner. He died in 1923, after a life as varied as the one he had invented and was buried as Louis Redmond—impostor to the end. □

If It Moves, Salute It

The streets of Berlin teemed with the bright blue tunics of Kaiser Wilhelm's army in 1906, when Prussian militarism was ascendant and a uniform commanded immediate obedience and respect. Thus, no one noticed that the small, sixtyish man in a baggy captain's uniform had a limp, needed a shave, and wore his cap insignia reversed. He arrived with a squad of armed soldiers one afternoon in the eastern suburb of Cöpenick and marched his men to the town hall, his overlong saber clattering on the cobblestones. After posting guards at the doors, he ordered the rest of his squad upstairs, where he arrested the mayor and the treasurer for suspected embezzlement and impounded the town's treasury—a mere 4,000 marks, less than $1,000. Outside, he ordered the soldiers to take the officials to military headquarters in Berlin. Then he vanished with the confiscated money. Later the saber was found in a train-station toilet and the uniform in a shed, but finding the impersonator—erstwhile petty crook and cobbler Wilhelm Voigt—took almost a fortnight.

That a man with the bearing of a bum could impersonate a Prussian officer simply by putting on a rented uniform brought sardonic comment from the world press, always at the kaiser's expense. "The worship of the military uniform," crowed one British newspaper, "which has been carried to such preposterously extravagant lengths in Prussia, never received so effective an exposure." Some spoke ominously of unquestioning obedience to uniformed authority as a German malady. "The uniform—our fetish!" lamented a Berlin paper. "They all lie on their bellies before a uniform."

All, perhaps, except Wilhelm Voigt. When finally arrested, he still had Cöpenick's cash and explained calmly that he had only wanted to be able to work and to leave his militaristic homeland. Germans not in accord with their nation's pervasive militarism made him a folk hero and followed his trial avidly, hoping for an acquittal. But the judge gave Voigt a four-year sentence, along with a handshake and best wishes. Voigt served only twenty months and was still a hero when he came out. A wealthy woman offered homage in the form of a pension of 100 marks per month, for life. Putting on the Prussian uniform again, the so-called Captain of Cöpenick became a popular music-hall act in Europe and America. He ended his days in 1922, aged seventy-two, in Luxembourg, having finally got his passport—and a pleasant kind of immortality as the little shoemaker who, the London *Review of Reviews* wrote, "kept the whole world laughing for a week." □

This 1906 cartoon was one of many celebrating Wilhelm Voigt, whose ill-fitting rented captain's uniform allowed him to command the town of Cöpenick—and ridicule the German awe of all military trappings.

Afternoon of a Fawn

Two decades after the little Captain of Cöpenick *(page 57)* tweaked the German penchant for uniformed authority, another imposture—this time of a deposed prince—put the sensitized nation back on the world's front pages. "OUR REPUBLIC," screamed a Berlin newspaper in 1927, "AGAIN THE WORLD'S LAUGHINGSTOCK." The trigger of this outrage had been another down-and-outer, a young Russian-born drifter named Harry Domela. In his imitations of minor aristocrats, monarch-starved Germans saw Prince Wilhelm, the kaiser's grandson and heir to the Hohenzollern line. In fact, the real prince was living comfortably in Potsdam, and Domela himself at first did very little to insinuate that he was Wilhelm. Indeed, he modestly traveled as "Baron Korff." But, as people seemed to want him to be the prince, he finally acquiesced in the charade and let them lend him money, entertain him in grand style, and introduce him to their daughters.

Having done time for several minor crimes, however, Domela feared discovery and decided to discard the royal identity. He had waited too long. A storm of publicity swept across the land, and snapshots of the "prince" appeared in newspapers, along with such headlines as "ALL GERMANY IS LOOKING FOR THE PRINCE OF IMPOSTORS," and "FALSE HOHENZOLLERN PRINCE FOOLS DIE-HARD MONARCHISTS." Domela quickly enlisted in the French Foreign Legion, hoping to endure five years of hard duty in North Africa instead of any more time in a German jail. But as he boarded the train for Metz, he was arrested by two detectives.

Despite his difficulties, Domela was widely viewed as a hero who had properly embarrassed the monarchists who had fawned upon him. A publisher offered him a 25,000-mark advance for his memoirs, which were an immediate success. At his trial, witnesses swore they had given him money willingly, and some had even profited from the presence of his bogus royalty. The judge let him off with the seven months he had already served. Harry Domela was free, popular, and rich from his book; he even starred in a film, *The False Prince.*

Unfortunately, Domela's happy ending presaged a bitter fate for his country. The German monarchists who had feted him, thwarted in their love of royalty, later handed their hearts to a truly dangerous interloper: Adolf Hitler. □

As Kaiser Wilhelm's equestrian statue looks on, false Wilhelm Harry Domela strikes a princely pose on Berlin's Unter den Linden.

Fly by Night

No one was more important to Canadian environmental awareness than the tall, gaunt man in the buckskins of the Ojibwa. He had come north from his birthplace in Hermosillo, Mexico, the blue-eyed son of a Scottish father and an Apache mother. He was first a hunter and trapper, then the man who would save the beaver. The Ojibwa, his adoptive tribe, called him *Wa-Sha-Quon-Asin*—He-Who-Flies-By-Night, or Grey Owl.

But Grey Owl's blue eyes did not exactly bespeak an Indian heritage, and even in 1906, when he first came to Canada at eighteen, braids, feathers, and buckskins had become largely ceremonial. Although he could hunt, track, and shoot with the best of them, he always seemed less the natural Indian than the white European's expectation of one. In fact, he had come to the Ojibwa not from Mexico and an Apache mother, but from the seaside English town of Hastings and a life no boy of spirit would have wanted. He was born

Archie Belaney in 1887, the middle-class son of a wastrel, lecher, drunk, and exile. When his father, whom he loved despite the man's destructive failings, left England, young Belaney was reared by aunts. He was a lone wolf from the beginning, drawn to the study of Canadian Indian lore. At eighteen, he persuaded his aunts to send him to Toronto, presumably to study farming, but actually to disappear into another, more comfortable identity—his evolution into Grey Owl was less a deception than a transformation from Englishman into Indian.

Once in Canada, Belaney went immediately to the North Woods, where he learned woodcraft from a guide and lived with an Ojibwa tribe. He married an Ojibwa woman, Angele, but his transmuted soul was restless and without direction. He soon went off wandering, earning his living as a trapper. In World War I, he served in the Cana-dian infantry and married an Englishwoman, Florence Holmes, whom he also abandoned.

Traumatized by the war, where he had found his niche as a sniper, he had begun by then to want less civilization about him. Back in Canada, he was horrified by what mining and timbering had done to his forests. Following the retreating frontier as guide and trapper, he married a town-reared Iroquois woman named Anahareo, who was to change his life. When they discovered two beaver kittens orphaned by his trap, she decided to raise them. The playful, intelligent ways of the kittens, called McGinty and McGinnis, settled what Grey Owl would be. "To kill such creatures seemed monstrous," he wrote later; "I would do no more of it." Instead of hunting beaver, he would restore them to the wilderness.

In the winter of 1928-1929, he started his first beaver colony and began to write and lecture on the wilderness, traveling with McGinty and McGinnis, and, after they had returned to the wild, with another beaver named Jelly Roll. His first book, *Men of the Last Frontier,* was followed by *Pilgrims of the Wild,* and—although he did not tell his growing audience—Anahareo was followed by a young French-Canadian, Yvonne Perrier.

His English publisher arranged a speaking tour in Britain, where ◊

Thirteen-year-old British loner Archie Belaney *(above)* grew up to be Apache-Scot naturalist Grey Owl *(right).*

Grey Owl was a sensation. A quarter of a million people thrilled to the tall, deep-voiced man of the woods, and money rolled in for his beloved beavers.

Not quite a decade later, his books took him back to England, where he was introduced at court. There he found two determined fans in the young princesses Elizabeth and Margaret. When Grey Owl finished his speech, the future queen jumped up and cried, "Oh, do go on!" He added an encore. But that tour, followed by an American one, exhausted him. Back in his North Woods cabin, he contracted pneumonia and died in April 1938, aged fifty.

Within a day of Grey Owl's death, like a genie escaping from a shattered jar, Archie Belaney came back to life. A noted nature writer wrote in the *Toronto Star* that he had known for years that Grey Owl was really a Briton named Belaney, since a government department had once traced the trail of documents left by the false Indian. Many came forward to refute the charge. Comrades-in-arms reported that only a true Indian could have crept through Flanders the way Grey Owl had, and Anahareo said she had known him only as a half-breed Indian. Tenacious reporters, however, soon turned up his aunts in Hastings, along with a birth certificate and early photographs. Then came word of his four wives.

In the end, however, Belaney was remembered sympathetically as a man who, the *Times* of London summed up afterward, "gave his extraordinary genius, his passionate sympathy, his bodily strength, his magnetic personal influence, even his very earnings to the service of animals." □

Doctor, Lawyer, Serbian Chief

When not in jail, Stanley Clifford Weyman lived in Brooklyn, a small, mild man with a strong resemblance to Charlie Chaplin and a genius for swift, flamboyant impostures. Born Stephen Jacob Weinberg in 1890, Weyman—one of many variations on a Weinberg-Weyman name scheme—seemed to have no identity of his own. He flickered like a candle flame, now a doctor, now a lawyer, diplomat, or warrior—anything but an obscure clerk. Ignoring the certainty of imprisonment, he carried out countless impostures, exercising the impostor's art for its own sake.

For his first role, in 1910, he became the U.S. consul delegate to Morocco, a country he never deigned to visit. Rather, his exotic posting took him no farther than Manhattan, where he went about bedecked in a resplendent purple uniform. Living up to his new status was costly, however, and a few unpaid bills in ritzy restaurants and the pawning of a stolen camera put Weyman in prison. The next year, he was out of jail and playing the Serbian military attaché, then an American naval lieutenant, guises that restored him to prison for two more years. When he returned it was as a Roma-

nian consul general holding the rank of lieutenant commander in the Romanian army. Dripping gold braid, he inspected a battleship, the USS *Wyoming*, as an envoy from the queen of Romania, after which he dined the officers in style at the Astor Hotel. The banquet was interrupted by his arrest, but the ship's captain remained impressed: "The little guy put on one hell of a tour," he said.

One of Weyman's favored names came to him when the United States entered World War I in 1917: Lieutenant Royal St. Cyr of the Army. The police intercepted him during his much-publicized inspection of the Forty-Seventh Regiment. In 1920, free on parole again, Weyman read that a doctor was needed by a company in Lima, Peru, and went for it with bogus credentials and his customary panache. He got the job and, not quite thirty, set out for Peru. There, far from the New York police, he rented a palace, bought a limousine on credit, and threw parties until his expense account brought exposure and recall.

The next year, now a self-styled naval liaison officer from the Department of State, Weyman took charge of a visit from Princess Fatima of Afghanistan. With her money, he took her to Washington in a private railroad car

Disguised as a U.S. Navy officer, Stanley Weyman *(far right)* helped Afghanistan's Princess Fatima *(center)* obtain an introduction to President Warren Harding.

and put her up at the swank Willard Hotel. Then, dressed more or less as a naval officer, he had her and himself received by the secretary of state and President Warren Harding. By the time inquiries were made, he was back in Brooklyn, in civilian clothes. Unfortunately, the princess's son saw Weyman's picture in the paper later, when he was posing as the Health Commission's representative in the New York clinic of a famous surgeon, and again he was put in prison. When he emerged, he was an authority on penal psychiatry and spoke on the topic to an admiring audience of professionals.

When film flame Rudolph Valentino died in 1926, the most stricken of all his admirers was actress Pola Negri, who came to New York in hysterics. Weyman grabbed his medical bag and rushed to her hotel. "Rudy," he told her, "would have wanted me to take care of you." He moved into her suite, dosed her with aspirin, and issued press bulletins as her personal physician. After his

exposure, Negri refused to file a complaint, saying he was the best doctor she had ever had or ever expected to have.

Weyman turned to the practice of law in the late 1920s, for which he served a few more years in prison. When World War II began, he became Dr. Stanley Clifford Weyman (again), this time offering consulting services for draft dodgers. He taught clients how to fake stupidity, impaired hearing, and heart trouble, and the Federal Bureau of Investigation prescribed another seven years. Back on the streets in 1948, Weyman went to the United Nations, where he worked as a reporter for two years before being discovered.

The compulsive impostor once said that "one of the first things an ambitious lad learns is that every opportunity for increasing his fame should be taken advantage of." But after a final arrest for obtaining $8,100 in fraudulent home-repair loans (he had no home to repair), Weyman seemed to lose his taste for those short, dramatic moments in the limelight, perhaps exhausted by the high price he had paid for them. At the end, he was working as a night manager at a Yonkers, New York, motel, playing no one but himself. One night in August 1960, the sixty-nine-year-old Weyman was held up by two men and shot dead defending the cash box—an imaginary man finally discovering the real hero within. □

Celebrity Crowd

George Robert Gabor was an artiste of imposture, a class act of irresistible polish and flair, capable of spinning as many illusory identities as a situation demanded. He was born, he claimed, in Hungary in 1906 and came to America in 1921. Over the next thirteen years, even with time wasted behind bars, he successfully posed as a German baron, an ambassador's son, a polo champion, an intrepid aviator, an assistant solicitor general of the United States, an undercover investigator, and a motion-picture magnate. A frequent guest of the rich and famous, he paved his way with calls and letters from important people—usually himself—and then arrived to charm his victims. They, accustomed to taking fellow celebrities at face value, gladly made loans and took checks to relieve the impostor's perpetual "temporary" financial embarrassment.

His best role may have been that of His Excellency the Baron Frederick von Krupp, Jr., son of the German munitions maker. As the baron, Gabor toured the country in a car Henry Ford gave him, visited the DuPont chemical plants, met Thomas Edison, and was royally entertained. But in Los Angeles, he overdid the part when he told a reporter that, as future director of Krupp, he would melt the guns into farming tools. When this assertion appeared in the international press, the Krupps exposed him. He was deported—but soon returned to America as an ambassador's son and daring aviator.

In 1935, the Federal Bureau ◊

of Investigation found Gabor working as the manager of a huge doll factory in Trenton, New Jersey, and of a large chain of movie theaters besides. After another stint in prison, he was deported for the fourth—and last—time in 1936. No one knows if the resourceful impostor, then only thirty, returned to the United States in another, impenetrable guise.

According to a man who made individual human histories his business, almost nothing is known about Gabor's real identity. Writing in the *American Magazine* in 1937, FBI director J. Edgar Hoover ruefully conceded that, whoever Gabor was, all that was known of him for sure was his record of prison terms and deportations. □

Occupation: Impostor

Perhaps no impostor in this century has played more roles, to greater effect, than the man born Ferdinand Waldo Demara, Jr., in Lawrence, Massachusetts, in 1921. Equipped with a formidable capacity for learning new skills quickly, he was an A student who could never squeeze himself into the behavioral mold of the classroom; much of his youth was spent searching for structure. He entered a Rhode Island monastery, then the U.S. armed forces, from which he deserted and was eventually dishonorably

discharged. By the time he was twenty-four, he had been in—and out of—twelve different Catholic orders, with many more to come. As Demara made imposture his vocation, however, he achieved a kind of great-

ness. At various times he was a deputy sheriff in Washington State, a civil engineer in the Yucatán, a college dean in Pennsylvania, and a teacher of languages and science across the land—former students still remember him fondly. He applied the lessons of an eighteen-month term in the navy brig at San Pedro (for desertion) to become a credible assistant warden at a Texas prison. A big, friendly, red-faced, hard-drinking man who looked like a linebacker and spoke pure South Boston, Demara easily donned the identity of Sunday-school teacher, lawyer, hospital orderly, public speaker, child-care expert, psychology professor, newspaper editor, cancer researcher, accountant.

The high point among his myriad short lives must have been the role of Dr. Joseph Cyr, surgeon lieutenant in the Royal Canadian Navy. In 1951, off Korea aboard the rolling destroyer *Cayuga*, Demara performed daring, complex, and successful surgery on a boatload of wounded Korean soldiers, although he had never even touched most of the instruments involved. Sweating with terror, and fortified with rum and prayer, he operated through the night and saved his patients. Later he helped more wounded Koreans and performed a difficult lung resection by following an article in a medical magazine. He was called a "miracle doctor" and became a hero—too much of one, as it turned out. When the resulting publicity reached the real Dr. Cyr,

Demara was exposed and drummed out of the Canadian navy.

Usually he brought on his own downfall by his unbridled enthusiasm and his pursuit of excellence in any life he undertook. He was called, and was, "pushy," seldom bothering with official permission for his plans. A detective who arrested him on a remote island off the coast of Maine, where he was teaching school as Martin Godgart, suggested that he expected too much of life and took on new identities to open new worlds. Robert Crichton, in his 1959 book, *The Great Imposter,* suggested that impostures were simply irresistible fun. For some, perhaps—but not for Demara. "Every time I take a new identity," he said, "some part of me dies."

Perhaps there was not much left

of him, then, when further publicity terminally cramped his style. A 1952 story in *Life* magazine exposed his impostures and haunted Demara for years as its reappearance brought lost jobs and blackmail attempts. Crichton's popular book, and the ensuing 1960 Tony Curtis film, applied the *coup de grâce.* Enduringly famous as Ferdinand Waldo Demara, Jr., he could become no one else; according to friends, the ebullient impostor sank into depression. From 1959 onward, he apparently lived under his own name, more or less—as Fred Demara—and turned his talents to performing good works. Before his death at the age of sixty, from heart failure, in 1982, Demara was a minister to the sick and dying in an Anaheim, California, hospital. □

Tinsel Prince

When an admirer chided Prince Dimitri Michael Obolenski-Romanoff for gaining illegal entry to the United States by bribing officials, the dashing little deportee replied in a reproachful Oxford accent, "Don't you know I never pay for anything?" In fact, he rarely needed to. His glittering circle of friends cheerfully loaned him money, with the treasures of the Romanoffs—deposed family of Russia's last czar—as security. Merchants and hotelkeepers accepted the checks he signed *romanoff* with the air of a man signing an autograph. When compelled to press charges against him, they did so regretfully. And when his benefactors learned that

he was merely Harry Gerguson—once the despair of various New York orphanages—they found him more delightful yet.

Romanoff somehow split the difference. On the one hand he maintained that he was a New York-born American citizen and not deportable; and on the other he said that he was Prince Michael, variously cousin, brother, or nephew of Czar Nicholas II, the ruler who was killed with all his family in 1918 by Soviet revolutionaries. Few agreed. Britain's Scotland Yard called him "a rogue of uncertain ◊

Although few people believed that he was a genuine Russian prince, Dimitri Michael Obolenski-Romanoff burnished his false claim to royal blood as the eccentric owner of Hollywood's celebrated watering spot: Romanoff's.

A Billy Tipton Trio publicity shot shows jazz saxophonist Tipton flanked by drummer Dick O'Neal *(left)* and bassist Ron Kilde.

nationality," possibly from Lithuania, who ran up a police record in Paris and London. Deported from America ten times, he made an art of returning as a stowaway, sleeping in empty first-class cabins and charming legitimate passengers in the first-class bar. He even charmed his way, briefly, into Harvard, wearing a monocle and claiming his college records had been destroyed in the revolution.

After officials grew tired of deporting him, Romanoff starred in a Broadway musical, *Say When,* and then went west to become what the *New York Times* called "one of the most beloved impostors Hollywood has ever harbored." In 1940, backed by celebrity admirers, he opened a Beverly Hills restaurant, modestly called Romanoff's and decorated with portraits of himself. For more than two decades, it was one of Tinseltown's favorite watering spots.

The ersatz prince, who never quite acknowledged his masquerade, ran his famous restaurant with regal arrogance, habitually dining alone with his two bulldogs, Socrates and Confucius, who daintily ate with napkins around their necks. Respectability triumphed in 1958, when an act of Congress allowed him to become a genuine and undisputed American citizen. He closed Romanoff's in 1962 and died in Beverly Hills of a heart attack nine years later—eternally the faker whose imposture had never mattered in the slightest to his celebrity friends. □

Blue Note

Billy Tipton's career as a jazz pianist and saxophonist spanned fifty years of American music, from the big bands of the 1930s and 1940s through the Billy Tipton Trio of the 1950s to club dates in Spokane, Washington. Well liked by fellow artists, Tipton was a scoutmaster and father to three adopted sons. In fact, the highly regarded musician had carried out a lifelong masquerade.

When Tipton died of a bleeding ulcer in 1989, the funeral director showed one of the musician's shaken sons "a little yellow piece of paper," a form where the box marked "sex" was checked "female." Claiming that he had suffered a sexually incapacitating injury, Tipton had lived with his ex-wife, Kitty, for nine years. She said she had never guessed his secret. No one had. Apparently, the person known as Billy Tipton had put on a man's identity to follow her talent into the rigidly male domain of instrumental jazz, where she won fame—and anonymity: No one knows who she really was. □

PRANKS AND PRANKSTERS

Often, some irrepressible element of the human spirit rises to pranks or to those who play them, attracted by the élan with which a trick is executed, the hilarious incongruity, the harmless game of confidence—and the innate good nature behind acts intended to trigger laughter, not destruction. Where many hoaxes are launched purely with an eye to revenge or profit, these more or less innocent deceptions are just humorous manipulations of perception and reality. Some spring from an ambush of props, costumes, accomplices, and clever scripts. Others are creatures of the instant, created by the prankster's sense that someone nearby is ripe for duping.

Often, a joker's genius is a large talent pressed into the service of a prank: Actors give brilliant performances in an offstage joke; journalists cleverly reclothe rubbish in the staid costume of The News. And in all great deceptions, the recipient of the jest should derive as much amusement from it as its author. In practical jokes there is a symbiotic relationship between the tricker and the tricked, and an implicit recognition that it is impossible to say which human appetite is greater: to be the fooler or the fooled.

Hookster

One of the more ambitious pranks of history was the so-called Berners Street Hoax, which was masterminded in 1809 by writer and prankster *extraordinaire* Theodore Edward Hook. His motive for the hoax has been muddied by time, but the spirit of the gag is feebly echoed by the modern joker who orders an armada of pizzas delivered to some unsuspecting victim in the space of an hour. In the social climate of Georgian England, however, and with a titanic prankster such as Hook in command, the trick assumed gargantuan proportions.

Hook spent six weeks laying the groundwork for an invasion aimed at a detested neighbor who lived across the street from him. Enlisting the help of friends, he sent out some 4,000 letters of an urgent and enticing nature to tradespeople, professionals, and politicians of all kinds, requesting an appointment with each on November 10, 1809, and signing off as Mrs. Tottenham of 54 Berners Street.

On the appointed morning, the drama opened in the gray light of predawn as an army of chimney sweeps descended on Mrs. Tottenham's door. From then on through the day, in wave after wave, visitors and merchants by the hundreds arrived, choking the street and inspiring this contemporary newspaper account of the events: "Wagons laden with coals from the Paddington wharves, upholsterers' goods in cart-loads, organs, pianofortes, linen, jewellry, and every other description of furniture, were lodged as near as possible to the door of No. 54, with anxious tradesmen and a laughing mob. About this time, the Lord Mayor arrived in his carriage." Everyone and everything imaginable, including a coffin—made to measure in Mrs. Tottenham's exact size—arrived at 54 Berners Street that day.

Meanwhile, a gratified Hook is said to have enjoyed a ringside view from his window across the street. Although Londoners had a fair suspicion as to who had caused all the fuss, Hook's biographer later noted that the hoax had been so well executed that "Theodore Hook, after a temporary visit to the country, returned unmolested, and more famous than ever, to his usual occupations."

But life played its share of jokes on Hook, as well. Four years after introducing Mrs. Tottenham to havoc, the twenty-four-year-old trickster acquired the post of accountant-general and treasurer of Mauritius, then a British colony. The job ruined him. Having neither arithmetic nor business sense, Hook was completely unable to manage the colony's accounts and came up thousands of pounds short. His property in Mauritius and England was seized by the Crown, and he spent two years in prison, after which he took up "the life of the hunted and harassed author," as one biographer put it, "and the scenes which had shone and sparkled were darkened by the great shadow of his unredeemed and unredeemable debt." Hook died in 1841, "done up," as he said near the end, "in purse, in mind, and in body." □

Theodore Edward Hook was drawn by Daniel Maclise for *The Choice Humorous Works, Ludicrous Adventures, Bon Mots, Puns and Hoaxes of Theodore Hook.*

Sothern Exposure

The famous nineteenth-century British actor Edward Askew Sothern is best remembered professionally for his creation of Lord Dundreary, a stereotypical English nobleman parodied in *Our American Cousins.* The play delighted audiences in New York and London. But for those who were exposed to Sothern personally, the actor may have been less memorable for his stage work than for his performances in an improvisational form of theater: the practical joke.

Born on April Fools' Day, 1826, the Liverpudlian player had a passion for pranks that amounted to a mania, which he pursued until his death in 1881. The British mail was a favorite medium for the gags that Sothern evidently pulled on an almost daily basis. One was to send a postcard addressed in pencil to a distant friend, with a plan for the card to be repeatedly erased and readdressed to a succession of far-flung correspondents. Eventually an unsuspecting friend of Sothern's—usually one living nearby—would receive the puzzling postcard, now bearing exotic postmarks from around the world. In another, simpler postal prank, Sothern would simply lift a stranger's letters from the post rack and scrawl an anonymous message—"I will bring the five peacocks with me on Saturday," for example—across the back of an envelope.

His own envelopes bore such disconcerting labels as "Boodles' Bee Hive," "Asylum for Confirmed Virgins," and "Troop Ship *Crocodile.*" Some, calculated to unnerve the recipient, contained small cloth samples, purportedly from "Southwell Smallpox Hospital" or the "Home for Incurable Itch." Sothern also liked to telegraph friends advising them of the demise—and impending arrival of the remains—of a total stranger.

Many Sothern pranks were elaborately staged, none more than a little drama performed for a compatriot, Philip Lee, on his first visit to New York, where Sothern was living and working at the time. Lee complained that he had seen no evidence of the wild American bohemian life one heard of in Europe. Sensing an opportunity for a good joke, Sothern explained that Lee had simply been mixing with the wrong crowd and generously offered to arrange a ◊

Edward Askew Sothern is shown costumed for his famous Lord Dundreary role at London's Haymarket Theatre in 1861.

dinner party at his hotel where Lee could meet some real bohemians.

When the visitor arrived at Sothern's private dining room, he saw nothing unusual in the assembled dinner guests. But as the soup was served, Lee noticed something ominous. One by one, each guest reached into his coat to withdraw a lethal weapon of some kind, which he then set casually on the table. Soon battle-axes, guns, billy clubs, and knives lay side by side with forks and spoons. "Keep quiet," Sothern warned the nervous Lee. "They are getting ready to discuss literature." The group, he explained, had quarreled earlier over the merits of a certain book; worse, they were all inclined to violence and had been drinking heavily. Inevitably, a raucous brawl broke out, replete with gunfire and flashing knives. "Defend yourself! This is butchery—sheer butchery!" cried one of the guests as he handed a long knife to the visitor. "Keep cool," advised the unflappable Sothern, "and *don't get shot!*" By then, the entire hotel had been aroused by the noise, and Sothern had to confess that his wild bohemians were all actors.

Although he loved elaborate pranks, Sothern was just as fond of tricks concocted spontaneously, in the course of daily life. Once, when a late arrival for one of his dinner parties was finally announced, Sothern told his other guests to hide under the table. "We'll give him a good shock," the host said. The guests complied, but then, when the latecomer walked in and asked where everyone was, Sothern gave the joke a last-minute twist. "Strange thing," he said. "The moment they heard your name they all got under the table." □

Humbug Himself

"Every crowd has a silver lining," P. T. Barnum, America's famous nineteenth-century showman, used to say. Indeed, if anyone could speak with authority on such a subject, it was Barnum. In a career that spanned almost six decades, the self-styled Prince of Humbug proved uniquely adept at stripping the silver from a crowd and lining his own pockets with it.

Born Phineas Taylor Barnum in Bethel, Connecticut, in 1810, the man who would eventually be dubbed the Shakespeare of American advertising inaugurated his special relationship with the American public at age twenty-five with an ad in a New York paper. He had discovered, he said, "Joice Heth, nurse to Gen. George Washington (the father of our country), who has arrived at the astonishing age of 161 years!" Heth, though dwindled now to a mere forty-six pounds, the ad continued, could relate many interesting tales of "the boy Washington." Any doubters were invited to examine "original, authentic and indisputable documents" proving her identity.

In the two weeks following the ad's appearance, 10,000 curious New Yorkers crowded the open-air Niblo Gardens to see a wizened, blind black woman whom Barnum had bought for $500 and promoted as Joice Heth. Local papers buzzed with controversy over the "living mummy," and one physician ventured that having made it to 161, the venerable nanny might be headed for immortality.

As Gotham's excitement over Heth inevitably began to wane, Barnum took his ancient wonder on the road. During her stint in Boston, an anonymous letter in a newspaper suggested that Heth might be a fraud. She was "not a human being," the letter said, but a "curiously constructed automaton" of whalebone and India rubber. Interest in Heth as a fraud soon had her packing the exhibition halls again.

The anonymous letter was, of course, the work of Barnum himself, typifying the strategies behind his lifelong belief that "the bigger the humbug, the better the people will like it." By 1841, Barnum was practicing hoaxes on a much grander scale at his new American

Museum in New York. Bright lights and banners drew people to the huge building where, for twenty-five cents, they could wander through 6,000 exhibits that included curiosities such as the Feejee Mermaid (an artfully sewn hybrid of a monkey and a fish), the Woolly Horse, and Chang and Eng, the Siamese twins—a term coined by Barnum. From a balcony outside the museum, a band of musicians blasted abrasive music that was calculated to send people scurrying inside, where a big sign reading THIS WAY TO THE EGRESS steered many hopeful egret lovers through a door that emptied

back onto the street. For another twenty-five cents, they could try the route again.

Among the most famous attractions that Barnum promoted at this time was Charles Stratton, a twenty-five-inch-tall five-year-old midget from Bridgeport, Connecticut. Barnum had dubbed Stratton General Tom Thumb and billed him as "a dwarf of eleven years of age, just arrived from England." The discrepancies between the truth and Barnum's claims about Stratton were typical of the fine-tuning in all

vintage Barnum illusions, where simple exaggeration gently closed the gap between what he had to offer and what his intuition told him the public would want. "It was my monomania to make the museum the town wonder and the town talk," Barnum would write in his autobiography, and by the mid-1840s he had done just that, tripling its annual income and amassing a huge personal fortune.

But in 1855, the master of humbug was himself swindled by a bad investment that left him bankrupt. In the tough years that followed, both Iranistan—Barnum's palatial Bridgeport estate—and his beloved American Museum burned to the ground. Then, like a creature that he himself might exhibit, Barnum rose from the ashes of financial ruin and—through hard work and a European lecture tour on "the Art of Getting Money" and "the Philosophy of Humbug"—rebuilt both his bank account and his museum. When the museum was again destroyed by fire in 1868, however, Barnum read the loss as an omen and decided to retire from show business—but not for long.

Two years later, the irrepressible huckster was back in business and bigger than ever with Barnum's Great Traveling World's Fair. By 1889, when Barnum and partner James A. Bailey took their three-ring circus to London, the troupe had established a worldwide reputation under the modest, enduring sobriquet the Greatest Show on Earth. Appropriately, the act that drew the greatest applause from admiring London crowds that year—two years before the great showman's death in 1891—was old Barnum himself, circling the ring in an open coach. □

Abyssinian Chats

A man who will take time out from his honeymoon to play a trick involving horse manure is a man who will do anything in the name of a practical joke. British-born William Horace de Vere Cole was just such an animal. On a spring night in 1919, he slipped away from his bride in Venice and, traveling by gondola, imported a load of manure from a suburban riding stable. This he distributed in small mounds around the famous Piazza San Marco. The next morning—not coincidentally, April 1—he had the satisfaction of seeing crowds of Venetians puzzle over this mysterious evidence of a nocturnal equine visitation to the horseless, canal-bound city.

The Venice caper was characteristic of Cole's pranks, which tended toward simple, high-spirited fun, executed with a confidence and style that

made him a legend among hoaxers. From a comparatively privileged background himself—born in 1881, he was the eldest son of a major in the Dragoon Guards—Cole often targeted his peers. For example, playing on the innate good manners of the well-bred English gent, Cole would pose as a surveyor on the street and politely ask a passing swell to help by holding one end of a string for a moment. Then the prankster would disappear around the corner, find another man to hold the other end of the string, and walk away.

He was also fond of spontaneous pranks. When he stumbled on a

road crew without a foreman one day, Cole leaped into the breach and directed the men to London's busy Piccadilly Circus, where he had them excavate a huge trench in the street. A nearby policeman obligingly redirected the heavy downtown traffic all day, and it was several hours before the city noticed the unauthorized hole.

But of all the hoaxes perpetrated in a lifetime of them, the most famous was one of Cole's first. Sometimes called the *Dreadnought* Affair, the elaborate gag took place in 1910. Cole and five young friends, posing as the emperor of Abyssinia and his retinue, arranged a VIP tour of HMS *Dreadnought,* the mightiest and most heavily guarded warship in the British navy. Cole chose for himself the demanding role of Mr. Cholmondeley, the Foreign Office official escorting the party, and assigned to his friend Adrian Stephen another major speaking part as interpreter for the group. The other four pranksters—Anthony Buxton, Guy Ridley, Duncan Grant, and Stephen's sister Virginia (later novelist Virginia Woolf)—undertook the primarily silent but elaborately costumed roles of the Abyssinian emperor and three princes.

After being welcomed aboard by the commander in chief, Admiral Sir William May, and a special honor guard, the bearded, turbaned troupe received a forty-minute tour of the latest in gun turrets, range finders, and wireless installations. "Bunga-bunga!" the royals exclaimed admiringly, while "interpreter" Stephen spouted translations to them in a hybrid of slurred Swahili, Latin, and Greek. The act must have been convincing, for even when Stephen and his sister found themselves face to face with an officer who was also their cousin, their disguises remained impenetrable.

Cole revealed the hoax to the newspapers the next day, outraging many. But the incident made its mark. Security rules aboard British warships were eventually tightened, causing Virginia—known aboard the *Dreadnought* as Abyssinia's Prince Mendex—to remark: "I am glad to think that I too have been of help to my country." And the mock-Abyssinian exclamation "Bunga-bunga" enjoyed a rush of popularity in London dance halls.

Cole died in France in 1936, aged fifty-four, reflective but still lighthearted to the end. □

Sarcophagal Scribe

When Charles Langdon Clarke, a reporter for Toronto's *Daily Mail and Empire,* got bored, he would sometimes amuse himself by rewriting stories from the Old and New Testaments as imaginary news items for two imaginary newspapers—the *Babylon Gazette* and the *Jerusalem Times.* On one Saturday in 1923, however, he decided to apply his creative journalism to current events. And he had a perfect target.

The papers that weekend carried rapturous accounts of the recently discovered tomb of ancient Egypt's King Tutankhamen. "This has been perhaps the most extraordinary day in the whole history of Egyptian excavation," a front-page *Mail and Empire* article had raved that morning, detailing at length the wondrous inscriptions and treasures and statues gracing the chambers of the tomb. It was "such a hoard as the most sanguine excavator can hardly have pictured, even in visions in his sleep."

Sensing the sweet scent of parody in such high-flown stuff, Clarke decided to flesh out this most sanguine excavator's visions. That same evening, in the *Mail and Empire's* weekend *Sunday World,* Clarke published a front-page story on King Tut's Golden Typewriter, which he said had also been discovered in the remarkable tomb. A blank sheet of papyrus was loaded in the resplendent machine, Clarke reported, and an alabaster cuspidor and other such luxurious desk accessories were found nearby, evoking, perhaps, an early

A rounded oblong box found in the tomb of Egypt's King Tutankhamen is capped with the royal name in hieroglyphics.

newspaper reporter's work station.

Early Monday morning, a reporter from a rival newspaper was sent to interview Dr. C. T. Currelly, a renowned Egyptologist, to get his opinion of the extraordinary artifacts found in the tomb. Currelly's actual remarks are lost to history, but he was not amused. □

Key players in the *Dreadnought* Affair: Standing from left are Guy Ridley, William Horace de Vere Cole, Adrian Stephen, and Duncan Grant; seated are Anthony Buxton *(right)* and Virginia Stephen (famous author Virginia Woolf).

Martians from Mercury

At 8:00 p.m. on October 30, 1938, Columbia Broadcasting System's "Mercury Theatre on the Air" played its familiar theme—Tchaikovsky's Piano Concerto in B Flat Minor no. 1—and announced that the night's drama was a radio adaptation of English author H. G. Wells's *The War of the Worlds.* Then, twenty-three-year-old actor-impresario Orson Welles began his now-fabled broadcast of a Martian invasion. Things moved in a slow pastiche at first; a rather scholarly lecture from Welles on extraterrestrials gave way to an announcer with the weather and then a rousing segment of dance music. Suddenly, the tone and tempo of the broadcast altered ominously, as the excited voices of Mercury players, using the recently introduced style of break-in news flashes, reported that a meteor had landed in Grovers Mills, New Jersey, killing 1,500 people. Soon, a report came in that the projectile had not been a meteorite at all. It appeared to be a metal cylinder, which began to open, and something emerged, "lurking out of the shadow like a gray snake. Another one and another one and another one," the rattled reporter blathered on. "They look like tentacles to me. I can see the thing's body. Its skin is like leather, but its face—ladies and gentlemen, it's indescribable."

No doubt, most of the audience was aware that this was theater, not news. But, at 8:12 that evening, a coincidence vastly magnified the impact of the Martian broadcast. The immensely popular act of Edgar Bergen and his urbane dummy Charlie McCarthy, broadcast in the same 8:00 to 9:00 p.m.

Sunday slot, temporarily went off the air while a little-known singer performed. Thousands of bored listeners twisted their radio dials, many of them to tune in Orson Welles on CBS, too late for the initial disclaimers. Unaware that they were hearing fiction, they lis-

tened transfixed. Apprised of the horrifying flaming deaths in New Jersey and New York from lethal "Martian rays," they ran screaming into the streets, convinced that their world was ending. No one seemed dissuaded by the impossible quantity of action by both Martians and terrestrials crammed into the forty-minute broadcast.

Vivid Hughes

When Brian G. Hughes died in 1924 at the age of seventy-five, his *New York Times* obituary hailed him first as "FAMOUS JOKER" and then, in much smaller letters below, as "Banker and Manufacturer." In fact, as a paper-box manufacturer and founder and president of the Dollar Savings Bank of the Bronx, Hughes had proved himself a shrewd businessman and enjoyed more financial success than most. But such sober, adult triumphs paled beside his glorious successes as one of the country's most creative practical jokers.

Typical of Brian Hughes's good-humored and well-prepared hoaxes was his playing Pygmalion to an alley cat bought for a dime. The scrubby feline was carefully groomed, installed in a gilded cage guarded by a uniformed attendant, and fed a royal diet of chicken and ice cream. Then, claiming he had one of the great Irish Brindles—namely, Nicodemus by Broomstick out of Dustpan Sweeper—Hughes entered his ten-cent stray in a prestigious New York cat show and took first prize. On another occasion, Hughes solemnly presented the Brooklyn Board of Aldermen with a piece of land for a permanent public park. The aldermen gratefully accepted, only to discover that the real estate in question measured two by eight feet and had cost Hughes a total of fifty-five dollars.

To feed his voracious appetite for pulling the public leg, Hughes kept a number of simpler jokes in more or less constant play. He sometimes posted large signs reading NOT FOR SALE on his various properties. In another favor- ◊

By morning, however, it was clear to everyone that the invasion had not been real, and a backlash of indignant anger rose against Welles and his players. In the prevailing atmosphere of impending global war, people were understandably skittish about any threats—even from Martians—and many felt manipulated by the stunt. Eventually, however, these negative feelings—like the false rumors of widespread panic suicides and injuries caused by the hoax—subsided, and Welles's name as a dramatic genius was made. The same glory, alas, did not befall other radio performers who decided to air their versions of *The War of the Worlds.* A similar 1944 broadcast in Chile caused widespread panic. Another, in Quito, Ecuador, in 1949, provoked retaliation by an angry mob that burned down the radio station, killing fifteen people.

More than fifty years after its execution, Welles's production remains a legend—not just for causing a monumental stir, but as a work of technical brilliance and as the occasion for a fascinating case study of social psychology. But its real distinction lies in the fact that the broadcast never intended to deceive. When he apologized a day after the show, Welles insisted that he had hesitated to air the play, not for fear that people might panic, but that they "might be bored or annoyed at hearing a tale so improbable." Scriptwriter Howard Koch was similarly distressed by the drab quality of the radio play, and five days before the broadcast he had tried to persuade his colleagues to abandon the project altogether. But the only alternative drama the troupe had in the works—*Lorna Doone*—seemed even drearier. In a last-minute rescue effort, editor John Houseman would later recall, the Mercury team decided to emphasize the newscast style of the play, spicing it heavily with "circumstantial allusions and authentic detail." The changes saved the play—and inadvertently spawned an enduring, first-rate deception. □

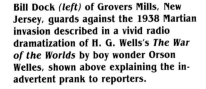

Bill Dock (*left*) of Grovers Mills, New Jersey, guards against the 1938 Martian invasion described in a vivid radio dramatization of H. G. Wells's *The War of the Worlds* by boy wonder Orson Welles, shown above explaining the inadvertent prank to reporters.

ite prank, he would leave an expensive umbrella hanging on a bar rail, as if abandoned there. Eventually some unsuspecting victim would pinch it. But opening the ill-gotten item advertised the crime: A large sign reading Stolen from B. G. Hughes, America, unfolded with the bumbershoot.

Like all pranksters whose feats pass into legend, Hughes has been credited with many escapades that have become somewhat fuzzy in

their facts. He is said, for example, to have once caused panic among officials at the Metropolitan Museum of Art by mischievously leaving a set of burglar's tools and several empty picture frames on the museum steps. Similar effects were produced with a bag of brass filings (labeled $50,000 gold, U.S. Mint) left by Hughes in New York's Ashbury Park, and a bag of fake jewelry planted on the sidewalk opposite Tiffany's.

Incorrigible practical jokers such as Hughes inevitably draw some return fire. Hughes got his in a scam in which he tried to give an old wreck of a home he billed as "the Lafayette House" to a historical association. New York's Archaeological Society solemnly accepted his offer, on the condition that he accept its counteroffer of a property it thought would be a suitable Hughes residence—a Connecticut insane asylum. □

Paper-box king and master trickster Brian G. Hughes stands with two pairs of dogs in New York circa 1914.

Deathless Ruse

"There is something in the human mind that turns instinctively to fiction," wrote critic H. L. Mencken *(below)*, "even journalists succumb to it." He made this assertion in 1926, in a column where—for the second time in print—the famous writer confessed that a history he had written of the bathtub in America was a total fiction. In the decades since, nothing has proved his point more powerfully than the persistence of this bathtub fairy tale. Although recognized as fiction by many, it still exerts its appeal on others, who continue to spread Mencken's story as fact.

First printed in the *New York Evening Mail* on December 28, 1917, the story lamented that December 20, allegedly the seventy-fifth anniversary of the "introduction of the bathtub into these states," had gone uncelebrated. The tale was an artful invention, rich with curious detail and full of heroes, villains, politics, and controversy.

Cincinnati merchant Adam Thompson had been the innovator of the American tub in 1842, Mencken said, and in 1851, President Millard Fillmore installed the first tub in the White House—thus ending a long dispute over the potential health hazards posed by such newfangled plumbing. "The example of the President soon broke down all that remained of the old opposition," he wrote, "and by 1860, every hotel in New York had a bathtub, and some had two and even three." Union General George B. McClellan, Mencken noted, introduced bathing into the army in 1862, and in 1870, a tub was used in a Philadelphia prison.

None of it was true. Mencken later explained that his bathtub history had been intended only as "a piece of spoofing to relieve the strain" caused by World War I. But by the time he made this disclaimer, his preposterous story had already been reprinted seriously in dozens of newspapers, in journals, and even in somber works of reference. In some instances, details of the story cropped up again as fact in the same newspapers that earlier had printed Mencken's confession that the bathtub history was a "tissue of absurdities." In 1952, President Truman used Mencken's chronicle in a speech to illustrate progress in public hygiene.

When Mencken died in 1956, his bathtub history still seeped into other writings on the subject. And as late as 1981, the cover for a new book, *Presidential Anecdotes*, featured a picture of President Fillmore—in his celebrated tub. □

Trojan Rhino

One snowy dawn, the inhabitants of the Cornell University campus, in Ithaca, New York, were puzzled by a curious phenomenon: A mysterious trail of a large animal's footprints led across the snow-covered campus to the edge of Beebe Lake. They appeared to be the tracks of a rhinoceros. A large hole in the ice fifty yards out on the frozen lake suggested that the poor, displaced beast had come to a frigid end. Because Beebe Lake supplied the campus with its water, news of the incident reportedly caused half the university's population to give up drinking tap water. The other half claimed it could taste rhinoceros. A few days later, to general relief and chagrin, a student named Hugh Troy revealed that the rhinoceros tracks had been nothing but a well-executed hoax.

Troy considerately kept the identity of the pranksters a secret at the time, but today the 1920s rhinoceros gag is known to have been an early brainstorm of Troy himself—one of many, for, over the years, Troy earned himself quite a name as writer, artist, and practical joker. Like all his pranks, the rhinoceros trick was conceived in an inspirational flash, then meticulously executed with a rhino foot a friend used as a wastebasket.

By 1962—two years before his death at fifty-eight—Troy had become so notorious as a prankster that *Washington Post* reporter Tom Wolfe—who would eventually become famous in his own right as a best-selling author—dubbed Troy "America's all-time free-style practical joke champion."

Most of Troy's early capers were perpetrated in New York. He ◊

Pasta Plantations

Well known for his sober and penetrating review of current affairs, British Broadcasting Corporation television commentator Richard Dimbleby moved easily between world events and the lighter topics of the day. "Spring has come early this year," Dimbleby reported on a 1957 edition of the BBC's "Panorama," and as a result the spaghetti harvest in Switzerland would be much earlier too. As violins soared in the background, the camera cut away from the somber anchorman to an Alpine scene where peasant girls gathered armloads of spaghetti from pasta-laden trees and spread it all to dry in the sun. Of course, Dimbleby continued, Switzerland's spaghetti farms were "not on anything like the scale" of those in Italy—most notably the vast plantations of the Po Valley. Curious viewers learned more about the stringy dish. For

once brought his own bench to a city park, feigned stealing it, and then waved his bill of sale in the arresting officer's confused face. He had a fire hydrant carved from balsa wood that he placed in front of his house to preserve his parking place while away—a trick exposed when a fire struck his block. Once he attached an artificial hand to his sleeve for the simple satisfaction of leaving his toll ticket and the false hand in the grip of a startled tollbooth attendant.

As a captain in intelligence during World War II, Troy parodied military paperwork by instituting Daily Flypaper Reports, which chronicled the number of dead flies per strip of flypaper—a practice soon required of other units.

Some of Troy's pranks seemed, as Wolfe put it, an attempt to "push a social trend clear over the cliff." When New York's Museum of Modern Art opened the first American van Gogh exhibition in 1935, Troy became annoyed with the huge crowds. Convinced that many were attracted by the lurid aspects of van Gogh's personal life, rather than by any real appreciation of his art, Troy carved an ear from a hunk of dried beef, mounted it in a blue velvet shadow box, and discreetly inserted it into the exhibition with the caption: "THIS IS THE EAR WHICH VINCENT VAN GOGH CUT OFF AND SENT TO HIS MISTRESS, A FRENCH PROSTITUTE, DEC. 24, 1888." As he expected, a mob gathered around the ear, and Troy was able to enjoy the paintings in peace.

In 1952, while living in Washington, D.C., he became disgusted with the flourishing trade of ghostwriting. He ran an ad for "GHOST ARTISTS," supposedly aimed at hardworking but artistic executives. "TOO BUSY TO PAINT?" the ad asked. "WE PAINT IT—YOU SIGN IT!" When the ad sparked several serious news stories, Troy just played along. "I know what we're doing is wrong, absolutely immoral," he confessed to one reporter. "Once they start coming to us, they can never stop." No doubt it was the same for this inveterate, lifelong prankster: Once he started, he could never stop. □

A frame from British television's "Panorama" spoof on April 1, 1957, shows a woman harvesting spaghetti in Switzerland.

example, the oddly uniform length of spaghetti was the result of years of dedicated cultivation, and—good news—the ravenous spaghetti weevil had at last been conquered. The report ended with scenes of merriment at the harvest feast.

More than 250 viewers jammed the BBC switchboards after the hoax aired, and amazingly, the majority were calling with earnest inquiries—where could they go to witness the harvest, where could they buy spaghetti plants? For those anxious to try their hand at homegrown pasta, "Panorama" producer Michael Peacock offered this helpful hint: "Many British enthusiasts have had admirable results from planting a small tin of spaghetti in tomato sauce."

In fact, the spaghetti harvest was one of the deftest and most celebrated of media hoaxes. But the two-minute feature had so engaged viewers that many ignored Dimbleby's cautionary sign-off: "That is all from 'Panorama' on this first day of April." □

Bald-Farced Lie

Russell M. Arundel loved fishing for bluefin tuna so much that in 1949 he bought a small island—Outer Bald Tusket—to support his habit. Located in the tuna-rich waters off the southwest coast of Nova Scotia, Outer Baldy, as fishermen called it, was a rocky forty-acre home to a few wild sheep when Arundel bought it for $750. But it was destined for a kind of greatness. One cold day when the fish refused to bite, Arundel waved his idle fishing rod scepter-fashion and rechristened his island the Principality of Outer Baldonia. He pronounced himself its regal leader, Prince Russell, knighted his fishing mates as honorary vassal princes, and promoted his fishing guides to six-star admirals in the Outer Baldonian Navy.

As mere whimsy evolved into a more elaborate fancy, Arundel—who when not fishing was a very successful businessman in Washington, D.C.—drew up a constitution that guaranteed his subjects the right to swear, lie, drink, and gamble, and promised freedom from shaving, women, taxes, and other such nagging bores. The prince then launched the paperwork for passports, stamps, and a basic currency—the tunar—for his kingdom and entered a listing in the Washington telephone directory: *Outer Baldonia, Principality of—DI7-2463*.

In short order, a man from the U.S. State Department called the number to ask about Outer Baldonia's principal exports. Then someone from Civil Defense offered Baldonians free leaflets about at-om bomb shelters, and the National Geographic Society wanted the principality's latitude and longitude. The tiny nation had become real, at least to some.

Most who heard of the minuscule island country where subjects were granted the right to "lie about fish and be believed" were charmed by Arundel's harmless fancy. But when the story reached Moscow, a Russian woman named L. Charnaya published a scathing article condemning Outer Baldonia, whose macho constitution, she felt, represented the "completest form of savagery." In a magnanimous show of good manners, Arundel waived his country's law banning women and invited Charnaya to his annual Outer Baldonia tuna tournament. However, Prince Russell added, "getting out of Russia," no mean feat in the late 1940s, "will be her own problem."

Arundel died in 1978 after bequeathing the island to the Canadian Nature Conservancy. □

Mike McGrady and "author" Penelope Ashe hold up a copy of *Naked Came the Stranger,* actually written by McGrady and twenty-four *Newsday* colleagues, eight of whom are shown here.

Jest Seller

As Mike McGrady sat up late one night in June 1966, he brooded—not for the first time—over what he considered the low standards of writing in many current best-selling novels. A columnist for the Long Island newspaper *Newsday,* McGrady decided that instead of getting mad, he would get even. He wrote an inspired memo to his fellow journalists: "As one of *Newsday*'s truly outstanding literary talents, you are hereby officially invited to become the coauthor of a best-selling novel," McGrady's missive began. "There will be an unremitting emphasis on sex," it continued, cautioning that "true excellence in writing will be quickly blue-penciled into oblivion." Twenty-four colleagues accepted the offer, agreeing to produce a chapter apiece for a steamy, sex-in-the-suburbs novel about a glamorous female radio personality: *Naked Came the Stranger.*

With the completed chapters in hand by June 27, McGrady complained that some of the writing was "much too good" and would require a lot of work to be made into bestseller material. Most of the coauthors, however, had risen—or sunk—admirably to the challenge. "Morton Earbrow waited for the sweat to dry," began one chapter; in another, a character in a lively sex scene worried that "the fillings in his teeth would melt."

A Vietnam assignment kept McGrady from following through on his project immediately. But three years later, in August of 1969, his composite masterpiece finally hit the stores. Supposedly written by "demure Long Island housewife" Penelope Ashe, a pretty brunette

pictured stroking an Afghan dog on the book's cover, the "scorching novel" sold more than 20,000 advance copies and drew inquiries for film rights from twenty producers within the first month of its publication. Ashe—really Billie Young, a Long Island housewife and McGrady's sister-in-law—made the rounds of publicity interviews, dutifully dropping stunning profundities such as: "A writer's gotta impale his guts on the typewriter."

But, like Frankenstein's monster, McGrady's raunchy creation acquired a life of its own—and refused to die even after the hoax

was exposed in mid-August. The hardback and paperback publishers, who had themselves been hoodwinked initially, laughed all the way to the bank as more and more copies sold. McGrady, who split all profits evenly among his twenty-four coauthors, insisted that the stunt had been an exercise in gullibility, although there was talk of a sequel. Instead, in 1970, McGrady published *Stranger than Naked; or, How to Write Dirty Books for Fun and Profit,* dedicated to another best-selling author of sultry sagas: "To Jacqueline Susann, with warmth." □

Raising Cain

Alan Abel's obituary was generous, running several column inches in the January 2, 1980, *New York Times*. The newspaper lauded the deceased as "a writer, musician and film producer who specialized in satire" and who had a flair for "challenging the obvious and stating the outrageous." The rest of Abel's fifty years was succinctly telescoped into a few paragraphs, accurate to a fault—except for one error. Abel, as the *Times* tersely announced two days later, was not dead. The obituary was simply fallout from yet another trick masterminded by Abel himself, a self-styled professional hoaxer.

Since graduating from Ohio State University in 1955, Abel has made it his life's work to concoct such hoaxes, supported by a succession of jobs in music, theater, and publicity, and by friends and occasional donors. Over the years, he has conned the world so often that his pleasantly plump face has become instantly recognizable to many—a fact that has forced Abel backstage for some recent antics. But in many of his earlier gags— his Society for Indecency to Naked Animals (SINA) caper, for instance—Abel performed center stage, deadpanning and ad-libbing with all the panache of a stand-up comic. SINA, as Abel explained when he appeared on television's "Today Show" with actor and fellow cutup Buck Henry in 1959, hoped to promote higher standards of decency by clothing naked animals and setting up a national system of animal restrooms. Many found the ideas odd, but most believed that Abel was sincere. One San Francisco woman even tried to donate $40,000 to the cause. Abel, who insists his pranks are for fun, not money, declined the gift by saying SINA could not accept money from outsiders.

In the 1960s, Abel found himself turning down contributions again when the world embraced a nonexistent presidential candidate that he had created with the help of his wife, Jeanne, a writer who often assists in Abel's scams. Jeanne introduced herself over the radio as independent candidate Yetta Bronstein, a Bronx housewife who promised that if elected she would establish national bingo, hang a suggestion box on the White House fence, and print a nude picture of actress Jane Fonda on postage stamps to "give a little pleasure for six cents to those who can't afford *Playboy* magazine." "Bronstein Headquarters" was an answering machine in the storage room of a Fifth Avenue office building. With her slogan of "Vote for Yetta and Watch Things Get Better," Bronstein drew media coverage that would eventually fill four thick scrapbooks. Although she failed in her bid for the presidency in 1964, Bronstein went on to run for mayor of New York and for president again in 1968.

Abel never stops very long at any one gag, as another inevitably appears on his quirky horizon. He has staged an engagement party for African ex-dictator Idi Amin, created Omar's School for Beggars, rented out bald heads as "miniature mobile billboards," and invented the fictitious First Topless String Quartet in 1965, followed by the nonexistent Sex Olympics in 1971. In 1990, he confected a totally fictional, $35 million New York State Lotto winner, the very attractive Miss Charlie Taylor.

In his Lotto scam, however, Abel was performing a charitable act, prompted by actress friend Lee Chirillo's complaint about the scarcity of work. "$35M AND SHE'S SINGLE" announced the front page of one New York paper when Chirillo, as Taylor, held a press conference in a rented hotel suite. "IT'S A HOAX," screamed the front page of a rival daily, whose reporter had recognized Abel in the hall. Having pitted two media monsters against each other, Abel simply let the publicity unfold—swamping Chirillo with job offers. □

Prankster Alan Abel flourishes a newspaper account of another Abel coup: his flattering 1980 obituary, published in the *New York Times*.

Par None

Many *Saturday Review* readers were shocked to learn, in the magazine's April 3, 1971, issue, of a foul plot afoot in Congress. Revealed in an almost full-page letter to the editor from K. Jason Sitewell were details of House Resolution 6142. This obscure bill, "introduced by Congressman A. F. Day and cosponsored by some forty members of the House," Sitewell said, would abolish all private parks of more than 50 acres and all public recreation areas of more than 150 acres that were used by fewer than 150 people a day, averaged over a week. The real effect of the bill, he insisted, would be to abolish all golf courses, both public and private.

Sitewell explained that he himself had been able to divine the true motive of the bill because he had grown up with Congressman Day.

Sitewell thus knew the long history of golf-related family tragedies —a grandfather who "perished in a sand trap," a feckless, golf-obsessed father who died of a coronary after hitting nineteen straight balls into a pond—that had set Day so vehemently against golf. "Everyone who knows what weekends are for," said Sitewell, "has the obligation now to act."

And act they did. Within the next two weeks, panicked constituents contacted dozens of congressmen. Golf clubs held emergency meetings, and the nation's leading weekly golf magazine reprinted Sitewell's letter under the headline, "A Frightening Bill." In the rush to halt the legislation, no one paused to consider the alleged congressman's name, A. F. (as in April Fools') Day, alongside the magazine's date or probed far enough to discover that H.R. 6142 was actually a bill to limit the liability of national banks for certain taxes. On April 10, *Saturday Review* fueled the fire by publishing a rebuttal from Representative Day stating that in an average year golf caused 75,000 coronary occlusions, 9,300 golf-cart fatalities, and 60,000 broken homes. Golfers did not blink at the horrifying statistics.

Within a fortnight, however, the *Wall Street Journal* exposed the antigolf bill and A. F. Day as an April Fools' spoof, and in a May 8 editorial, *Saturday Review* editor Norman Cousins *(left)* confessed that he himself was K. Jason Sitewell. Indeed, Cousins had used the same pseudonym—an imperfect anagram for "It's a joke, son"—in several spoofs he wrote in more than thirty years as editor of the magazine. □

Staged Secrets

The so-called Pentagon Papers—a massive, secret government report on the background of the Vietnam War—were leaked to key newspapers, including the *New York Times*, in the summer of 1971 and published in defiance of a government order. A chilling peek behind the apparatus of war, the documents helped to erode public support of an already-unpopular conflict. Hardly had the ink dried on the original, however, than another set of revealing documents cropped up—not in the liberal press, but in the printed voice of American conservatism.

"THE SECRET PAPERS THEY DIDN'T PUBLISH," shouted the big, bold cover headline on the July 27, 1971, issue of *National Review*—a right-wing magazine then owned and edited by forty-five-year-old William F. Buckley, Jr. *(above, right)*, a pundit, author, and television personality. In the magazine, *Review* readers found fourteen pages of memos and correspondence on the Vietnam War, most of them signed by high-ranking government and military officials. Among them were former Secretary of State Dean Rusk and one-time chairman of the Joint Chiefs of Staff Admiral Arthur Radford. The documents took a hard line on the war, urging a "demonstration drop" of a "nuclear device" over North Vietnam and the closing of North Vietnamese ports. Newspapers and broadcasters across the nation swiftly reported the *National Review* exposé, accepting the story as fact.

Buckley was unavailable for

comment when his magazine appeared, having coyly left word that he was "hiding with Daniel Ellsberg"—the former Pentagon aide suspected of leaking the earlier Pentagon documents. But the next day, Buckley called a press conference in New York and, smiling broadly, announced that the memos had been a hoax. The idea for the scam had come to Buckley and five of his colleagues over dinner two weeks earlier, and they had quickly written the documents and gone to press. The point, Buckley claimed, was to prove that "forged documents would be widely accepted as genuine, provided their content was inherently plausible."

But the hoax also tweaked the papers that had published the real Pentagon report. *National Review* had "proceeded in something of an ethical vacuum," Buckley admitted, tongue characteristically in cheek. "The *New York Times* has instructed us that it is permissible to traffic in stolen documents, but they have not yet instructed us on whether it is permissible to traffic in forged documents." □

Upper Crust

When Miss Venetia Crust first surfaced among London's debutantes, she seemed, to *Evening Standard* readers, a breath of fresh air. Here was a girl with style—and, apparently, dazzling good looks to boot. The 1958 season's usually predictable and stodgy parties, reprised in society editor Jeremy Campbell's "In London Last Night" column, seemed to spring to life when they included tidbits about the green-eyed, deliciously wicked newcomer. She reportedly glued money to the pavement "outside the Dorchester" so that she could pour champagne on the poor souls who tried to pick it up. She delighted readers by betting £1,000—set aside by her father for a coming-out party—on a horse race. And she exhibited a charming, if unsequential, brand of wit. "I don't mind the country," the stiletto-heeled socialite once remarked, "I've been in Holland Park [a London suburb] twice this year, and it's still only May."

But Miss Crust was better and worse than trivial and wicked: She was false. In June 1959, a competing London newspaper, the *Daily Mirror*, exposed Venetia and Arnold, her charming fair-haired father, as total fabrications. "Presenting Miss Upper Crust!" cried a *Mirror* headline, which was followed by the real story of the "deb who never was." Placing an announcement in the staid *Times* of London to mark Venetia's coming-out party had doomed the gag, which quickly unraveled. Jeremy Campbell *(below)*, the dubious deb's real parent, was briefly suspended for his prank, although his career survived. He went on to become the *Standard*'s man in Washington, D.C., and to write several books—about science, not high society. □

Bills
WILLIAMSPORT

Heading For Cooperstown

1988 Game Program

Our most famous Bill, Dave Bresnahan

$1.00

Potato Sack

Minor-league baseball player Dave Bresnahan had always wanted to try something, and, one night in August 1987, he decided the time had come. As catcher for the Williamsport Bills in Pennsylvania, Bresnahan was playing a club from Reading in the 137th game of a 140-game season; his Class AA Eastern League team was seventh in its division, and the ballpark was not exactly bristling with excitement. During the fifth inning, Reading put runner Rick Lundblade on third base. Bresnahan signaled to the umpire that he had a problem with his mitt and disappeared into the dugout. When he reappeared, he held a peeled potato carefully concealed in his hand. On the next pitch, he caught the ball in his mitt, then sent the potato hurtling wildly over the head of his third baseman in a calculated imitation of an errant pick-off throw. Lundblade, of course, sprinted home, only to have the crafty catcher tag him out with the real ball.

The potato trick had worked, but officials were not amused. Lundblade was ruled safe, and Bresnahan was charged with an error and fined fifty dollars. His team fired him the next day. Shocked by the outcome of his little hoax, the twenty-five-year-old Bresnahan delivered fifty potatoes in lieu of his fine. "I guess he just decided to retire himself," one colleague remarked of the erstwhile catcher, who had racked up a modest .149 batting average in thirty-two games that season. But his hoax had left its mark. Two days after his vegetable improvisation, Bresnahan's former ball club pro-

moted Potato Night, admitting any fan with a potato for only one dollar. Ex-catcher Bresnahan worked his way through the bleachers, autographing potatoes with the inscription "This spud's for you." A year later, Bresnahan, then an Arizona real estate agent, was invited back to Williamsport to recreate his potato trick—but no one has asked him to play ball. □

Wherefore Art?

A noted spotter of new trends, the *Washington Post*'s "Style" section scooped its rivals on May 2, 1986, with news of a remarkable new diet plan. A New Yorker named Joe Bones, it said, was marketing a slimming system called the Fat Squad. "It's the newest strategic advance in the ongoing Battle of the Bulge," the article announced as it described how—for $300 a day for at least three days—Bones's Fat Squad "commandos"

could be hired as around-the-clock guards to keep dieters on the straight and narrow. "We're finding out that people simply need to be told what they can and cannot do when it comes to their eating habits," Bones explained to the *Post* reporter. "In many ways, they're reliving their childhood." Although they wished to remain anonymous, two former Fat Squad clients attested to the effectiveness of the commandos' intimidating presence, and Bones's business was hailed as a "thriving enterprise."

Other newspapers quickly picked up the unusual story. On May 13,

Joe Bones and six of his amiable but strict commandos appeared with a former Fat Squad client named Stephanie Martin on ABC-TV's "Good Morning America," then hosted by actor David Hartman. "The interview with David Hartman," Bones would recall later, "was very serious."

But not, perhaps, as serious as the earnest television personality might have wished. "We were had, in spades," Hartman said the day after the Bones interview aired. He made his retraction after the *New York Post* exposed Joe Bones and his Fat Squad as players in yet an-

Joey Skaggs points out kitchen features
in his $1,500 fish condominium on
TV's "Good Morning America" in 1984.

other hoax by veteran media prankster Joey Skaggs, a forty-one-year-old Greenwich Village artist and college instructor. Ironically, Skaggs—who adopted the alias Joe Bones for his Fat Squad stint—had appeared on Hartman's show only a year or so earlier to promote another of his gags: fish-tank condominiums, replete with living rooms, bathrooms, and kitchens, for "upwardly mobile guppies."

Skaggs claims to have used several aliases and masterminded scores of hoaxes in the name of social and political commentary over the years. Some of his earlier works included advertising a celebrity sperm bank, hanging a fifty-foot bra on Wall Street, and announcing a bordello service for canines—the so-called Cat House for Dogs that caused one gullible television station to chide him for animal abuse. With hoaxes such as the Fat Squad story, Skaggs has said, he was targeting the faddish personal health field, hoping to highlight both the irresponsibility of the press and the credulity of the public. As he put it, "I use the media as a medium, as a painter would a canvas."

An earlier poke at the American health fixation in 1981 cast Skaggs as the "world-famous entomologist" Dr. Josef Gregor, who declared that he had developed a miracle vitamin from hormones extracted from a superstrain of cockroaches bred in his laboratory. The vitamin was said to cure arthritis, acne, anemia, and menstrual cramps; it also immunized against the side effects of nuclear radiation. Skaggs, who hired about seventy actor friends to pose as converts to the pill, called his outfit Metamorphosis and wore a giant cockroach on his T-shirt. Although many called to buy Dr. Gregor's pills, no one caught the allusion to Franz Kafka's story "The Metamorphosis," in which the protagonist, Gregor Samsa, inexplicably turns into a giant beetle.

Finally Skaggs leaked the truth to the *Wall Street Journal,* and Dr. Gregor faded into history—for the public at least. Some time later, Skaggs told a reporter he suffered from "a recurring nightmare that two guys dressed in Raid cans are going to come with straitjackets and carry me away." □

Dan's Papers Capers

The Hampton villages on the east end of Long Island have long been popular as a chic summering spot, but people have tended to overlook some of the area's winter holidays. According to the October 5, 1990, *Dan's Papers,* one of several complimentary Hampton weeklies published year-round, the Hamptons have several "Little-Known Winter Holidays" that could make them hot even in chilly January and February. Among the festive options: a champagne celebration of the Real Estate Equinox on January 6, when the falling real estate market hits bottom and begins an upward climb; a "houses from the outside tour" of boarded-up summer homes; and an Eel Festival featuring eel burgers, eel pie, and "a women's jump rope contest where the jump rope is a live eel."

But the event that really appealed to readers—so much so that the paper was soon deluged with calls for more details—was the January 26 Flight to Portugal. Billed as the third annual flight, it was described as a competition in which "a wooden ski jump is erected at the top of the cliff at the Montauk lighthouse, and hundreds of our local young men, in a display of courage and derring-do, drive old automobiles off it and into the sea a hundred feet below."

The Flight to Portugal, like all the other winter holidays, was the creation of *Dan's Papers* editor and publisher, Dan Rattiner, who routinely prints a number of imaginary "news" stories each year. A native of Montauk, the island's easternmost village, Rattiner began publishing his first summer giveaway newspaper, the *Montauk Pioneer,* in 1960. With little interest in hard news, he has opted to offer his bemused readers more creative concoctions: a plea from a local police chief for raw meat donations, to curb the consumption of tourists by a hungry killer shark lurking offshore; imaginary legislation restricting parking to Mercedes, Audis, and BMWs only, to ease a local parking shortage; and an emergency law, passed by the County Board of Supervisors in a 5-to-4 vote, prohibiting fat tourists from the area as of May 1, 1984. This last was the follow-up to another colorful Rattiner gag, in which an alleged Seismological Institute of New York report claimed the area had sunk more than an inch because of the weight of the two million tourists who visit every year.

"I believe the line between fiction and reality is obvious," says Rattiner. Not everyone would agree, especially those who had their hearts set on watching "gaily painted" junkers plummet into a wintry sea and only reluctantly accepted that the Flight to Portugal was a hoax. Although Rattiner—nicknamed the Hoaxer of the Hamptons—has since published a piece explaining that his special holidays were made up, he says he will not be surprised if environmentalists contact him, upset by the idea of old cars littering the ocean floor. □

CARS BLOCKING DRIVEWAY MORE THAN 1 MIN. BECOME PROPERTY OF DANS PAPERS PARK IN BACK

HOAX GOES TO WAR

The high art of warfare lies in gulling one's enemy so thoroughly that he is subdued with little fighting or none at all. Even before the ancient Greeks played their legendary horse trick on the Trojans, clever warriors were dreaming up subterfuges in hopes of sparing their own blood and that of their comrades in arms.

Every fine stratagem of war invokes timeless principles. Many modern leaders, from generals to politicians and executives, are apt to be familiar with the 2,500-year-old writings of Chinese soldier-scholar Sunzi (Sun-tzu), a peerless master of the uses of deceit. "All warfare is based on deception," he declares. "Therefore, when capable, feign incapacity; when active, inactivity. When near, make it appear that you are far away; when far away, that you are near. Offer the enemy a bait to lure him; feign disorder and strike him. When he concentrates, prepare against him; where he is strong, avoid him. Anger his general and confuse him. Pretend inferiority and encourage his arrogance."

Greek Gift

The most famous hoax in military history ended the ten-year siege of ancient Troy, according to legend, and it entered the language as a synonym for deception: A Trojan horse can be any deadly decoy. Despite its fame and lingering cautions about Greeks bearing gifts, no one knows if the horse ever really existed or was itself a fake—an arresting narrative invention by the poets whose verses are the only extant history of the fall of Troy.

The existence of classical Troy (in Latin, Ilium), at the site known as Hissarlik on the coast of Asia Minor, and its ruination by fire and sword in about 1250 BC, is well documented by archaeology, and by ancient poems, the most notable being the two epics attributed to the blind Greek poet Homer. The *Iliad* unfolds over about two months of conflict between the attacking Greeks and the besieged Trojans. The end is described in the *Odyssey,* Homer's account of the postwar adventures of the wily hero Odysseus, who conceived the subterfuge that destroyed the Trojans: a giant hollow wooden horse filled with warriors.

But it was not enough to imagine the ploy. Before Odysseus could proceed with his fraud, according to the account of the fourth-century poet Quintus of Smyrna, he first had to convince his compatriots that employing guile was not dishonorable; deception was considered by most of the other Greek warriors an unmanly way to fight. Neoptolemus, the son of the fallen hero Achilles, vocally opposed the scheme. But the majority of the war-weary Greeks favored any plan that would let them go home quickly—as victors.

A craftsman named Epeios built the wooden horse, by some accounts in three days, "tall as a hill," according to Virgil, the Roman poet whose *Aeneid* chronicles the adventures of the Trojan survivors who, legend holds, founded Rome. Whatever its true dimensions, the beast had room for thirty men and their weapons inside. When the decoy was ready, its retinue of armed soldiers entered the wooden body at night, sealing the door behind them. The remaining Greek forces, encamped on the shore not far from the city walls, burned their shelters and sailed off—to hide on the far side of a nearby island.

One Greek stayed behind in plain sight: Sinon, a warrior who allowed himself to be captured by the Trojans. He explained that the horse was intended as a peace offering to the gods in exchange for safe passage home. It was made necessary, he said, because Odysseus and another warrior had desecrated a shrine dedicated to the goddess Athena; the sacrilege had pushed the already dispirited Greeks into giving up their siege. In fact, Sinon told the Trojans, he had been intended as part of the sacrifice himself, until he escaped. In some accounts, Sinon's story was quickly accepted; but in others, his captors tortured him horribly, cutting off his ears and nose. Sinon bravely stuck to his story, however, and at last most of the Trojans believed him.

Among the few who still did not buy the tale was the Trojan priest Laocoön. He declared the horse was a ruse, hurled a spear into its flank, and urged that the creature be burned. "Have no faith in the horse!" he cried, according to Virgil, adding, "Even when Greeks bring gifts I fear them, gifts and all." To silence this doubter and undermine his credibility, those of the gods who favored the Greeks sent two great sea serpents up on the beach to kill Laocoön and his twin sons. Cassandra, a daughter of Troy's King Priam, also saw the deception clearly, as she did all things, but could give no credible warning: She was doomed by the god Apollo, her spurned lover, always to tell the truth but never to be believed. The Trojans, afraid to leave the potent figure where it was, dragged it—and its thirty hidden soldiers—through a breach in their city's walls.

Under cover of darkness, the Greek fleet returned to the beach and put ashore its soldiers. When deep night fell, the hidden warriors climbed down from their hideout, opened the city gates, and let in their comrades. Betrayed by the enemy within, Troy sank into blood and fire—and the "unmanly" use of decoys and deception became a fixture in human warfare. □

No Pain, No Gain

Suspicions run so high in wartime that any deception must somehow defeat the enemy's heightened skepticism. Throughout history, a favorite means to this end has been to plant a false turncoat in the foe's camp to gull the adversary into a fatal misstep. Of history's several great pseudodefectors, none approached the willingness of Zopyrus, a Persian nobleman of the sixth century BC, to sacrifice himself—and others—in the name of duplicity, on behalf of his true master, Darius the Great.

Darius had taken the throne in 521 BC at a time of chaos in the Persian Empire, deposing a pretender who had held power for seven months. The new ruler first turned his attention toward the empire's subjugated eastern provinces, which were aflame with wars of independence. The most serious uprising was in Babylon, which held out against the Persian forces, according to the Greek historian Herodotus, for a year and seven months. Rebels joked that Darius would triumph only when mules, the sterile offspring of horses and donkeys, bore foals.

They did not reckon on Zopyrus, son of one of Persia's barons who had helped crown Darius—or on his mules. When one of his pack animals foaled, according to Herodotus, Zopyrus heeded the omen and designed a scheme for winning the Babylonian campaign. Determined to infiltrate the enemy military, he knew he could win the Babylonians' confidence only by using extreme measures. His first step was to mutilate himself horribly by cutting off his nose and ears; then he shaved his head, had himself whipped, and presented himself to a bewildered King Darius. His purpose, Zopyrus said, was to convince the Babylonians that he had been wrongfully punished by his monarch and sought a military command from the Babylonians to gain revenge. But more sacrifice would be needed, he told the king: For his plan to succeed, 7,000 Persian soldiers would have to be sent to certain death.

The first 1,000 men, he suggested, should be posted in front of a specified gate of the besieged Babylon ten days after his defection. They should be dressed for war but carry only daggers. Zopyrus hoped by then to have taken command of a Babylonian force that would destroy them. A week later, 2,000 more Persians, similarly armed, should be sent to meet the same fate. Finally, twenty days later, the remaining 4,000 should be sacrificed. Immediately after that, he said, the rest of the Persian army should begin an assault, with special attention reserved for two specific city entrances.

With Darius's concurrence, Zopyrus let himself fall into Babylonian hands, where his mutilations convinced the rebels he was indeed a turncoat. As he had predicted, they gave him a troop command, which massacred the sacrificial Persian soldiers, bringing him the reward of increasing levels of trust and responsibility. Right on schedule, Zopyrus was named master of the city's defenses. And right on schedule, he opened the gates to Darius, who swiftly conquered Babylon—and let Zopyrus rule it for the rest of his life. □

The Sun Also Ruses

About 500 BC, the timeless Chinese strategist Sunzi (Sun-tzu) observed: "Know enemy, know self; one hundred battles, one hundred victories." Something over a century after his death, his maxim was verified in a brilliant act of military revenge—by a great infantry general who had no feet.

The man who came to be called Sun Bin was born in the modern-day province of Shandong. Said to be a descendant of Sunzi, he studied military theory with another aspiring general, Pang Juan, who profoundly envied his more talented rival. When Pang became commander of the army of the state of Wei, he tricked Sun into a secret visit, then brought false charges against him, causing authorities to cut off Sun's feet, brand his face, and throw him into captivity. The mutilated tactician was rescued by an ambassador from the neighboring state of Qi, who spirited him home. In Qi, Sun's strategic abilities brought him the second-ranking post in the army, and he became known as Sun Bin—Sun the Footless.

About fifteen years later, Qi invaded Wei, and the rival schoolmates faced each other again. Sun Bin had studied the Wei forces; they were known for fierce impetuosity and contempt for the warriors of Qi. "They consider Qi to be cowardly," he reportedly mused. "The skillful fighter will take this circumstance into account and plan his strategy to profit from it." Knowing his old enemy inside out, the footless general tailored a deception to Pang's weaknesses.

As the Qi forces advanced across Wei, Pang Juan and his army moved to intercept them. On the first night of the Qi incursion, Sun Bin advised his soldiers to light 100,000 campfires; on the second night, 50,000; on the third, 30,000. Learning about the dwindling points of light, and already convinced of his foe's cowardice, Pang Juan concluded that the enemy was deserting. He and his lightly armed vanguard outstripped their heavy forces and at evening reached a road through a narrow gorge. In the gloom, they saw a tree with writing on its trunk. Pang lit a torch to read the inscription, a message from Sun Bin: "Pang Juan dies under this tree."

The kindled torch was the signal for Sun's carefully laid ambush. Hundreds of concealed archers rained arrows into the gorge and tore Pang Juan's forces to shreds. The man who had used lies to destroy Sun Bin was now a victim of deceit. With defeat in sight, he committed suicide. Finally avenged, Sun Bin rushed on to destroy the laggard Wei army. □

Footless Chinese general Sun Bin, depicted in this Qing dynasty woodblock print, used a false retreat to lure an old rival to his doom.

Cool Han Lute

Not all classical strategists agree that war is mainly deception. Some, including the third-century-BC Confucian philosopher Xunzi (Hsün-tzu), have maintained that the only tactic worth considering is that of using superior forces, adequately supplied, to crush an enemy. To Xunzi, a tactic based on the hope that the enemy will be deceived is worse than no tactic at all.

And, of all military deceptions, the most repugnant is also the riskiest: a bluff, in which one tries to win against superior power by concealing one's true weakness. Ironically, without the teachings of Xunzi, warfare might have been deprived of one of its grandest bluffs—the day that Zhuge Liang (Chu-ko Liang) routed 150,000 men while armed only with a lute.

A legendary warrior of the second-century-AD Han dynasty, Zhuge Liang is regarded by many experts as the foremost Chinese strategist of his era, a formi-

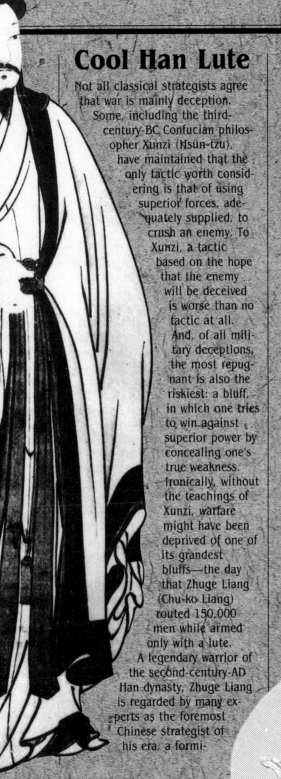

dable but prudent military man and an earnest believer in the concept that a small force is easy pickings for a larger one. But conceptual tactics meant nothing when, remaining with a skeleton force at a remote fort while his army maneuvered far away, Zhuge found himself threatened by an overwhelming enemy force. The Han general kept his nerve. After considering the nature of his opponent, whom he knew, he acted decisively. He ordered his troops to take down all their flags and hide, then had the gates thrown open. His fort helplessly exposed to the intruders, Zhuge, dressed in a religious robe, sat on a wall and, in plain view of the enemy, serenely plucked at a lute.

The oncoming general was flabbergasted by the man's nonchalance. He, as Zhuge Liang knew, also adhered to the advice of Xunzi and knew that Zhuge would never try anything so risky. A bluff was inconceivable. Instead, the enemy general reasoned, the lute-strumming figure reclining on the wall must have devised a trap that guaranteed certain victory. Sure that his cause was lost, the enemy general withdrew his host. And the relieved Zhuge, from all accounts, resumed his policy of playing only from strength. □

Zhuge Liang, a legendary Chinese general of the Han dynasty, is portrayed in a Ming dynasty woodblock print. The general routed 150,000 of the enemy by calmly strumming a lute.

The Princely Dupe of Joppa

Pharaoh Thutmose III was in an empire-building mood during the mid-fifteenth century BC, and his armies made frequent forays into neighboring Palestine. During one campaign, his high commander, General Thoth, laid siege to the port city of Joppa. When the city's ruling prince decided to seek a settlement, he ventured out to the enemy camp, where, perhaps to his surprise, he was received cordially by the general. Well lubricated with wine, the negotiations seemed increasingly convivial, and after an hour, Thoth declared that he would hand himself, his wife, and his children over to the Joppans as tokens of Egypt's surrender.

Although the prince should have smelled a rat, he was apparently too drunk to think straight. Rejoicing in victory, he demanded to see the staff the pharaoh had given Thoth as an emblem of royal power. When it was brought in, Thoth stood up and said, "Look at me, O enemy of Joppa!" And with that he struck a blow to the prince's forehead that knocked him to the floor.

With the prince bound and helpless, Thoth turned to the next stage of his ruse, directing 200 soldiers to hide in baskets. The prince's charioteer, unaware of the fate of his master, was asked to go into the city and deliver the news to the princess of Joppa that the captured Thoth, his family, and 200 baskets filled with tribute would soon be at her disposal.

The charioteer was as gullible as the prince, and the princess no less so. He rattled off to Joppa, and when 300 Egyptians bearing 200 baskets arrived at the city, its gates stood open to receive them. Once inside, the soldiers burst out of their baskets, and the 500-man force overwhelmed the Joppans.

That night, Thoth crowed in a letter to his pharaoh that the god Amon "has given you the enemy of Joppa, along with all his people, as well as his city! Send men to take them away as plunder, so that you may fill the house of your father Amon-Re, king of the gods, with male and female slaves, who are fallen under your feet forever and ever." The army scribe who recorded the campaign noted with emphatic satisfaction, "IT HAS COME TO A HAPPY ENDING." □

Sound and Fury

Darkness is disorienting, and loud flashes and noises in the dark even more so. One of the first great generals to take advantage of those deceptive tools was Gideon, who sowed confusion among the Midianites and won one of the Old Testament's most famous victories. It happened around 1176 BC, when a mere 300 Israelites vanquished thousands of their nomadic foes.

The Midianites were the bane of Palestine for seven years, raiding and pillaging the holdings of the agrarian Israelites. Gideon, a man of relatively humble origins, appears to have had instinctive military genius. First he organized an uprising against the invaders, drawing some 33,000 men to his standard. Then he chose the 300 best by means of a famous test: leading them to water and watching how they slaked their thirst. The smartest, wariest, and most disciplined were those who did not fling themselves down to drink but instead crouched carefully, keeping one eye out for enemies and one hand on their weapons while they lapped water from the other hand.

Around this warrior corps, Gideon began to build one of the great masterpieces of military deception. He knew the Midianite fighters were essentially a guerrilla force, uncomfortable with fighting pitched battles, even in daytime. Playing to this weakness, he reportedly foreshadowed his attack with word of the 33,000-man force he had originally raised. Dividing his compact elite corps into three companies of 100 men each, he gave each soldier three tools for the hoax: a torch to provide light, a pitcher to hide the light until the last minute, and a trumpet—the instrument used even into modern times to issue battle commands to large hosts of men.

On the night of his attack, Gideon personally scouted the enemy camp, where the nervous chatter of the Midianites convinced him the enemy was ripe for panic. His men stole to their places on a carefully prearranged timetable. Gideon waited until around midnight before giving his signal to attack: That was the time, he had already learned, when the Midianites usually changed sentries. Finally, he gave the famous password: "The

sword of the Lord and Gideon."

Suddenly, the enemy camp was surrounded by hundreds of lights and a clamor of trumpets blaring commands. The jarring illusion convinced the marauders that they were surrounded by a force many times larger than their own. In the confusion, the Midianites began fighting with one another before scampering away. The Israelite forces never had to strike a blow in their attack. Only when the disorganized Midianites were on the run did they fall by the tens of thousands

to Gideon's relentless pursuit.

So devastating was the victory that the Israelites were profoundly confirmed in their belief that divine providence was at their side. According to the Old Testament, Gideon, renamed Jerubbaal, reigned for forty years as king of Israel—unmolested by the enemy he had stampeded with a clever nocturnal hoax. □

Gideon's small Israelite force stampedes the Midianites in this 1620s canvas by French artist Nicolas Poussin.

Modest Archer

The annals of military deception are filled with accounts of using false information to make weak forces look strong, and small ones large. But few strategists have had the brass to try to rout an enemy—as an ancient Persian king is said to have done—by claiming to be the worst warrior in the land.

Bahrām V, king of Persia from 420 to 438, was anything but inept. One of the more energetic members of the expansionist Sasanid dynasty, he warred against the Byzantine Empire in the first years of his reign, then issued an edict of tolerance to Christians in Persia. In 427, he crushed an invasion of Mongols and extended Persian influence into Central Asia. Bahrām appears often as a dashing and romantic figure in classical Persian folklore, an indication of his popularity, and his deceptive exploits are set down, with some embellishment, in a fourteenth-century Arabic compendium of deceit, *The Subtle Ruse.*

During the war with the Mongols, according to this account, the monarch received word from his spy network that an enemy prince had begun pillaging the frontiers of his kingdom, giving every indication of permanently undermining Bahrām's authority. The king's closest advisers were unnerved, and, as they were no help, Bahrām helped to drive them away from court by pretending his own wits were addled.

Once his claque of courtiers was gone and he could act in secrecy, the king disguised himself as an old peasant, then stole from the palace at night and traveled to his new enemy's territory. Close to a track where the insurgent's scouts would find him, he drew forth a bow and arrows and began killing with deadly precision every bird and beast within range. Soon discovered, he was taken to the enemy camp, where he told his captors he was the slave of a groom, abandoned to fend for himself.

Word of the captive got back to the marauding prince, who demanded a demonstration of Bahrām's superior bowmanship. Greatly impressed at the result, the invader was dismayed when Bahrām confessed that he was "the most pathetic and pitiful and puny bowman in the kingdom." The disguised monarch then confided to his captor that things were not what they seemed. "Our king is making fun of you," said Bahrām. "You are in a trap and he is preparing to attack you because he knows you cannot escape." The lack of organized Persian opposition was merely a lure to cut off retreat, the bogus archer said. Then he asked, "If I can hit a thousand enemy soldiers with a thousand arrows, what do you think will be the fate of anyone attacked by our king with 400,000 archers?"

Suitably unsettled, the invading prince withdrew, without even stopping to plunder. Bahrām returned to his court three days later, where he revealed how a little modesty had saved the day. □

Ill Bread

Long before Napoleon uttered his celebrated observation that an army marches on its stomach, an Eastern potentate demonstrated a related axiom: One man's wheat is another's poison. A medieval Arab document, *The Subtle Ruse,* tells the unsettling tale of a besieged sultan who turned to his vizier for a way out of their predicament. The minister's solution: to load a camel caravan with 100 sacks of grain, laced with the powdered root of a twining plant known as scammony, which acts as a powerful cathartic. The vizier told the leader of the caravan to steal out of the city for two days' travel, then wend his way back through the besieging host, so that he could be captured. As planned, the enemy seized the returning caravan and expropriated the cargo, which was baked into bread. Shortly thereafter, the attacking army became excruciatingly ill, with some soldiers even dying of the effects of the tainted loaves. Having tricked the enemy into taking poison, the sultan sallied forth to crush the surviving foe—and to add another recipe for deception to the desert's military lore. □

War of the Words

The deceptions of warfare have created hidden languages that have often been as ingenious as the stratagems themselves. The historian Herodotus relates that a Greek visitor to the court of Persian monarch Darius the Great sent home sensitive information by shaving a servant's head, writing a message on it, then letting the man's hair grow back. When the Medean general Harpagus conspired with Cyrus the Great of Persia against the king of Medea, he stuffed his message into a dead hare and sent it with a messenger disguised as a hunter. In Rome, the poet Virgil mentions messages written on leaves that were plastered over the putrid "ulcers" of a disguised beggar. Ovid refers to secret messages inscribed on the bearer's flesh. The preferred language of deception is no longer a message secreted on a messenger, however, but one hidden in the tangled symbols of a code or a cipher.

In the thirteenth century, the Republic of Venice invented modern diplomacy, and along with it its distinctive encrypted language. By the sixteenth century, the cipher of Michel, the Venetian ambassador to the court of England's Queen Mary Tudor, was so complicated that it was not decoded until 1868. Not that the cipher did much good. Fighting guile with old-fashioned bribery, the French ambassador to England paid Michel's secretary sixty crowns per month to let him read the Venetian reports in plain Italian. Spanish codes were equally complicated and almost as useless. Often, diplomatic records in Madrid were filled with marginal notations that demanded another, intelligible dispatch, or read: "Cannot be understood."

Because secret messages must be comprehended by the right person at the right time, they have always offered little margin for error and thus grand possibilities for disaster. The British general Sir Charles "Chinese" Gordon, trapped by the Sudanese in 1884 in the city of Khartoum, learned this the hard way. Instead of using a relatively simple cipher— an easily memorized transposition of letters, numbers, and words—he relied on an elaborate code. When a siege was imminent, he kept his code books from the enemy by shipping them out of town on the last boat down the Nile. But when plans for the city's relief were smuggled to him, written in his code, Gordon could not decipher them. Unable to coordinate with the relief column, Gordon fought on, Khartoum fell, and he was massacred.

Few people have fumbled a sensitive encryption as badly as Arthur Zimmerman, German foreign minister during World War I. Anxious to pin down American troops if the United States entered the conflict, Zimmerman sent a famous message to Mexico, offering the states of Arizona, Texas, and New ◊

A spy who was captured during the First World War, and shorn *(far right)*, bore a secret message on his scalp.

Mexico as booty if the government entered the war on Germany's side. Unfortunately, he sent the message over a transatlantic cable routinely tapped by the British, who had broken Zimmerman's code. The incendiary cable then made its way to the German embassy in Mexico City. When the British finally convinced President Woodrow Wilson of the ploy, an enraged United States declared war—just five weeks after Wilson published Zimmerman's message.

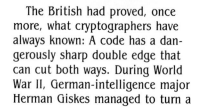

The British had proved, once more, what cryptographers have always known: A code has a dangerously sharp double edge that can cut both ways. During World War II, German-intelligence major Herman Giskes managed to turn a code against its creators during an incident in Holland. After arresting one British agent in March 1942, Giskes was able to extract the cipher and begin transmitting German signals to London in the British code. The captured agent had used a security check in his messages—a prearranged coding mistake—to guarantee their provenance. Incredibly, the British listeners across the North Sea did not notice that the bogus German messages lacked this crucial feature and accepted them as real.

Using his secret ace in the hole—and the captured Briton to transmit his distinctive Morse dots and dashes—Giskes was gradually able to compromise the entire Dutch underground, while London spymasters ignored signals that might have given away the Nazi game. The captured agent transmitting the messages finally flashed: "CAUGHT CAUGHT CAUGHT." His words were lost on London.

A second captured agent tried to warn London, using the grapevine of the Gestapo prison where he was being held. Then, worried no one had received his warning, he managed to escape and, after running for three months, reached safety at Gibraltar. But, back in England, he was quickly jailed as a double agent.

The British, however, had finally grown suspicious and ended their operations in April 1944, two years after the Germans had broken their code. In that time, the Germans had collected thousands of air-dropped weapons and a small fortune in Dutch currency. The real cost of the deception—and Britain's inability to see it—was in human life: Forty-seven British agents and 1,200 members of the Dutch resistance were lost to the cruel hoax within a hoax. □

Bluff at the Bridge

On November 12, 1805, French marshals Jean Lannes and Joachim Murat halted their armies within sight of a large wooden bridge over the Danube River near Vienna and contemplated their orders from Napoleon. The bridge must be captured, but captured intact: Serious damage to it would slow the advancing French troops, and time was of the essence. Lannes and Murat were rushing to join the emperor, who expected an early confrontation with the combined armies of Russia and Austria on the far side of the Danube and needed every French soldier he could muster. Well aware of the bridge's strategic value to the French, the Austrians had sprinkled the span with mines and stationed artillerymen at its Vienna end.

Lannes and Murat put their heads together, disappeared briefly, then returned in ceremonial uniforms encrusted with medals. Followed by several aides, the marshals walked to the bridge and, calling "Armistice! Armistice!" to

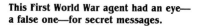

The British had, once

the amazed Austrians, crossed the river with perfect composure.

The local Austrian commander, General Auersperg, put in a belated appearance, and Lannes and Murat declared that the armistice's terms called for him to yield the bridge to them. As the marshals were pulling wool firmly over the bewildered general's eyes, French grenadiers and sappers emerged and advanced on the bridge. An Austrian tried to put a torch to a mine, but Lannes snatched it from his hand, then boldly sat down on the nearest cannon. His move worked. Before the startled gunners could fire, the first French troops had crossed the river.

Hopelessly outwitted, General Auersperg handed over the bridge to the marshals and their men. Three weeks later, the clever tricksters Lannes and Murat helped Napoleon humiliate the far larger forces fielded by his enemies at Austerlitz. □

Perfectly Frank

One of the most successful deceptions of the American Civil War was carried out not by hardened soldiers, but by a young Canadian who hoodwinked both sides in the conflict for nearly two years, outwitting the Confederacy as a spy behind rebel lines. Throughout the years of secret work as soldier and spy, however, the daring operative kept another, deeper secret: Despite the masculine disguises, she was a woman. Her name was Sarah Emma Edmonds.

Edmonds had been carrying on her gender masquerade for some time before she joined the Union Army. Born in 1842 on a farm in New Brunswick, where she felt oppressed by an inflexible, authoritarian father, she was inspired to dress up as a man and seek escape in fantasies of some freer, more venturesome life. At age nineteen, she left the family farm and, calling herself Frank Thompson, immigrated to the United States and took up selling Bibles for a Hartford, Connecticut, firm. The roving job took her to Michigan, where, five days after hostilities broke out between North and South, Frank Thompson joined a Michigan volunteer regiment as a field nurse.

Her transition to espionage came suddenly when a New York regiment returning with prisoners brought news that a Federal spy was about to be shot in Richmond. The devoutly religious Edmonds had befriended a camp chaplain, ◊

who asked if the young nurse wanted to undertake a "situation of great danger and of vast responsibility." Restless, Edmonds agreed to take the dead spy's place behind the lines. Her qualifications were validated by a phrenologist who examined the bumps on her head and declared that the youth's organs of "secretiveness and combativeness" were highly developed.

However unscientific the yardstick, the examiner was right. Edmonds's first mission was to travel through Confederate lines at Yorktown and report on troops, fortifications, and enemy plans. She dyed her head, neck, hands, and arms black, slipped on a wig of black hair, and posed as a field hand. But her disguise backfired. Confronted by rebel troops at a fortification, she was forced onto a work gang, doing hard labor as, ominously, her skin dye began to fade. On the evening of the third day, she slipped back through the lines. Although she would return once more in the guise of a black woman, she vowed she would never go back as a male who could be pressed into hard labor.

On her next mission, near Williamsburg, she posed as an Irish peddler woman—using her true gender as a disguise—and tended to a dying Confederate officer on her journey. In all, she made eleven spy trips for the Union before moving on to a related line of work: counterintelligence. As Union troops occupied Kentucky, she posed as a clerk for a Louisville merchant with rebel sympathies. In that guise, she flushed out three Confederate agents.

Edmonds served in some capacity or another at both battles of Bull Run and at Williamsburg, Fair Oaks, Antietam, and Fredericksburg. But at the Battle of Vicksburg in 1863, the strain of her many-sided imposture began to take its toll, and her Frank Thompson mask began to slip. "All my soldierly qualities seemed to have fled," she wrote in her autobiography, adding that she did little but weep. "All the horrid scenes that I had witnessed during the past two years seemed now before me with vivid distinctness, and I could think of nothing else." Edmonds asked to be discharged from the army, and her surgeon gave her a certificate of disability, releasing her from duty as "Nurse and Spy in the Union Army"—the title that she took for her autobiography, published in 1864, while the Civil War still raged.

Once away from the conflict, she dressed as a woman for the first time in years and resumed work as a nurse. In 1867, she married; eventually, she had three children and in 1884, after prolonged petitioning, won a twelve-dollar-a-month pension for her war effort. She died in 1898, a woman who had found a way to serve her adopted country by living a monumental lie. □

Photographed in Fort Scott, Kansas, Frank Thompson, a Union soldier, nurse, and spy during the American Civil War, was really a courageous Canadian named Sarah Emma Edmonds.

Von Rewrite

Hoaxes have often helped decide the outcome of wars, but only rarely has one nation duped another into starting one. One such occurrence came in the late nineteenth century, when Prussia provoked a war with France by means of a single, perfect hoax—and unified the Teutonic kingdoms under a single crown.

The ruse was the work of Count Otto von Bismarck, chancellor of Prussia and father of modern Germany. In July 1870, the fifty-five-year-old statesman's fortunes and spirits were at an ebb. For one thing, his royal master, King Wilhelm I, had just been humiliated by the aggressive French emperor Napoleon III, who had threatened war to keep Wilhelm's cousin Leopold off the Spanish throne. On July 12, Bismarck heard that Leopold had bent to the pressure. Dining at home the next night with Prussia's top military commanders, a dejected Bismarck discussed the possibility of his resignation.

His brooding was interrupted by the arrival of a telegram from Wilhelm, who was vacationing at Bad Ems, a spa northwest of Frankfurt. In the coded wire, Wilhelm said he had been approached by the French ambassador to Berlin, Vincent Benedetti, with another demand from Paris. It had not been enough for Napoleon III that Leopold had stepped aside from the immediate Spanish succession. Now the French wanted assurances that Leopold would *never* accept the Spanish crown. In his carefully worded message, Wilhelm said he had declined to give the guarantee but left it to Bismarck to decide if the demand and response should

A Friedrich Emil Klein portrait of Count Otto von Bismarck, painted about a decade after the crafty statesman edited a royal telegram in order to provoke the French to declare war.

be revealed to the Prussian diplomatic corps and the press.

In the midst of his gloom, Bismarck saw a sudden opportunity. With his guests watching, the inventor of realpolitik edited the telegram down to two terse sentences describing the French demand and the Prussian king's cold rejection. No words were added or changed, but the final effect of the textual message was very different. What had once sounded like bland diplomatic backing and filling had taken on the tone of bold and dashing defiance.

Bismarck's hope, he wrote later, was that publication of the altered Bad Ems telegram would "have the effect of a red rag upon the Gallic bull." His cynical calculation proved exactly right. In Paris, Na-

poleon decided to take the telegram as a cause for war—easily his worst decision. Expecting quick victory, the French declared war on July 19 and almost immediately began to suffer a string of catastrophic defeats. The conflict culminated in a five-month siege of Paris, and Napoleon was deposed. Various southern Teutonic duchies, which had followed their northern cousins to war against the common enemy, united with them into a single nation. On January 18, 1871, Wilhelm I was proclaimed emperor of Germany at the Palace of Versailles. Bismarck's great dream had been achieved—and the stage was set for the bloody wars to come—with a few deft strokes of a great statesman's figurative blue pencil. □

Rebel Quell

No sooner had the United States wrested the Philippines from Spain in the war of 1898 than it was faced with a prolonged insurgency. Thousands of Americans—and tens of thousands of Filipinos—died before the tide was turned by the daring deceit of a feisty U.S. Army officer from Kansas.

The Treaty of Paris, which handed over the Philippines to Washington, was especially bitter to Emilio Aguinaldo, a Chinese-Tagalog founder of Filipino nationalist resistance to Spain. Aguinaldo had returned from exile in Hong Kong in 1898 to help defeat his old enemy, Spain. But he found that his country was no sooner free of the Spanish yoke than it became a territory of the United States. Aguinaldo refused to accept this state of affairs, declared himself president of a new Philippine Republic, and on February 4, 1899, launched an uprising against occupying American troops.

The Philippine insurgency was an ugly conflict, involving as many as 70,000 American soldiers. Countless atrocities were committed by both sides, but the insurgent army was systematically worn away until only a guerrilla force remained. Emilio Aguinaldo retreated into the remote fastness of the main island of Luzon to direct his remaining rebels in what seemed an eternal conflict.

Then, on February 4, 1901—the second anniversary of Aguinaldo's revolt—a voluble American brigadier general named Frederick "Scrapping Fred" Funston had a stroke of luck. His troops intercepted a courier with a message from Aguinaldo to a field com- ◊

American General Frederick Funston *(left)* relaxes aboard the USS *Vicksburg* after posing as a prisoner to capture Philippine rebel leader Emilio Aguinaldo, shown below gamely saluting the victor's colors.

mander,
asking for reinforcements at the nationalist leader's secret headquarters in Palanan, a small village in the most isolated region of northern Luzon. The settlement could be reached only by marching through dense jungle populated by rebel sympathizers.

To Funston, it was a chance for a bold stroke. He proposed to the American commander, General Arthur MacArthur, that loyal Filipino soldiers pose as the requested rebels. Funston and four other U.S. officers would command them—but would travel disguised as captives. Funston chose eighty-five members of an ethnic group known for its hostility to Aguinaldo's Ta-

galog forces, gave them a crash course in their foe's language, and issued them the blue uniforms, rifles, and bolo knives used by the rebels. On captured insurgent stationery, Funston had a clerk forge a message to Aguinaldo, announcing the troops' impending arrival. On March 14, the false rebels and their fake captives sailed as close to Palanan as they dared, then began their long jungle trek. Back in Manila, only five U.S. Army officers knew of the adventure.

As they neared Palanan, the troops were almost foiled by the security-conscious leader of a rebel outpost, who had been ordered by Aguinaldo to hold the prisoners at a village six miles away from his hideout; there was no point in letting them see his headquarters. Funston quickly had one of his men forge a counterorder from Aguinaldo rescinding the quarantine. Gaunt and weak from lack of

food, the American-led force finally reached Palanan on March 23. The trip had been arduous, but the ruse worked; Aguinaldo welcomed them. Then, as he engaged the "commanders" in conversation, the "reinforcements" opened fire. Aguinaldo was grabbed and subdued. Funston emerged from hiding in the nearby jungle to claim his dazed prisoner of war.

Once returned to Manila, Aguinaldo ordered fellow rebels to lay down their arms. Some did, but many did not; the war sputtered into the following year. But the backbone of resistance had been snapped. Aguinaldo generously hailed the deceit as a "bold plan, executed with skill and cleverness." Funston, at no loss to his small force and with only two killed and three wounded among the enemy, had effectively ended a war, after conventional tactics had cost thousands of lives. □

Doped Dupes

World War I is largely remembered as a brutal bloodbath, but it also was lit by flashes of deceptive brilliance. No campaign was more guileful, perhaps, than the British assault in Palestine by General Edmund Allenby, aided by Captain Richard Meinertzhagen, a thirty-nine-year-old intelligence officer with a knack for tactical trickery.

Before Allenby's arrival in 1917, British troops fighting the Turks and their German allies were stalled in the southern part of the barren, hilly Holy Land for eight months. To break this deadlock, the new commander planned to send a small feinting force northward toward Gaza, a heavily defended Turkish position, and to send another, stronger force some thirty miles east to Beersheba, to seize the smaller town and its priceless water wells. Then, he reasoned, they could strike westward at the soft eastern flank of the Turks' Gaza defenses and retake that city as well. To make sure the Turks and Germans were thinking along the right lines, Allenby turned to Meinertzhagen, whom he later hailed as "largely responsible for my successes in Palestine."

The son of a London banker, Meinertzhagen was a trickster par excellence who had already wiped out a variety of enemy agents in the region and had served with distinction in campaigns against the Germans in East Africa. In 1910, he had wangled a conducted tour of a secret Russian fort in the Crimea, mapping the fortifications as he posed as a British bird watcher. Now, not content with the purely military elements of a faked attack on Gaza—misleading artillery barrages and the like—the captain wanted to plant a real red herring where the enemy could find it. Accordingly, he confected a dummy notebook, in the name of a nonexistent staff officer, that contained, as he put it later, "all sorts of nonsense about our plans and difficulties." Among other things, the phony record suggested that

any British troop movements around Beersheba would be mere reconnaissance efforts.

When two agents failed to plant the notebook with the Turks, Meinertzhagen did the job himself. He rode out near Beersheba until he met a Turkish patrol. Then, pretending to be hit by a bullet, he dropped a knapsack with the tainted information—the notebook and other articles, all stained convincingly with horse's blood. He reported the loss to British troops who had not been apprised of his ruse. They scurried to retrieve the documents, failing, but in the process convincing the Turks the notebook was real.

In the week before the October 31 attack began, the wily captain reinforced his hoax. Radio messages were sent disclosing that General Allenby would be away from the front from October 29 to November 4. Other transmissions—all in a cipher the Turks could read—emphasized the innocuous reconnaissance mission at Beersheba. When the British forces struck, the flat-footed Turks complained that their reserve forces had not even been called up; they had expected no attack until nearly a month later.

As the British prepared the second stage of their assault—the westward thrust at Gaza—Meinertzhagen had a final trick ready. For months, British warplanes had flown over Turkish lines on his orders, dropping small packets of cigarettes with propaganda messages. The bemused but tobaccoless Turks had grown used to the bounty. Despite Allenby's moral objections, Meinertzhagen laced a ◊

Royal Army intelligence trickster par excellence Richard Meinertzhagen poses for a photograph at the 1919 Paris Peace Conference.

load of cigarettes with opium and dropped them to the Turks on November 5. Preceded by their soporific gifts, the British swept through the befuddled Turks with ease. Allenby pretended not to know about the insubordination. But years later, in offering his aide a cigarette, he reassured him: "They aren't doped." □

High Spirits

It all began with a homemade Ouija board, constructed to help ease the endless tedium of life in a prison camp. Its inventor was a lieutenant named E. H. Jones, a Welshman who, along with a number of captured British comrades, was waiting out World War I in Yozgat, a Turkish town where prisoners were quartered. Isolated in the primal fastness of the mountains, Yozgat offered little opportunity for escape. So, stuck there, the prisoners put most of their energy into outwitting their most available and formidable enemy—boredom. Hence the Ouija board.

For true believers, the device is a conduit for messages from the world beyond. Supposedly under a spirit's control, a person moves a pointer around a board or a disk inscribed with the alphabet until "instructed" by spirit forces to stop. The nearest letter is recorded, and the process is continued until a message appears in the string of letters.

Jones played fair: He moved the pointer randomly with his eyes closed, and the letters added up to nonsense. The results failed to amuse his audience, so he decided

to cheat. He memorized the arrangement of the letters and after a little practice could produce "messages." Before Jones knew what was happening, several men became convinced he was a genuine medium—a conduit between this world and the next. It seemed too late to confess his innocent deception, and word of his uncanny abilities spread to the Turks.

Suddenly, Jones found himself with an enthusiastic clientele. The camp interpreter, whom the prisoners had dubbed the Pimple, showed up for a consultation about his love life. He liked what Jones's spirit guide had to say and became a regular. The Pimple also offered some useful information: Kiazim Bey, the camp commandant, was an ardent spiritualist.

Jones was a clever fellow, and before long it struck him that Kiazim's credulity might be the key to freedom. If the commandant could somehow be made the unwitting accomplice to an escape, he might provide some means to lead Jones out of the mountains. Better yet, a cooperative Kiazim would not dare

punish inmates left behind in the camp lest the incident trigger an incriminating inquiry by the Turkish War Office.

Details of a plan eluded Jones for a time, but the Pimple once again supplied the germ of an idea. Was it possible, the translator asked, for spirits to find buried treasure? The locals believed a rich Armenian had hidden a treasure on his grounds, now part of the camp, shortly before his people were massacred by the Turks in 1915. Indeed, avowed the elated Jones, the spirits were most reliable at finding treasure. The bait was set.

On a September afternoon in 1917, Jones set off in search of treasure, accompanied by the Pimple and a man called Cook, who was the commandant's manservant. The trio looked most peculiar. Jones scampered nimbly over the hills, while the Turks demonstrated an odd, stiff-legged gait that called to mind Frankenstein's monster. Warming to his mediumship, Jones had told his credulous captors that the spirits had rules for successful treasure hunting: One was that each of the Turks had to wear an unsheathed sword inside one pant leg. This stratagem, Jones said, would lead first to a weapon guarding a fabulous treasure, then to the treasure itself.

Pretending to be in a trance, the Welshman led the Turks a merry chase, finally pausing beside a garden wall. With the Pimple and Cook as witnesses, he performed a ritual before searching for the guardian weapon. Over a small fire of twigs, Jones chanted, *"Gwyn fyd na chai Cymru ei diwifr eihun,"* a safe bet, since the Pimple and Cook were unlikely to recognize a Welsh love song. Presumably at the spirit's behest, Jones then dug beside the wall and turned up a rusty revolver, and the overjoyed Pimple rushed to report the find to the commandant.

Although pleased with his progress, Jones decided two heads would be better than one in translating spirit power into freedom. He confided in Australian pilot and amateur magician Cedric W. Hill, who immediately signed on as a partner. Jones's equal in show-

manship, Hill worked up a mind-reading act that deceived the Pimple and the commandant thoroughly. Abandoning the Pimple as his informant and go-between, Kiazim appealed directly to the mind-reading mediums for help in finding the treasure. They acquiesced, and Hill came up with the perfect twist to the plot. Since prisoners never attempted escape, the commandant permitted chaperoned ski outings. Hill concocted two related clues to the cache's location and planted them when he went skiing.

The spirit guide then obligingly contacted two late friends of the treasure's owner, each of whom had buried a clue to the loot. These were duly retrieved. There was, according to the dead pair, an essential third clue that had been given to yet another friend. Unfortunately, he was still alive, so the spirits could not reach him for more information.

No problem, Jones and Hill assured Kiazim: They could still learn everything they needed to know about the clue by reading its possessor's mind. Unfortunately, he lived on the coast, and it was impossible for them to establish contact from Yozgat. The surrounding mountains, they explained, interfered with mind waves as well as radio waves.

Kiazim was eager to get Hill and Jones to the coast, but he needed a reason that would satisfy the Turkish War Office. Jones's resourceful spirit provided it: The commandant would claim that the two prisoners had gone mad and should be sent to Constantinople, where English hospital ships were allowed to pick up desperate cases.

The War Office bought the story, and in May of 1918, Hill and Jones

were put aboard a train with the Pimple as their escort. As they came into the lowlands near Constantinople, Jones and Hill slipped into what seemed to be a joint trance. Their mumbling thrilled the Pimple. Tuning in the right mind waves, they described the location of the last clue; it was in a garden in the prison camp.

The spirit told the excited Pimple to write to the commandant describing where to find the clue but warning him to wait for the translator to return so that the two could conduct the search together. Jones and Hill picked up some worrisome hints from the spirit world that fellow prisoner E. J. Price had already dug up the clue, but Jones's otherworldly guide cheerily discounted them as false.

As soon as he could, the Pimple rushed back to Yozgat, and Hill and Jones were locked up in Turkish mental wards in Constantinople to fake madness and await a British ship. Six weeks later, a miserable Pimple came to see Jones. Price had found the clue, he said, a gold piece wrapped in a scrap of paper with some words he could not read—and he had lost it! The spirit guide spoke up: He had made Price lose it, to punish the commandant for starting a search as soon as he received the Pimple's letter from Constantinople.

As the curtain fell on the comedy, the commandant and the Pimple were left to brood about the treasure that had almost been theirs. After playing at being madmen for six months, Jones and Hill sailed away from Constantinople in late October—only two weeks before the armistice was declared and all the prisoners of Yozgat were set free. □

British lieutenants E. H. Jones (*near left*) and Cedric W. Hill flank a drawing of the homemade Ouija board that they used to conjure an escape from a Turkish prisoner-of-war camp.

Vanishing Act

The British and their allies were getting trounced. In April of 1917, they had sailed across the Aegean Sea and begun landing a massive force on the beaches of Turkey's Gallipoli Peninsula. Over the summer, the contingent would come to number 332,000 men. Their objective was to advance some 150 miles and capture Constantinople. But seven months after the initial landing, the Allies had moved only one mile toward their goal—and that at a staggering cost of 214,000 casualties, as Turkish fire rained down from the hills on soldiers exposed on the beaches.

The impasse at Gallipoli became the talk of London as the British cabinet debated abandoning the feckless offensive. The cost had been far too high and the gains far too meager, proponents of withdrawal argued. Besides, many said, World War I would be won in the trenches in France—not on some far-flung and ill-considered second front in the Middle East. Opponents of retreat feared losing face, and they also had a more concrete concern: Withdrawal would almost certainly mean a bloodbath. Soldiers would have to leave what little cover they had managed to dig or build in order to make their way to evacuation ships. The troops would be cut to pieces.

In December of 1917, a compromise was reached: Three Allied beachheads had been established—at Suvla Bay, Anzac Cove, and Cape Helles. The 83,000 troops at Suvla Bay and Anzac Cove would be evacuated. At Cape Helles, the most strategically important site, the remaining soldiers would stay and fight.

The plan was not entirely to the liking of Lieutenant General Charles Monro, who had just taken command at Gallipoli a month earlier. After spending his first day making a whirlwind tour of the three footholds, Monro fired off a message to the British war minister recommending that all three be abandoned. Nevertheless, the commander set about making the best of the compromise.

Instead of plotting a textbook withdrawal, in which troops are moved en masse while the enemy's attention is focused on a feint, Monro decided to play a different kind of trick: Night after night, men would slip away by the hundreds to board waiting boats, yet the Turks would not notice their absence because the beachheads would appear unchanged.

Monro and his officers had begun working out the operation even before the cabinet voted for only limited withdrawal. At Anzac Cove, for instance, they made a trial run of the "silent stunt," which was meant to desensitize the Turks to the growing quiet of a vanishing army. For fifty-four hours straight, the Allies held their fire, and sounds were muffled as much as possible. Blankets were spread in the bottoms of trenches, and the men wrapped their boots and clanky metal objects in sacks. When a few curious Turks crossed no man's land to see what had become of the enemy, they were quietly bayoneted.

After sundown on December 10, the evacuation began in earnest.

The paths from the camps to the water's edge had been marked with flour, and hooded lanterns were set in trenches. For ten nights, thousands of men filed on muffled feet to a flotilla of little boats waiting to whisk them away. The Turks were oblivious to the nighttime parade and apparently saw nothing suspicious during the day. It was not the silent stunt alone that had thrown the enemy off the scent. The Turkish government had concluded that the well-publicized withdrawal wrangle in Britain was merely a smoke screen designed to hide the true Allied intent to continue the offensive. Passed down the chain of command, this misinterpretation made the officers and troops alert to battle preparations—not to withdrawal.

Keeping up appearances kept the remaining Allied soldiers hopping. They tended an unchanging number of campfires, set up dummy soldiers, drove supply wagons laden with empty cartons, and spread themselves thin among the bivouacs to give the camps an air of liveliness. A clever tin-can mechanism was rigged to fire unmanned rifles at random intervals.

At 4:00 a.m. on December 20, soldiers at Anzac Cove set fire to a huge pile of equipment and jumped into the last boat. Within moments, a large Allied mine exploded, and the Turks let loose a barrage of fire. But they were too late, for every man escaped from the beachhead with his life.

The scenario was played out simultaneously at Suvla Bay with equal success. From a safe distance offshore, the last troops to embark watched the Turks spill from the hills and scurry like confused ants on the beach. The audience broke into cheers, tears, and laughter when a navy ship opened fire on the scuttling figures.

With Suvla and Anzac abandoned by the Allies, the Turks moved their main defense force to Cape Helles, and the British troops there found themselves overwhelmingly outnumbered, twenty-one divisions to four. Because of the hopeless odds—and because Monro's ruse had worked so well at the first two beachheads—the decision was made to evacuate Cape Helles. Between January 1 and the dawn of January 9, 35,000 men were withdrawn. Not a single Allied soldier was left behind, and the Turks sprang to their guns only when the Allied ammunition dumps started to explode.

Because of Monro's mastery of deceit, there was no bloodbath at the Gallipoli retreat. In fact, not one Allied life was lost. □

Making Major Mincemeat

Major William Martin of the Royal Marines made his first public appearance on April 30, 1943, off Spain's southwestern Atlantic coast when a fisherman spotted his body bobbing and drifting in the water. Summoned to take charge of the morbid catch, a Spanish naval officer sent it to the coroner in the nearby town of Huelva for autopsy. It appeared from the examination that the major had drowned some five days earlier, and officials surmised that he had been a courier aboard an airplane that crashed and sank without a trace.

In London, Lieutenant Commander Ewen Montagu anxiously waited at Admiralty headquarters to learn whether Major Martin had reached Huelva according to plan. On May 3, a message arrived from the British naval attaché in Madrid describing the major's fate. After the autopsy, Martin had been given a military funeral and buried in the local cemetery.

This news was splendid, prompting smiles rather than sorrow among the handful of men in on a fiercely guarded, incredibly complicated secret. In the inky predawn of April 30, a British submarine had surfaced 1,600 yards offshore near Huelva. Working quickly, the commander and four officers opened a coffin-size canister packed with dry ice and pulled out a body. The commander inflated the Mae West life jacket the corpse wore over his Royal Marine uniform and checked the dead officer's briefcase. Everything was in order, and the men pushed their grisly cargo overboard. ◊

Trapped on Gallipoli Peninsula during World War I, Australian soldiers casually play cricket under Turkish guns as part of an elaborate illusion of normalcy— cover for the safe retreat of more than 118,000 Allied troops.

Issued in lieu of Nₒ 09650 lost.

Page 2.

Surname MARTIN

Other Names WILLIAM

Rank (at time of issue) CAPTAIN, R.M.
(ACTING MAJOR)

Ship (at time of issue) HQ
COMBINED OPERATIONS

Place of Birth
CARDIFF

Year of Birth 1907

Issued by

At ADMIRALTY

Date 2nd February 1943.

Page 3.
Navy Form S.1511

NAVAL
IDENTITY CARD No. 148228

Signature of Bearer
W. Martin.

Visible distinguishing marks
NIL.

A naval identity card bears the likeness of Major William Martin, World War II's Man Who Never Was—a phantom used by Allied intelligence to pass false invasion plans to Axis agents.

The body was quite real, but Major William Martin, Royal Marines, was a total phony—the Man Who Never Was, as Montagu titled his history of Martin's strange odyssey. The false identity and fake secret papers tucked into the corpse's pockets and briefcase had been painstakingly concocted to hoodwink the Germans about the coming Allied invasion of southern Europe. Martin's chief creators were Montagu and Flight Lieutenant Charles Cholmondeley, members of a high-level British security committee charged with keeping prospective Allied operations under wraps. If a leak was detected or if enemies appeared to anticipate an operation in the works, the committee sought a scheme for throwing them off the track.

As early as the summer of 1942, Allied strategists were already plotting the invasion of southern Europe. They zeroed in on Sicily as the attack point because of its proximity to North Africa, which finally came under Allied control in the spring of 1943. Sicily's southern shore bristled with Axis aircraft and artillery, ready to hail explosives on Allied convoys bound for the eastern Mediterranean.

The advantages of conquering Sicily at the invasion's outset overwhelmed any alternative target. Prime Minister Winston Churchill put the security committee's tricky task in a nutshell when he remarked, "Anybody but a damn fool would *know* it is Sicily." Only the most watertight of deceptions could persuade the Germans to relax their defenses in Sicily and strengthen them elsewhere.

Montagu and his confederates chose two targets for their fictitious invasion: the island of Sardinia in the western Mediterranean and the Peloponnesus in southern Greece. If the Germans fell for it, they would be planning not for one operation but two, centered some 800 miles apart.

Given this message, the committee had to come up with a medium. It was Cholmondeley's brainstorm to use a dead man to deliver false documents. The lieutenant's colleagues bought the plan, which they dubbed Operation Mincemeat. The intelligence team accepted as a given that the Germans would eventually gain access to the corpse; although officially neutral, Spain was full of German spies and collaborators. The real key to Operation Mincemeat was the most scrupulous attention to detail, for the suspicious Germans were sure to scrutinize the evidence with extreme care. Montagu consulted various specialists noted for their expertise and their clamlike ability to keep their mouths shut. A pathologist, for instance, was enlisted to describe causes of death compatible with an air crash at sea; it was essential that the corpse pass its postmortem with flying colors. When and where to launch the body toward shore was pinned down after studying data about winds and tides.

War produces a surfeit of bodies, but it took diligent searching to find the right one—a young man who had died of exposure and pneumonia, since the chances were good that the fluid in his lungs would be mistaken for seawater. With the body in cold storage until needed, the committee selected his name, service, and rank. Getting a usable photo for his identity card was not easy. The obvious tack did not succeed. "It is impossible to describe," Montagu wrote, "how utterly and hopelessly dead any photograph of the body looked." By chance, Montagu met an officer who bore a strong resemblance to Martin. Without giving the game away, Montagu persuaded the man to sit for a photo.

Telling props were assembled to breathe life into the dead major—theater ticket stubs, an invitation to a London nightclub, a notice of an overdrawn bank account, a snapshot of his fiancée, two love letters, a grumpy note from his father concerning fuel rationing.

Montagu had to dream up and subtly communicate a good reason for Major Martin to carry a top-secret document from an official of the highest level to a commander in North Africa. The solution: Make Martin an expert in landing craft on the staff of Combined Operations chief Lord Louis Mountbatten, then detach the major temporarily to run a training course in Algiers, the Allied headquarters for Africa. In a letter cooked up by Montagu, Lord Mountbatten asked Andrew Cunningham, commander of the Mediterranean Fleet, to send Martin back to London "as soon as the assault is over. He might bring some sardines with him."

Warming to the art of fiction, Montagu was pleased with his arch little joke about Sardinia. The Germans would get the point when they read the most vital of the documents, the letter on which British hopes were pinned. In this chatty, old-boy masterpiece of deceit, Vice-Chief of the Imperial General Staff Archibald Nye purports to bring his colleague in Tunisia, General Harold Alexander, up to date on critical War Office decisions about Brimstone, the code name for the Sardinian invasion, and Husky, the operation in the Peloponnesus. Sicily is to serve as the cover for Brimstone, Nye writes, adding that there seems to be a very good chance of making the enemy "think we will go for Sicily—it is an obvious objective and one about which he must be nervous." The crafty author signs off with a chummy "Archie."

Within two weeks after the delivery of Major Martin's corpse, there were signs that the security committee had a hit. Someone in the Spanish navy had certainly taken a peek into the major's briefcase, for when a naval officer delivered it to the British attaché in Madrid, the key was in the lock. And it was the navy that filled in German intelligence about Major Martin.

When the major's effects reached London, a scientific examination of the letters showed that they had been opened, then carefully resealed. Whatever the Germans might make of the contents, the committee was pleased that its carefully laid information pipeline had sprung such a fine leak. Conferring in Washington with President Roosevelt, Churchill received a succinct message: "Mincemeat Swallowed Whole."

The message was borne out on July 10 when Allied forces landing on Sicily's southern coast met little resistance from the Germans. Montagu's committee soon learned that the Germans had shifted their defensive strength from the south to the west and the north—the areas most likely to be assaulted in conjunction with an invasion of Sardinia.

Documents seized after Germany's surrender were the proof of the Mincemeat. An intelligence memo from the files of Admiral Karl Dönitz, head of Germany's navy, states flatly, "The genuineness of the captured documents is above suspi-

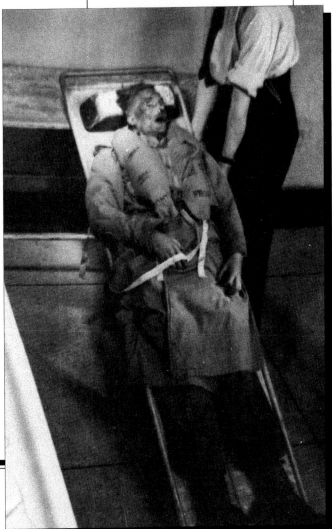

cion." The admiral's diary entry for May 14, 1943, records a major disagreement between Hitler and Mussolini: "The Führer does not agree with the Duce that the most likely invasion point is Sicily. Furthermore, he believes that the discovered Anglo-Saxon order confirms the assumption that the planned attack will be directed mainly against Sardinia and the Peloponnesus." How wrong he was.

As for the dead hero of Operation Mincemeat, the man who never was, was also never known. The real identity of the corpse that became Major Martin remains a secret to this day. □

The corpse of "Major Martin," keystone of an operation code-named Mincemeat, is loaded into a canister for its voyage to Spain aboard a British submarine.

Abdul Hamid Bakkush *(center)*, the Libyan prime minister deposed by Colonel Muammar Qaddafi, sits calmly at a 1984 Cairo press conference as Egyptian officials display photos used to convince Qaddafi that Bakkush had been killed.

Death on the Nile?

Not a man to deal gently with his political enemies, Libyan dictator Muammar Qaddafi decided in 1984 to have one old foe killed. The intended victim was Abdul Hamid Bakkush, who had been Libya's prime minister before Colonel Qaddafi seized power in a coup in 1969.

Keeping himself well insulated from the planned assassination, the Libyan strongman had several layers of intermediaries. The first was his ambassador to Malta, who in turn promised four terrorists a handsome payoff to find and hire yet another band of terrorists to actually pull the trigger. Bakkush was living in Egypt, so, in due course, the four recruiters journeyed to Cairo and found several locals to do the dirty work.

On November 12, Bakkush vanished. Four days later, Libya's official radio jubilantly announced that the "stray dog" had been executed by a death squad devoted to liquidating enemies of the nation's revolution. But Qaddafi's triumph over the stray dog was short-lived. On November 17, Egyptian president Hosni Mubarak announced that Abdul Hamid Bakkush was alive and well. Within hours, the former prime minister proved it by appearing at a news conference. Accompanying him was the Egyptian minister in charge of police, who revealed that his country's officials had gotten wind of the plot even before the first terrorist arrived in Cairo. And forewarned enabled the Egyptians to be ingeniously forearmed.

The plot was an affront to President Mubarak, who was no friend of Qaddafi's and who was, after all, Bakkush's host and protector. Various forms of retaliation were suggested; one hotheaded adviser even suggested that Mubarak bomb a Libyan airfield to express official displeasure. The president, however, was attracted by a cooler proposition: Egyptian undercover police would get acquainted with Qaddafi's terrorist recruiters and get themselves taken on as the hit men, then carry out their own version of the assassination.

The police remained mum on how they pulled off the first stage, but after the ringers were hired, officials popped the real terrorists into jail and hustled Bakkush off to a safe hideout. The Libyan ambassador had demanded that his assassins provide photographs of the dead Bakkush, so with fine dramatic flair the intended victim flopped onto the floor and was liberally doused with the Egyptian equivalent of ketchup while the camera snapped away. His pale suit was a mess, probably unwearable thereafter, but a necessary sacrifice to realism.

A "hit man" flew to Malta, where he handed over the gory photographs to Qaddafi's intermediary, along with a letter, purportedly from one of the recruiters, asking prompt payment and praising the work done by the "local cousins." From the ambassador the news flashed to Muammar Qaddafi. His triumphant crowing stopped abruptly when, like a well-aimed slapstick cream pie, the Egyptian news conference smacked him squarely in the face. □

Splotched with fake blood, Bakkush's "corpse" was photographed to show Qaddafi that his order to kill his political foe had been carried out.

IN THE NAME OF SCIENCE

For science, presumably the temple of ultimate truth, fraud can be a deadly intruder: It survives by destroying the great mutual trust that scientists must share. Often, the perpetrators of scientific deception are scholars and technicians of the first rank who, for their own unfathomable reasons, opt to spend their careers running just ahead of a breaking wave of exposure. Some scientists, titanic thinkers among them, more compelled by their own theories than by empirical truths, march backward from foregone conclusions to experimentation, tailoring results to fit along the way.

As with everything human, hoaxes perpetrated in the name of science offer dramatic extremes. On the one hand, there is that innocent itch to bamboozle, which becomes especially intense around the first of April, when the high seriousness of science cries out for an inoculation of witty nonsense. On the other, a cold-blooded hoax may distort an entire line of scholarship until the fakery finally comes to light, as it seems inevitably to do—and destroys the guilty savant in the ensuing glare.

Not Quite the Greatest

Around AD 145, Claudius Ptolemy, a Greek scholar at Egypt's famed Alexandria Library, produced one of history's most enduring astronomical works, *Mathematikes syntaxeos.* The observations and supporting mathematics put forth in this work essentially shaped for centuries the human view of the universe: an Earth-centered system in which the planets and the Sun moved like lights on the cars of a Ferris wheel, against a spherical backdrop of stars. The Ptolemaic model prevailed for more than a thousand years, during which the Arab scientists who had inherited Ptolemy's tome renamed it *Almagest*—Greek for "The Greatest." Even when the alternative design of a Polish canon named Nicolaus Copernicus replaced Ptolemy's geocentric system with a more realistic Sun-centered one in the sixteenth century, Ptolemy kept his reputation. Now, according to some scholars, it looks as if he was not only wrong—he was something of a fraud as well.

One of the technical beauties of the *Almagest* was its extensive compilations of planetary and solar motions and stars. But modern astronomers, calculating planetary motion back through the centuries, find that many of Ptolemy's so-called observations are too good, a sure sign of numbers fudged to square with theory. Errors in the timing of solstices (the extreme northern and southern points in the Sun's annual track across Earth's sky) and equinoxes (when the Sun appears to cross the

Earth's equator) suggest that Ptolemy simply invented the numbers.

There is also evidence, put forth by astronomer Dennis Rawlins at the University of California, San Diego, that Ptolemy did not map the stars himself but simply copied data obtained two centuries earlier by Hipparchus of Rhodes. The tip-off: Alexandria is five degrees of latitude south of Rhodes, which

means that Ptolemy could have observed five degrees of southern sky that were invisible to Hipparchus, but none of the 1,025 stars in Ptolemy's catalog come from that part of the sky. Moreover, many of Ptolemy's celestial-motion solutions are based on the latitude of Rhodes, not Alexandria. The *Almagest* may have been the greatest, but it was not the truth. □

Newton's Fudge

When Isaac Newton published *Philosophiae Naturalis Principia Mathematica*—the seminal work known simply as *Principia*—in 1687, he established the principle that scientific theory and experimental evidence must coincide exactly. As one historian put it, a Newtonian universe of precision replaced a world of more or less.

Newton spun a formidable tangle of mathematical computations to make his theories fit the real world, and he seemed to do so with extraordinary precision for his day. His proof of his theory of universal gravitation—crucial to understanding how the universe works—carried out calculations of lunar orbit and other dynamic features to accuracies of about one part in three thousand, astonishing for the seventeenth century. Incredibly, his computed speed of sound almost exactly matched the 1,142-foot-per-second value measured by colleagues. And, in calculating what is called the precession of the equinoxes—the eastward drift of the Sun's apparent point of crossing the equator in March and September, about fourteen thousandths of a degree per year—he again achieved an accuracy of about one part in three thousand.

Modern scholars have found, however, that Newton was not marching through his jungle of mathematics empirically; he was marching backward from his already-hardened theories. Thus, the impressive calculations on which his law of gravitation rests were made after the fact, drawn not from observations but from conclusions. His computed speed of sound at first fell some 20 percent below measured values and was gradually pumped up by inventive mathematics in successive editions of the *Principia*. To make his precession of the equinoxes fit the real world, Newton had to make a 50 percent adjustment in a key value, and shave about thirty-two miles off the planet's circumference. Nevertheless acknowledged as the father of modern science, Newton is now seen as the perfecter of one of science's vital tools: the fudge factor. □

Sir Isaac Newton, shown here in a 1702 painting by Sir Godfrey Kneller, sometimes juggled numbers to guarantee a good fit between observation and theory.

Moonshine

A penny New York newspaper called the *Sun* broke the astonishing news in August 1835: Life had been discovered on the moon. It was not life as earthlings knew it, but a strange population of blue unicorns, beavers that walked upright, and humanlike creatures with wings. Talk of the discovery echoed from New York to Boston. Some proclaimed it the herald of a new era. And everyone clamored for copies of the *Sun.*

The story of lunar life began on August 25, when the *Sun* published what purported to be a special supplement to the *Edinburgh Journal of Science,* containing a report of some amazing discoveries. These were attributed to Britain's Sir John Herschel, who was then working at an observatory on the Cape of Good Hope.

The English astronomer, as the scientific community knew, had sailed to the Cape of Good Hope in 1833 to set up an observatory. But the *Sun* seemed to have obtained the only known results of his expedition. Before sailing for southern Africa, according to the August 25 issue, Herschel had built a remarkable telescope based on "an entirely new principle." The newspaper described the telescope as having a twenty-four-foot focal length and the capability of magnifying objects 42,000 times—comparable in size to the largest telescopes of the day, but with seven times their magnifying power. Herschel, the paper stated, had turned his gigantic refractor toward the lunar surface in January 1835—and a wondrous landscape of luxuriant forests and rolling plains, deep rivers and white sand beaches had sprung into view.

The *Sun*'s incredible lunar story continued through August 31. In the early episodes, readers learned that the moon's rich landscape was inhabited by "herds of brown quadrupeds" whose eyes were shielded from the fierce sun by a flap of hairy skin; an antelope-like animal of "a bluish lead color," with a "*single horn*"; and a creature resembling a beaver that carried "its young in its arms, like a human being," lived in well-built huts, and used fire.

With successive installments, demand for the *Sun* grew. Running its presses ten hours a day, the tabloid barely kept pace with the demand. On August 28, publisher Benjamin H. Day proudly announced that daily circulation had reached 19,360, the largest in the world, surpassing even that of London's venerable *Times.* That day's installment also answered readers' most eagerly asked question: Were there humans on the moon? Yes, said the *Sun*—and no.

According to the paper, the moon was inhabited by a species dubbed "the Verspertilio-homo, or man-bat." The creatures "averaged four feet in height, were covered, except on the face, with short and glossy copper-colored hair, and had wings" that lay "snugly upon their backs, from the top of the shoulders to the calves of the legs." Although their faces resembled those of orangutans, they wore more human expressions, and their gait was "both erect and dignified." The *Sun* described some of their activities but discreetly kept silent on others that "would but ill comport with our terrestrial notions of decorum."

Competing eastern newspapers praised the *Sun*'s coverage of the lunar discoveries; even the respected *New York Times* called them "probable and plausible." European papers, meanwhile, faithfully recounted the story without mentioning its source.

For many readers, the discovery of life on earth's satellite was less a surprise than a fulfilled expectation. Several European astronomers and theologians had already expressed belief in lunar life. A practitioner of both disciplines, Thomas Dick, proposed that geometric symbols large enough to be visible 240,000 miles away on the moon be laid out on Russia's Siberian plains as a way of making contact with the moon folk.

Two professors from Yale University, named Dennison Olmsted and Elias Loomis, were so excited by the story that they made a personal trip to New York. They wanted to see the forty pages of mathematical calculations "on which a great part of the established lunar theory depends"—highly technical material that the *Sun* had not reproduced. But upon their arrival, *Sun* reporter Richard Locke regretfully informed them that the only copy of the Edinburgh supplement had been sent to a printer and directed them to the printing office. Unfortunately, that printer had shipped the journal elsewhere. After an unplanned tour of several offices in New York City, the bewildered Olmsted and Loomis returned to New Haven empty-handed. And Locke, the true author of the moon chronicle, breathed a sigh of relief.

The Great Moon Hoax, as it came to be known, was science-fiction writer Locke's magnificent creation, spun from a blend of fact, pseudoscience, and fantasy. Astronomer Sir John Herschel, for example, really had been ensconced at the Cape of Good Hope, using a telescope, though smaller than the one the paper described. The deception had begun soon after Locke joined the *Sun*'s staff and found the two-year-old paper struggling against older, better-established competitors. He offered to write a story that would seize public attention and boost circulation. Publisher Day agreed, and the moon hoax was born.

But Locke's goal was more than deception; he wanted to satirize the intense, but often misguided, public interest in extraterrestrial life. A Cambridge graduate with an interest in astronomy, he was well acquainted with the beliefs of astronomers and theologians such as Thomas Dick and used his spurious lunar report to roast them. A year after the Great Moon Hoax was exposed, an unamused Dick responded by writing a sermonette in his book *Celestial Scenery* that placed Locke squarely "in the class of liars and deceivers."

In the end, it was not the journalist's guile but his generous spirit that exposed his lunar charade. Locke had evidently confessed the truth to a friend at the *Journal of Commerce* to save the man from the embarrassment of reprinting the story—and this friend seems to have repaid him by informing his employers of the truth. In early September, the *Journal* told all.

The *Sun* itself held out until mid-September before admitting the hoax. But it offered no apology. Instead, the paper took credit for entertaining the public and fooling its competitors. As for astronomer Herschel, he thought the whole story very amusing— although, he added, he feared that his real discoveries would not prove half so interesting. □

Fossil Lies

It is common knowledge today that fossils are the naturally preserved remains or imprints of animals and plants from prehistoric times. But in the early eighteenth century, many scholars thought fossils were the remains of creatures destroyed in the biblical flood. Others believed them to be the stone offspring formed from animal sperm that had seeped into the earth. Fossil theories were almost as numerous as the scholars who wrote about them, among those Dr. Johann Bartholomew Adam Beringer, respected physician and faculty member of Germany's University of Würzburg.

Fossils from all over Europe graced Beringer's display cabinet, including some from the duchy of Franconia, where he lived. Not satisfied with this collection, the doctor hired some local youths to dig the surrounding hills for him. On May 31, 1725, the diggers, working on nearby Mount Eivelstadt, uncovered three distinctly uncommon stones. All bore figures in raised relief: One figure represented a sun and its rays, the others, worms.

An excited Beringer sent the boys back for more. They labored from June until November, exhuming 2,000 stones with raised figures: exotic and everyday animals, delicate flowers and herbs, fiery comets and distant stars. Even more amazing were stones bearing Arabic, Hebrew, and Latin characters, some forming words. Beringer believed his incredible find to be fossils of a type never seen before and hastened to inform the world about them.

In order to explain the discovery, Beringer first needed a theoretical framework that would account for both the figured stones and the lettered ones. He consulted a number of language experts, who told him that the letters and words referred to the name of God. This led Beringer to embrace a theory, proposed by earlier scholars, that the fossils were *lusus naturae*, or "pranks of nature"—nature, in this case, being God. Beringer inferred that the letters and words were manifestations of "the one and only author of these wondrous stones." In essence, he concluded that God had been playfully sculpting rocks—and had signed his work.

The professor labored throughout the winter on a book about his finds, commissioning expensive plates to reproduce the figured stones. As he rushed to complete his tome, however, two Würzburg colleagues, J. Ignatz Roderick, a geography professor, and Georg von Eckhart, the university librarian, started a rumor that the stones were fakes. To prove their point, they laid a trap for Beringer. Roderick, who had learned carving from his father, created stones similar to Beringer's, then sent Christian Zänger, one of Beringer's diggers, to sell them to the doctor as fossils. The unsuspecting Beringer bought them, as he had bought all the other figured stones. Roderick and Eckhart then triumphantly revealed the new stones' true origin—proof, they suggested, that all Beringer's figured stones were fakes.

To the blindly convinced professor, however, their trap proved nothing. There had always been "counterfeiters and money spoilers" in the world, he said, but that did not mean all money was suspect. In one entire chapter of his book, Beringer described the two men's efforts to destroy his reputation and nullify his great work with their false charges. "Their clever efforts might have succeeded," he boasted, "had not my vigilance discovered the deceit and throttled it at birth."

Sure of himself and his theory, Beringer published his book, *Lithographiae Wirceburgensis*, in early 1726, and fellow scholars rushed to buy. Then, suddenly, the author was discovered anxiously trying to recover every single copy of his paleolithic masterpiece. Having spent a fortune publishing his work, Beringer now spent a second fortune to retrieve it. Something had brought him to the belated realization that his famous fossils were indeed fakes. One possibly apocryphal story claims that, after publishing his book, he had found one more stone

with the singular inscription: *Beringer*.

Humiliated by the hoax, Beringer requested a judicial hearing to find the perpetrators. At the April 1726 proceedings, the digger Zänger was persuaded by officials to reveal the truth. The stones were indeed "pranks," he confessed, but not of nature: They were the malicious forgeries of Roderick and Eckhart, the same men who had tried to trap Beringer earlier. At the hearing, officials learned that the two, thinking their colleague arrogant, had set out more than a year before to destroy his academic reputation. They had carved hundreds of the figured and lettered stones, then hired Zänger to help polish and bury them on Mount Eivelstadt. Then, perhaps having second thoughts about the far-reaching consequences of Beringer's forthcoming publication, they tried to prove the stones were fake, without confessing their part in the deception. But Beringer had been too enamored of his theory to under-

stand their warning, and he proceeded to destroy his professional reputation himself.

The two guilty academics received punishments tailored to scholars. Roderick lost his position at the university. Eckhart managed to retain his but was denied access to the archives he needed to complete his history of the duchy of Würzburg. He died four years later, his work still unpublished. As for Beringer, he achieved a kind of immortality—though not quite what he had envisioned. In 1767, a second edition of his figured-stones book was published, not for the edification of colleagues but for the public's amusement. Today it is a collector's item—and Beringer remains forever one of science's great dupes. □

Running on Empty

John Worrell Keely was born in Philadelphia on September 3, 1837, and grew up to be a powerfully built carpenter whose poise and certitude inspired immediate confidence. In 1872, when he was thirty-five, Keely began to apply his considerable natural talent for mechanical invention to a succession of so-called Keely Machines, powerful devices capable of running on very little. Keely boasted that his engines would one day drive a train from coast to coast. They never did. But they were able to propel their inventor, usually in some style, for more than a quarter century on nothing at all.

As he recalled later, he had drawn his 1872 inspiration from watching the vibrations of a tuning fork, which suggested a new source of motive energy. His "hydro-pneumatic-pulsating-vacu-engine" would use vibrations in a device he called a liberator to disintegrate a few drops of water, freeing nature's basic "etheric force." This energy source, put to work by his motor, would power a steamship from New York to Liverpool on a gallon of water. Because water was known to contain hydrogen, an energetic, explosive light element, Keely's claims had a quirky kind of credibility. A research-and-development check for $10,000 was immediately forthcoming from investors.

During the winter of 1873-1874, Keely demonstrated a sort of prototype of his motor that seemed very powerful indeed. Its pressure gauge registered 50,000 pounds per square inch, and the machinery it drove ripped apart cables, twist-ed metal bars, and fired bullets through several inches of wooden boards. The press excitedly saluted the achievement, and speculators, including many poor ones attracted by the mirage of eventual wealth, flocked to the inventor. When the Keely Motor Company was formed soon afterward, it had five million dollars capital with which to continue development.

For years afterward, Keely parried stockholders' queries, always promising the practical motor he saw on the horizon—but unable to deliver it. Conservative Philadelphia newspapers finally turned on him and brought in prominent scientists to discredit his idea. Eventually, the Keely Motor Company itself withheld funds for its delinquent president's further experimentation. By 1881, Keely was described by press reports as starving and close to despair.

News of his plight touched one reader, Clara J. Bloomfield Moore, the widow of a wealthy paper manufacturer. She offered Keely her support. Flush once more, he embarked on the second phase of his motor-development career but kept clear of the perfidious Keely Motor Company that had cut off his funds. On December 14, 1886, he announced that he had discovered a new, improved form of energy. The former etheric force, he said, had failed to live up to expectations after all—and he had gone on to something better. The new force depended on the vibrations of a previously unknown fluid between atoms in the ubiquitous, if ill-defined, substance called ether.

Sued by disappointed stockholders, Keely went to jail rather than explain the difference between the former force and the present one. An expert witness, however, examined the apparatus and testified that it was indeed different from the Keely motor built a dozen years earlier, and the inventor was soon released. Set up in his Philadelphia workshop, Keely's new machine was large and dangerously powerful. It comprised the motor itself, the vibration transmitter, and a hollow brass sphere on a metal platform, all connected with wires and a bristling phalanx of steel rods. To start the machine, Keely stood on the platform and played a musical instrument—a violin, harmonica, zither, or plain tuning fork. Aroused, the machine then demonstrated its power by ripping apart a cable.

Clara Moore was Keely's staunchest supporter, but over the protests of her son, Clarence. In 1895, forced to respond to litigation concerning the handling of her late husband's estate, the widow Moore sought an expert's opinion of the Keely motor. The task went to E. Alexander Scott, an electrical engineer, who was allowed to examine Keely's machines and swiftly identified the mysterious motive force: compressed air. The seemingly solid rods connecting different parts of the machinery, he discovered, were in fact hollow conduits for pressurized air from a hidden source in the building. Asked by his benefactor in May 1896 to repeat his experiment with one of these "solid" rods cut, Keely refused—as Scott had predicted he would. Her belief shattered, Clara Moore cut Keely back to an allowance of $250 a month.

Keely died on November 18, 1898, aged sixty-one. When Clara Moore learned of his death, she reportedly said, "I hope that he imparted the secret to someone before he died." On January 5, 1899, she, too, passed away.

In fact, Keely had shared the details of his motor with no one, not even his wife. Soon after his mother's death, however, Clarence Moore rented the North Twentieth Street property. The motor itself had been removed by Keely's friends, who hoped to cash in on his discovery. Moore had experts from the nearby University of Pennsylvania rip the empty place apart—and exposed the details of Keely's dirty pneumatic secret.

Keely had conducted his demonstrations in a second-floor room in the narrow two-story building. The floor, Moore's examiners discovered, had been honeycombed with hidden hollow tubes, which could be opened and closed by Keely's foot, keeping time with the music he used to activate the machine.

Downstairs, the ground floor was false—in effect, a stage, filled with hidden pipes. In a back room to which no one had been admitted, the investigators found a three-ton, forty-inch-diameter iron sphere with valved fittings. Evidently, Keely had charged the vessel, tested to a pressure of 28,000 pounds per square inch, with compressed air, which he could then divert as needed to power his machine. Admittedly a kind of engineering masterpiece, the motor had actually done very little—except keep Keely in style.

Even with the evidence of fraud laid out before them, many Keely followers kept their faith in the inventor, despite their hero's professed preference in epitaphs: "Keely, the greatest humbug of the nineteenth century." □

Peasnik

In 1865, Gregor Mendel, an Augustinian monk, read a paper—"Experiments in Plant Hybridization"—before the Natural History Society of Brno, in what is now Czechoslovakia. In a series of breeding experiments with peas, he reported, he had discovered a previously unknown hereditary principle. His plants had demonstrated that the units of heredity (which Danish geneticist Wilhelm L. Johannsen would name genes in 1909) were transmitted from parents to offspring without change, generation after generation. Some inherited characteristics, he said, recurred in most offspring; others tended to be knocked out of the hereditary picture by what ◊

Nineteenth-century inventor and con man John Worrell Keely sits in his Philadelphia laboratory with a model of one of several machines he claimed could produce vast energy from little fuel.

Gregor Mendel at forty, two years before he explained genetic inheritance.

are now called dominant strains. Experimenting with some 28,000 plants over a decade, he had obtained a ratio of three to one: In experiments with tall and dwarf plants, for example, in every four offspring, three would breed tall and only one would breed a dwarf.

His findings were largely ignored. Mendel died in 1884, bitterly disappointed by this scientific cold shoulder. Not until sixteen years later did European scientists realize that his Brno paper had identified the hereditary mechanism that was missing from Darwin's concept of species evolution.

And not until 1936 did anyone notice that Mendel's figures were too good to be true.

Before the rediscovery of Mendel, scientists believed that the inheritance of parental characteristics by offspring was a process of blending. With each offspring, many traits were stirred together to produce the new individual. But in 1867, two years after Mendel read his crucial paper, Edinburgh engineer Fleeming Jenkin noted that, logically, such blending tended to reduce, not promote, difference—and could not support the chance variations on which evolution depended. In effect, the performance of Mendel's peas rescued the idea of evolution from its enemies, for it offered a rigid mech-

anism for inheritance that could be modified through random mutations. In England, the champion of Mendelism—and the man who gave genetics its name—was William Bateson.

But Mendelian genetics, like a game of dice, operates not on absolutes, but statistical probabilities. Most of the time, results should follow the three-to-one ratio, and offspring should tend to reproduce the dominant line. Curiously, Mendel's pea plants showed a steady ratio of three to one, without the exceptions that should occur. In 1936, British statistician Ronald A. Fisher scrutinized Mendel's numbers—and decided that they fell impossibly close to theory. "The data of most, if not all, of the experiments," he wrote, "have been falsified so as to agree closely with Mendel's expectations."

Apparently, the good monk's hypothesis had been too good to be disturbed by experimental reality. But so popular had the formerly neglected researcher become that most scientists were inclined to give Mendel the benefit of the doubt. As so often happens when such discrepancies come to light, they were blamed on the great man's hapless assistant. And the obscure monk, ignored in his own time, remains a revered founding father of modern genetics. □

Chiselers

The bald giant's gray face wore just the faintest trace of a smile, but his great naked body was twisted, as in a final painful contortion at the moment of death. Apparently ancient, the ten-foot four-inch figure lay in a shallow excavation, where the interment of centuries seemed to have transformed him into stone.

Two well diggers uncovered him on October 16, 1869, on the struggling farm of one Stub Newell, near the upstate New York town of Cardiff. Word of the find soon drew a local crowd. A practical man, Newell erected a tent over the megalithic humanoid and began charging half a dollar for a fifteen-minute look at him. As word spread, viewers came by the hundreds to be awed by the astonishing figure. "As one looked upon it he could not help feeling that he was in the presence of a great and superior being," wrote one reporter. "The crowd as they gathered around it seemed almost spellbound. There was no levity."

The Cardiff Giant, as the ossified man was called, offered something to everyone. To scientists, he was a paleolithic discovery of the first magnitude. To the clergy, he was proof that, as the Bible said, there once had been a race of giant humans. And to a tall, powerfully

made Binghamton cigar maker and all-around rogue named George Hull, he was both a marvelous prank and a money tree.

Some three years earlier, Hull had visited his sister in Iowa, where the unbelieving New Yorker had an opportunity to argue biblical truths with a passing evangelist. The preacher maintained that the giants of Genesis 6:4 had really existed—a race of men, he estimated, at least twice as tall as their modern counterparts. The conversation, Hull would recall later, had started him thinking about just such a man—a petrified one. Hull pondered all this ◊

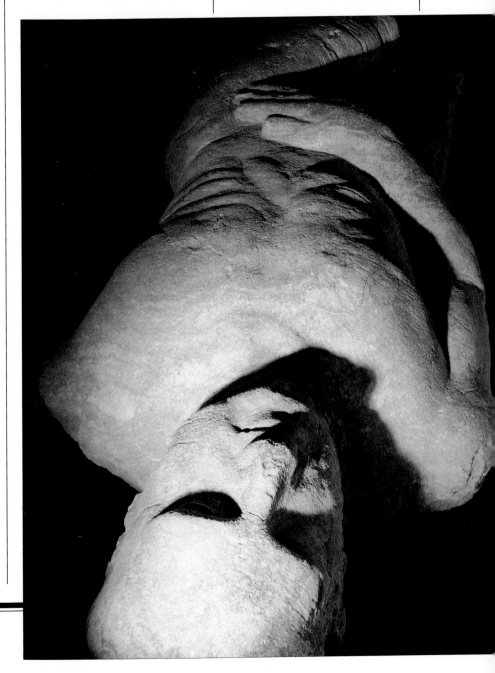

Modeled after its creator, confidence artist George Hull, the Cardiff Giant was carved by two Chicago sculptors from a twelve-foot slab of Iowa gypsum.

on his return to Binghamton and in June 1868 decided on a plan.

He and a colleague visited a quarry in Fort Dodge, Iowa, and after numerous false starts, found a twelve-foot oblong of gypsum four feet wide and twenty-two inches thick. With some difficulty, they transported the ton-and-a-half block to a railhead and shipped it to Edward Burghardt, a marble cutter in Chicago. There, two sculptors, Henry Salle and Fred Mohrmann, chiseled the block into a reclining giant racked by terminal agony. According to a close friend of Hull's, the giant was "the perfect image" of its creator, who not only supervised the sculptors, but modeled for them as well.

For greater realism, Hull put hundreds of darning needles into a wooden block, with which he hammered simulated pores into the stone skin. He also produced a believable skin texture by rubbing the gypsum with sand and a wet sponge, then aging it with a rinse of sulfuric acid. In November 1868, he had the statue shipped to upstate New York, then carted over a circuitous rural route to the farm of his cousin, Stub Newell. The giant was buried behind the Newell barn and left to age for yet another year. The whole enterprise had cost Hull some $2,600—a mere week's take, once the Cardiff Giant was discovered.

But belief in the gypsum goliath was short-lived. Initially taken to be an authentic petrified human being, the figure had retained soft external parts that leave no trace in natural fossils. Perhaps, supporters said, it was not an ossified human but an ancient statue. And maybe, as some experts declared, it was an out-and-out fraud. Paradoxically, the more fraudulent the giant seemed to be, the greater became its popularity, causing the legendary showman P. T. Barnum to offer Hull $60,000, a huge sum for 1869, for his petrified man. When Hull declined the offer, Barnum had his own figure carved out of stone and billed it as the real Cardiff Giant. Then Hull sold a three-quarter interest in the statue to a group of city fathers in Syracuse for $37,500. After they had made their profit, Hull took his giant on the road, where, hoax or not, the enormous figure drew enormous crowds.

In the meantime, however, Hull's creation had fallen from favor with the press. Reporters discovered that Stub Newell had not really needed another well after all, and they heard about George Hull's traveling around New York State with a giant-size wooden crate a year earlier. Other journalists detected the flow of money from Newell to his cousin and picked up Hull's trail back at the Fort Dodge quarry. The stonecutters were identified in Chicago and confessed. His hoax exposed, George Hull stayed resolutely in character: He laughed and told all. The revelation in no way damaged either Hull or his creation. The giant's popularity had been waning somewhat. Now thoroughly debunked, Old Hoaxey, as he had come to be called, toured to renewed profits and revived acclaim. □

Second Son

Near the village of Beulah, Colorado, William Conant recounted later, he and his son had noticed a rocky protuberance, which, when uncovered, was seen to be a man's foot. Further excavation revealed a giant stone figure lying in a shallow grave. The seven-and-a-half-foot body weighed some 600 pounds and had a smallish, simian head and extraordinarily long arms. It was, observers agreed, either a petrified example of the elusive missing link between apes and humans or a statue of great age. But it was most certainly real. "There can be no question about the genuineness of this piece of statuary," proclaimed Denver's *Daily Times* for September 20, 1877. "The stone shows the effects of time, and the circumstances of

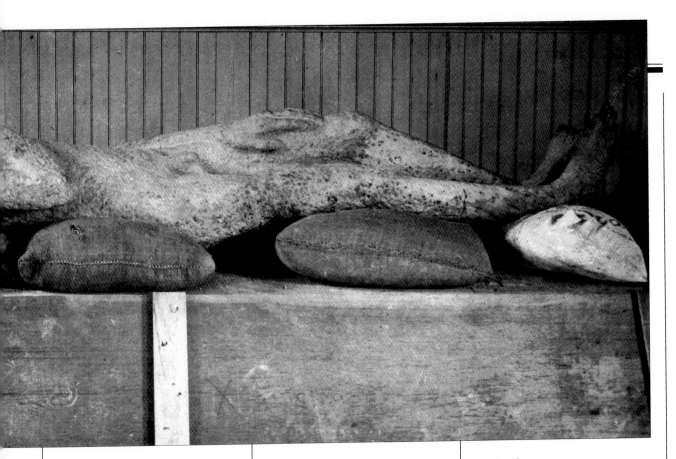

the discovery are such as to preclude anything like a repetition of the clumsy Cardiff Giant fraud."

In fact, the Solid Muldoon, as the figure soon came to be known, was the fake giant's little brother, fathered by the same George Hull. Now fifty-three, Hull had decided to surpass himself with a new stone man. Over a period of some three years, a figure was sculpted from a mortar of pulverized stone, clay, plaster, ground bones, blood, and meat, then kiln-fired for several weeks to produce a suitably ossified hominid. Strapped for funds, Hull was able to secure financial help from showman P. T. Barnum, Conant's former employer. Then, Conant, Hull, and a few others planted the massive figure near Beulah several months before Conant's feigned find, hoping to cash in on the fact that Colorado's year-old statehood would add luster.

But, like its predecessor, the Solid Muldoon hoax was short-lived. While the stone giant was being exhibited in New York, one of Hull's unpaid creditors revealed the forgery to the *New York Tribune*, which exposed it on February 2, 1878. The Solid Muldoon disappeared without a trace, leaving behind a monument on a low mound familiarly called Muldoon Hill since his discovery there.

It also left a more enduring mystery: Why was it known as the Solid Muldoon? The *Pueblo Chieftain* reported soon after the figure's discovery, " 'MULDOON, THE SOLID MAN' is what the boys have christened Mr. Conant's discovery," and began referring to it as the "Solid Muldoon." Another paper thought the name had come from an old Irish song about a Muldoon

Another George Hull creation, the Solid Muldoon, was "discovered" near Pueblo, Colorado, in 1877.

who was a "solid man." In 1981, Western novelist Louis L'Amour wrote the Colorado Historical Society to identify the Muldoon in question. The song, he said, had been written about William Muldoon, chairman of the New York Boxing Commission from 1921 to 1923—and before that a famous wrestler and strongman. "He was enormously popular," recalled L'Amour, "almost as popular as Babe Ruth was later, and he was variously referred to as The Iron Duke, The Old Roman, AND The Solid Man"—the sobriquet he was using when Conant "found" the Solid Muldoon. □

Scam of the Cave Bear

In the summer of 1873, Konrad Merk, a young Swiss schoolteacher, was hiking through the high country near Thayngen, on the German border, when he chanced on a cave opening hidden by overgrowth. The cavern, called Kesslerloch (Kessler Hole), tantalized him: Like many of his contemporaries, he had a keen interest in geology, sparked by the remarkable discoveries in France. There, in 1845, a cave at La Chaffaud had yielded bones engraved with images of two does, the presumed work of Stone Age cave dwellers—primitive hunters whom no one had thought capable of such artistry.

Merk returned to Kesslerloch that December with a teaching colleague and two students and began to explore the cave. The cavern proved a paleontological trove, littered with flints and bone tools from the Old Stone Age—the so-called Magdalenian period, which began some 15,000 years ago. Most exciting to Merk, however, were two bones, one etched with the likeness of a grazing reindeer, the other bearing a wild horse and the head of a musk ox. When the pieces were shown to Albert Heim, a geology professor at the University of Zurich, they caused great excitement. Heim joined Merk at Kesslerloch, hiring two Thayngen workers to help with the excavation.

Early that spring, one of the helpers, Albert Stamm, presented Merk with two more illustrated bones. One bore the profile of a bear, sitting like a circus animal, the other a three-quarter view of a seated fox—both very unlike the conventional side views found on most Stone Age relics.

When Merk published his description of the Kesslerloch finds in 1875, he noted that the bear and fox lacked the other drawings' "grace and correctness." But no one thought they were less than genuine. In the opening speech at the meeting of the German Anthropological Society in August, the chairman praised the Kesslerloch discoveries and said that they were undoubtedly authentic.

His words were aimed in part at a distinguished scientist in the audience, Ludwig Lindenschmitt, a prominent

A seated bear (above) and a fox (right) etched in blackened bones found in a Swiss cavern in 1874 were believed to be the work of Stone Age artists until someone noticed their similarity to these illustrations from a German children's book about animals.

prehistorian, founder of the Roman German Central Museum in Mainz, and a determined nonbeliever in Stone Age art. Lindenschmitt returned fire a year later. Just before the next meeting of the society, in 1876, he published a paper that called the Kesslerloch fox and bear engravings fakes—and took the opportunity to smear Konrad Merk as well. "There are many more caves and masses of bones," he sneered, "waiting to be copied."

Lindenschmitt had not detected the forgery himself. His son had picked up a copy of *Globus* magazine and was reading an illustrated article about the Thayngen excavations when the bear and fox images caught his eye. Somewhere, he realized, he had seen those drawings before—in a children's natural history book. As his father told the story later, "without saying a word," his son placed the magazine article and the children's book side by side before him. The forgery was immediately obvious.

The unfortunate Merk, stigmatized by the fraud, had actually played no part in the deception. Albert Stamm, hoping to earn the customary bonus paid for extraordinary finds, had asked a young friend named Konrad Bollinger to draw animals on two pieces of bone from the cave. Bollinger had turned to his copy of the children's book for models.

Stamm's deception was far more destructive than he intended. The senior Lindenschmitt used the Kesslerloch fakes to discredit all such discoveries, with some success. Although Merk's reputation survived the scandal, paleontology almost did not. Three years later, for example, beautiful animal paintings were discovered on the walls of caves near Altamira, Spain. But the fear of Stone Age fakery was then still so acute that the images were taken to be the work of forgers. More than twenty years elapsed before these magnificent creations were accepted as the work of talented cave dwellers. □

Light Fantastic

According to contemporary newspaper accounts, the remarkable device called the diaphote—an instrument that transmitted light as telephones transmit sound—was first shown at an 1880 meeting of the Monacacy Scientific Club of South Bethlehem, Pennsylvania. There, diaphote inventor H. E. Licks reportedly exhibited a prototype diaphote said to be capable of sending images by wire over hundreds of miles. The device consisted of a receiving mirror, transmitting wires, a galvanic battery, and what the inventor called the reproducing speculum. Licks explained that light altered the chemistry of the mirror, which in turn modulated the electrical current to produce corresponding changes in the remotely located speculum.

During a demonstration of his invention, Licks had members transmit images of an apple, a penknife, a dollar bill, and the like from one room to the receiving mirror, which had been put in another part of the building. After the meeting, the club's president, Professor L. M. Niscate, described the many possible applications of image transmission—even the possibility of printing British newspapers in New York a few hours after they appeared in London.

Word of the diaphote quickly spread. "The imagination almost fails," effused the staid *New York Times*, "before the possibilities of what the diaphote may yet accomplish." Newspapers around the country carried the story, which soon surfaced in Europe. Besides engendering general wonder, the ◊

diaphote inspired its share of diaphote-like inventions: Two Pittsburgh men tried to patent their "telephole," which would permit telephoners to see each other while they spoke, and a German inventor reported a device that permitted viewers in one city to read a newspaper held up to his instrument in another. In 1914, the *New York Times* reported that a Dr. A. M. Low had lectured on seeing by wire. "Perhaps," wrote H. E. Licks, "Dr. Low is on the right track, and if his apparatus becomes a verity, then he should give proper credit to Dr. H. E. Licks by calling it the diaphote."

From the beginning, however, a few—including the *New York World*—had sensed that the diaphote had been designed less to enlighten than to deceive. Surely, Licks, in real life a distinguished civil engineer from Connecticut named Mansfield Merriman, had never intended it to be taken very seriously. Among other things, the people assembled in South Bethlehem by Licks included the too aptly named Professor M. E. Kannick and Colonel A. D. A. Biatic, of "the Brazilian Corps of Engineers," along with club president L. M. Niscate, whose surname evokes the term "lemniscate," a horizontal figure eight. And H. E. Licks himself might have been named for the resulting innocent spiral—or helix—of deception. □

Missing Links

For nearly a decade, Charles Dawson, an amiable British solicitor and respected amateur in geology and archaeology, had poked around in a gravel pit at Piltdown Common, near the Sussex village of Uckfield. In 1908, the shallow trench yielded a tantalizing handful of interesting objects: fragments of an ancient human skull, bits of tooth from extinct hippopotamuses and elephants, and crude stone tools. But these were more than old bones and flints: They were the seeds of history's most enduring scientific hoax.

In February 1912, Dawson wrote Arthur Smith Woodward, the distinguished and impeccably honest keeper of the Department of Geology at the British Museum, to say that he had come upon an interesting site. On Piltdown Common, in rock laid down near the very dawn of man, Dawson reported, he had found some "cranial fragments" that appeared to be from the same skull as those found in 1908, along with part of a hippopotamus tooth.

On June 2, an excited Woodward joined Dawson and his friend, French Jesuit Pierre Teilhard de Chardin, who was destined to become a noted paleontologist in his own right. The trio began sifting the gravel more systematically. Soon, Dawson came up with another skull fragment, and Teilhard found a crude implement and a piece of elephant molar. Incredibly, these puzzle pieces began to suggest that, some 500,000 years ago, an early humanlike creature had coexisted with mammals long vanished from the British Isles.

Then, late in June, after Teil-

hard's departure, Dawson and Woodward chanced upon what amounted to a keystone: a powerful lower jaw, or mandible, of a hue that matched the skull's. Most significantly, its molars were worn, indicating that the jaw had come from a human, not an ape: Simian jaws do not grind down the back teeth as human jaws do. By autumn, Woodward was able by inference to reconstruct the mysterious creature's skull. It had a thick, remarkably big brain case—almost the size of modern man's—looming incongruously over the large, primitive jaw of an ape. Evidently, an enlarged brain was an early evolutionary gift to humans. Woodward called this unique creature, which seemed to bridge between apes and humans, *Eoanthropus dawsoni*—Dawson's Dawn man.

On November 21, the *Manchester Guardian* reported that Woodward had proof that, very early in the Pleistocene period (now known to have begun about two million years ago), human beings had already separated into divergent stocks: the degenerate low-browed Neanderthal discovered in Germany and the larger-brained Piltdown man. Woodward unveiled his reconstructed skull at a Geological Society meeting in December, to mixed reviews. Some thought that his reconstruction was on the mark and that the assumed age of the skull must place it in the early Pleistocene.

But others—in particular, Arthur Keith, an anatomist and museum conservator at the Royal College of Surgeons—saw profoundly greater implications. Woodward and Dawson, Keith declared, had discovered more than they knew. *Eoanthropus*, he said, must be

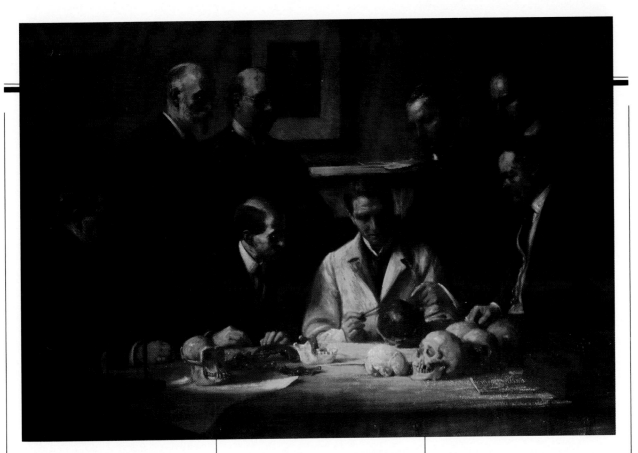

from the earlier Pliocene period, an era believed to predate modern human development. Still, the simian jaw was troublesome. Keith lamented that no fossil canine tooth had been discovered.

Conveniently, while poking around the Piltdown site with Dawson the following August, Teilhard found a canine tooth that proved a perfect fit. Nearly a year later, the researchers turned up additional rhinoceros and mastodon teeth, and a paddlelike bone object that appeared to have been carved with stone tools. Then, in January 1915, Dawson discovered what he called "Eoanthropine" frontal bones in nearby Sheffield Park; more than six months later, he found a molar to fit. Woodward presented the remains of this second skull—Piltdown II—in 1917, as proof positive that *Eoanthropus* was real.

Dawson could not share the glo-

ry. He had sickened with anemia during the first part of 1916 and died on August 10. Still, for the next thirty-seven years his immortality seemed assured by his discovery of an early link between apes and men.

In 1949, anxious to verify the presumed great age of Dawson's fragments, Dr. Kenneth Oakley of the British Museum's geology department got permission to use his newly developed method of dating samples by their fluorine content, which was known to increase with time. He found that the mastodon and elephant bones taken from the Piltdown site contained about two percent fluorine, but that the skull fragments contained barely a tenth as much. This reduced the estimated age of Piltdown man from 500,000 to 50,000 years. *Eoanthropus* could not have been a link, scientists concluded, but an

isolated blind alley of human evolution. In a way, the enigma of Piltdown man had only deepened.

But Oakley's findings also cleared up a larger mystery. The skulls of early hominids being discovered in Africa and Asia suggested that humans had evolved their large brain case later rather than sooner. With Piltdown man out of the family tree, these results began to make sense. In 1953, at a meeting organized by Oakley to discuss those finds, *Eoanthropus* was hardly mentioned. He was on some scientists' minds, however.

Sharing a dinner table with Oakley and others, South African anthropologist Joseph Weiner, then working at Oxford University, idly raised a question that had been bothering him: Why, he asked Oakley, had there been no systematic search of the area where the crucial Piltdown II remains had ◊

been discovered? The disturbing reply: No one knew exactly where it was. Weiner decided to probe further, believing at first that the truth lay in some coincidental placement of ape and human fossils. The idea of a forgery was, he said, "repellent."

But further microscopic, radiological, and chemical tests of the Piltdown bones disclosed the repellent truth. The worn molars had been deliberately filed down, the bone fragments deliberately stained. The jaw had come from a more modern ape (1980 tests indicated a contemporary orangutan), and the teeth had been ground to human shape. The skull fragments had been stained to resemble true fossils, the crucial canine tooth shaved to fit the jaw. The bone implement had evidently been shaped by a steel knife. Piltdown man was a fake, an invention. Even the site was bogus: The gravel was not what geologists call fossiliferous; everything discovered there had been a plant.

"From the evidence which we have obtained," Weiner, Oakley, and British anatomist Wilfrid Edward Le Gros Clark announced on November 21, 1953, "it is now clear that the distinguished paleontologists and archaeologists who took part in the excavations at Piltdown were the victims of a most elaborate and carefully prepared hoax." The scientific sleuths had uncovered a crime—but not a criminal.

Most researchers believe that Dawson was involved, and some believe he arranged the entire deception, perhaps to ridicule a complacent establishment or perhaps to ensure his own induction into the professional ranks of the Royal Society. While hardly anyone holds Dawson completely innocent, however, few believe he had the technical wherewithal to carry off the illusion. Who, they have asked for nearly half a century, was the missing expert?

Suspects have included almost all of the scientists connected with the Piltdown discovery. Harvard science historian Stephen Jay Gould has fingered in particular the Jesuit, Pierre Teilhard de Chardin. It was he who found the crucial missing canine tooth at Piltdown, and he indicated later that Dawson had shown him the remains called Piltdown II, which Dawson himself mentioned only in 1915. Teilhard was then serving with the army in France; therefore, he must have been in on the forgery from the beginning. Gould also points out Teilhard's silence regarding Piltdown during the rest of his distinguished career. The Frenchman, Gould believes, had intended the hoax as a youthful prank but had watched in horrified silence as it evolved into a career-wrecking scandal.

Not everyone is convinced by Gould's argument. In 1990, Frank Spencer, an anthropological historian with Queens College of the City University of New York, using his own research and that of Ian Langham, an Australian colleague who died in 1984, published another compelling—but still controversial—theory. His distinguished suspect, Spencer writes in *Piltdown,*

Bone fragments from Piltdown *(dark areas)* suggested a modern skull joined to an apelike jaw.

A Scientific Forgery, was ambitious, socially adroit, and a courageous taker of intellectual risks. He advanced the idea that modern humans characterized by large brains had appeared even before the early Pleistocene—a hypothesis that discounted the hominid remains found in Africa and Asia, and boosted his own career. Most incriminating, the suspect's 1912 diary revealed that he had written an anonymous essay about the Piltdown discovery two days before Woodward officially revealed it, suggesting that the man had detailed prior knowledge of the site. His diary, Spencer adds, also implied a private agenda for the Piltdown remains that was duly played out between 1913 and 1917.

The hoax, according to Spencer, was not a prank that spiraled out of control, but a deliberate use of fraud to alter the entire course of paleontology. The man behind Dawson: Arthur—later, Sir Arthur—Keith, who had claimed from the start that Woodward did not know what had been found at Piltdown. □

Hot Water

On April 11, 1916, a group of reporters gathered at the Farmingdale, Long Island, home of a man named Louis Enricht. "I have learned to do what chemists have been dreaming of for years," the seventy-year-old Enricht told his skeptical audience. "I have discovered, gentlemen, a substitute for gasoline that can be made for a penny a gallon." With that simple declaration, the demonstration began.

First, Enricht shoved a long stick into his car's gas tank, wiggled it around, then displayed it to the reporters. It showed not a trace of gasoline. The tank was "dry as a bone," he declared. The journalists checked the car, satisfying themselves that there was no false bottom to the tank. Enricht then filled a porcelain pitcher from a garden hose and offered it to a reporter for taste testing. "Pure water," the newsman pronounced. Now the inventor produced a small vial of greenish fluid, which he stirred into the water. He poured this mysterious concoction into the car's tank. His son, Louis, Jr., cranked the engine, and, to the reporters' amazement, it roared to life. News of Enricht's miraculous gasoline substitute spread across the country and to Europe.

Meanwhile, the now-famous inventor was explaining how his formula worked. "My chemical has an affinity for oxygen in water and is able to separate the hydrogen, thus producing hydrogen at- ◊

oms," he claimed. Supposedly, the hydrogen then combined with oxygen atoms in the air, "producing an explosion of power." Thomas Freas, a respected Columbia University chemistry professor, dismissed Enricht's formula as an impossibility. "No chemical can be added to water that will make it combustible," said Freas, who was quickly seconded by other chemists. Enricht scoffed at their skepticism, observing that there were always naysayers when an important new discovery was made.

One man who did not dismiss the possibility of a breakthrough was tycoon automaker Henry Ford. On April 24, thirteen days after Enricht's initial demonstration, Ford traveled to Farmingdale and met secretly with Enricht in his back bedroom. When spotted by vigilant reporters, the millionaire manufacturer refused to comment.

But just three days after the Ford-Enricht meeting, a New York newspaper splashed Enricht's surprising and colorful past across its pages. The self-styled inventor had no background in science, but an extensive one in swindling. Over the past few decades, the newspaper reported, he had taken money for a railway he never built, sold 45,000 acres of land he did not own, and persuaded an English syndicate to buy a formula for making artificial stone—a formula that evidently did not work.

Ford closeted himself with Enricht that night. The next day, he declared that Enricht was a reformed man and that he, Ford, would go forward with their negotiations. In exchange for exclusive rights, Ford would give Enricht a new Model T and funds to continue research on the fuel formula.

But events soon proved Ford's faith in a reformed Enricht premature. On April 29, 1916, the Maxim Munitions Corporation of New Jersey claimed that *it* had exclusive rights to Enricht's formula. Enraged, Ford brought suit, later dropped, to reclaim his Model T. Meanwhile, Maxim suddenly reversed itself, denying any connection to Enricht.

Curiously, although Ford and Maxim had publicly dissociated themselves from Enricht, Enricht seemed not to want for money. He began building a laboratory and a new house, and said he would soon build a factory. Many supposed he was taking time to perfect his gasoline substitute. But no more information was forthcoming from Enricht, and the fantastic fuel story slipped from the news.

It reappeared suddenly in November 1917, when railroad financier Benjamin Yoakum accused Enricht of treason. Yoakum, evidently the secret source of Enricht's funds, had completed a deal with Enricht on April 12, 1917, six days after the United States entered World War I. Yoakum had then begun negotiating with the United States and England for shipments of the substitute fuel. The talks disintegrated, however, when Enricht refused to turn over the formula while the war was going on. His suspicions aroused, Yoakum engaged private detectives to ferret out the truth. They reported that, in the summer of 1916, the old man had met secretly with the former military attaché to the German embassy, Captain Franz von Papen (later Adolf Hitler's vice-chancellor), who had been expelled from the United States in 1915 for espionage.

"We have grave fears," Yoakum declared, "that Enricht has already disclosed his secret to the German government, and that the seeming plentifulness of gasoline in that country is due to the fact that they are manufacturing Enricht's liquid on a large scale."

Enricht admitted to meeting with von Papen but claimed the Germans wanted his formula for artificial stone, not fuel. In fact, he added, the fuel formula no longer existed—he had burned his only copy. The U.S. attorney general did not have enough evidence to indict Enricht, and Yoakum was forced to cut his considerable losses and drop the matter.

Enricht, unrepentant, turned to another swindle. In the early 1920s, the old con man was caught trying to sell yet another secret process for manufacturing a fuel substitute, this one using peat. When Enricht failed to produce anything but dark smoke and a foul odor in a courtroom demonstration, he ended up in Sing Sing.

But his most successful hoax— the successful demonstration on April 11, 1916—remained a mystery. One engineer has hypothesized that Enricht's secret formula was really acetone, a volatile, inflammable liquid then used in smokeless gunpowder. The treated water would have carried the acetone into the car engine, causing it to fire long enough for a convincing demonstration. Others have speculated that perhaps the car had an undetected second fuel tank hidden somewhere in the chassis. And some few still believe Enricht's discovery was genuine. But no one really knows. In 1924, Enricht took his deceptive secrets with him to the grave. □

Nasal Passage

In 1957, a remarkable German discovery was brought to light in a lengthy paper authored jointly by Professor Harald Stümpke, museum curator for the Darwin Institute of Hi-Yi-Yi, and Gerolf Steiner, a zoology professor at the University of Heidelberg. Largely the result of research carried out earlier by Stümpke, the paper, "Bau und Leben der Rhinogradentia"—in English, "The Habitation and Life of the Snouter"—described a species of small mammals that had evolved remarkable noses that carried out a host of activities, from propulsion to grasping and trapping prey.

Snouters were first reported by an escaped Swedish prisoner of the Japanese, Einar Petterssen-Skämtkvist, who washed up in the Pacific's Hi-Yi-Yi archipelago in 1941. Although he infected all of the native human beings there with what proved to be for them a fatal head cold, he was able to endure and compile the first observations of the Rhinogradentia.

Apparently, the little creatures had evolved from a small, furry, shrewlike primitive snouter, *Archirhinos haeckelii* (named for their later discoverer, Haeckel), that walked on four legs and lacked the highly developed "nasarium" seen in more recent variations. From this humble beginning, the snouter adapted to fill every niche in its ecological domain. One branch, the *Hopsorhinidae*, evolved a large, springy snout used to propel the creatures in backward leaps covering several inches and were ubiquitous on

Snouters include *Ranunculonasus pulcher (below)*, which uses a floral snout to trap insects, and *Nasobema lyricum (left)*, whose snouts are used for walking.

their native island. The so-called earwing, *Otopteryx*, had an iridescent pelt and flew backward, driven by large, Dumbo-like ears. *Carbulonasus* had evolved a petal-like snout that permitted it to pose as an open flower to catch unsuspecting insects. A relative, *Orchidiopsis rapax*, imitated an orchid attached to a tree branch. One snouter's snout became six squid-like tentacles. And, stalking rapaciously among its cousins, the sharp-fanged *Tyrannonasus imperator* made its terrible way.

Before these fascinating creatures could be studied further, Steiner recounted in an epilogue, they were extinguished by a ghastly accident, along with their chronicler, Professor Stümpke, and their unique habitat. A secret nuclear test 125 miles away, Steiner wrote, had caused a tectonic disturbance that submerged the entire Hi-Yi-Yi archipelago, wiping out every trace of the remarkable fauna described by Skämtkvist and Stümpke.

Since its publication in German, the snouter study has appeared in French (1962) and English (1967). But its greatest impact may have come from partial publication in *Natural History* magazine, which was followed by scores of letters that lamented the snouters' passing, expressed disbelief, earnestly sought more information, or protested the bomb test that had destroyed Hi-Yi-Yi. Largely ignored was the fact that the magazine had published its snouter article on April Fool's Day, 1967. The 1957 original had been a charming zoological joke carried out, in the Germanic tradition, with a gravity as bogus as the delightful little creatures it created. □

Charades of the Gods?

In the early 1960s, according to Dr. Janvier Cabrera Darquea, a surgeon and professor in the village of Ica, Peru, people searching for shards of ancient pottery began turning up remarkable artifacts: carved stones that told an astonishing story. Hundreds of thousands—perhaps millions—of years before, the doctor would explain to visitors, the original civilization of the region had left a record of its achievements carved in rocks. Some of the illustrated stones depicted the surgical replacement of a human heart, others showed men peering skyward with great telescopes, and still others suggested the coexistence of humans and dinosaurs, believed to have lived tens of millions of years apart. If genuine, the engravings suggested that scholars needed to rethink nothing less than the entire history of the world.

Cabrera has collected thousands of the engraved rocks for his Library of Culture in Ica, but he does not show them to just anyone. Even so, in 1973 he let French writer Robert Charroux take a look. The stones, Charroux reported, were black or gray, some weighing hundreds of pounds, and were covered with engravings etched, Cabrera insisted, by Atlanteans—the lost people of Atlantis—whom he called Ica's "Unknown Ancestors."

Charroux's account of his Ica visit drew a Swiss hotelier and former convict named Erich von Däniken to Peru. In his view, such artifacts, and the mysterious giant figures drawn in the dry earth of the Nazca Plain, suggested that Cabrera's Unknown Ancestors were not from the lost world of Atlantis but from outer space. His excited speculations—in books such as *Chariots of the Gods?*—attracted a worldwide audience and gave von Däniken an enormous popular celebrity, along with such journalistic sobriquets as "the Clifford Ir-

Father Carlo Crespi *(above)* poses with "ancient Egyptian musical instruments," as Dr. Janvier Cabrera, of Ica, Peru, *(above, right, in glasses)* shows a visitor a stone supposedly etched with scenes of an ancient brain transplant.

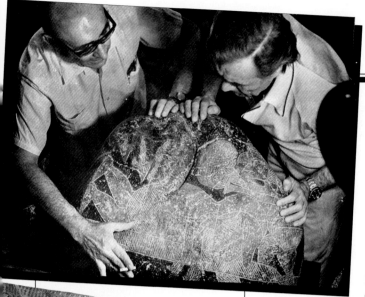

ving of the Cosmos'' *(pages 29-30).* His theory: that Earth was explored more than once by extraterrestrials who mated with early hominids, imparting the gift of intelligence. Von Däniken proposed that these extraterrestrials may have built such monumental structures as Egypt's great pyramids and that they were sometimes like Jehovah in their wrath—Sodom and Gomorrah, he speculated, were destroyed by this powerful ancestor's nuclear weapons.

He was also drawn to the region by tales of dazzling artifacts collected by Father Carlo Crespi in the Ecuadoran village of Cuenca, some 800 miles to the north. Then in his eighties, with impaired sight and hearing, Crespi had once been an amateur archaeologist of some

note; he believed that pre-Columbian art had come to South America with migrant Egyptians. Over the years he had acquired what was reputed to be a priceless collection of gold and silver artifacts: paddles, musical instruments, book covers, sarcophagi. Years earlier, in 1969, a visiting expert had pronounced the artifacts to be recent and made of brass. Two Canadian psychiatrists, visiting in 1971, confirmed that the objects were like pieces routinely sold to tourists in Cuenca. Evidently, the local artisans had found their own gold mine—in the form of Father Crespi's fixation on Egyptian ancestors and, later, von Däniken's on galactic ones.

Few believe that the Swiss pop scientist was taken in by the fake artifacts in Father Crespi's collection, although he did celebrate them in subsequent writings. As for the Cabrera stones, they did not transform human history after all. A film crew from the British Broadcasting Corporation, on location in Ica for a documentary, *The Case of the Ancient Astronauts,* received a stone as a souvenir from Cabrera. A London laboratory confirmed that the object was both local and contemporary—but too late. The film crew had already met an Ica artisan named Basilio. Basilio had produced Cabrera's stones and had a thank-you note from the doctor to prove it. □

Painted Mice

By 1970, thirty-five-year-old William T. Summerlin had become almost a celebrity among doctors in the field of organ transplantation, a procedure that the body's immune system is designed to defeat. A body's own cells are chemically marked as friendly in a code that the immune system's killer cells can read. But intruders carry alien proteins that the immune-system soldiers read, usually correctly, as the enemy and mobilize to destroy. Thus, attempts to transplant organs, skin in particular, usually require the suppression of the host's immune-system response. But this technique is risky. With the host's immune system lulled, a common cold can become a fatal illness, and immune-system cells in the donated organ may attack the weakened system of the host. Summerlin tried to circumvent this difficulty in a 1969 experiment. While working at Stanford University, he placed skin in a nutrient solution for several weeks before trying to transplant it—and found that the transplant took without suppressing the host's immune system. His most dramatic success had been to transplant cultured white skin on a black patient—without rejection.

The young doctor from South Carolina had come to Stanford with solid credentials. He had graduated from Emory University Medical School in 1964, interned at the University of Texas Medical Branch in Galveston, then served two years at Brooke Army Center near San Antonio—the army's renowned burn-treatment hospital. He moved to Stanford in 1967 as a resident in dermatology and ◊

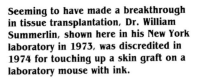

by 1970 had become chief of dermatology at a veterans hospital in Palo Alto. His reputation brought Summerlin an offer, which he accepted, from Robert Good, the distinguished pathologist-director of an immunology laboratory at the University of Minnesota. When Good became director of New York's Sloan Kettering Institute in the spring of 1973, he brought Summerlin with him.

Throughout this period, Summerlin had continued his search for ways to reduce the rejection of skin grafts, using tissue cultures between donor and host. Although no one knew why his technique appeared to work, experts guessed that the culture must somehow remove the donated cells' foreign flags. Summerlin reported success in grafting supposedly incompatible human skin, skin between white and gray mice, human corneas into the eyes of rabbits, and adrenal glands among different genetic strains of mice.

At Sloan Kettering, he continued his research while at the same time taking on the scientific management of a research lab and serving as head of clinical service at the associated Memorial Hospital. Apparently, the combination of responsibilities stretched him to the breaking point. At the same time, colleagues began having trouble reproducing Summerlin's results in their labs, and journal articles to that effect loomed on the scientific horizon. Then, in the autumn of 1973, as Summerlin later recalled, "I had no new startling discovery, and was brutally told by Dr. Good that I was a failure in producing significant work."

On Tuesday, March 26, 1974, Summerlin had a 7:00 a.m. appointment with Good, to show him the progress of an experiment involving skin grafted between genetically dissimilar mice. Among the samples Summerlin selected were two albino mice with grafted skin from black mice on their backs. On his way to the meeting, Summerlin looked at the two white mice to see how their grafts were progressing. The culture preparation had bleached the black skin to a nondescript gray. Acting on impulse, as he described it later, Summerlin darkened the grafts with a black felt-tip pen—an act that would destroy his research career and add something to the language: *Painted mice* became a synonym for scientific fraud.

As it turned out, Good did not even look at Summerlin's mice. After a forty-five-minute meeting, the imperiled researcher returned to the laboratory building and handed the bin of mice to senior laboratory assistant James Martin, in charge of getting the right animals into the right cages. But as he handled Summerlin's mice, Martin noticed the blackened skin patches on the two albinos. A quick alcohol swab revealed that they had been inked, and word of the deception swiftly spread through the laboratory. Before the morning ended, Good talked to Summerlin, who admitted touching up the grafts with ink, and the young dermatologist was suspended. Subsequent hearings brought other apparent discrepancies to light and led to his dismissal.

Summerlin's reputation never recovered from the ensuing blitz of publicity. The former rising star of transplantation took up quiet practices in rural Louisiana and Arkansas, and has kept well clear of transplantation research, a field that took some time to recover from his impulsive doctoring of two albino mice.

Ironically, however, Summerlin's line of research may yet prove fruitful. His early work at Stanford appears to have been verified by further experiments there, and a former colleague at Sloan Kettering has found that culturing skin does seem to reduce its chances of rejection. But such work is being carried out with knowledge and techniques that were not available in Summerlin's day. It may be that the man who became notorious as America's "mouse-painting doctor" was less a fraud than a harried scientist ahead of his time. □

Heal Thyself

Cyril Lodovic Burt *(overleaf)* was England's first true psychologist and, until his death at eighty-eight in 1971, one of its most distinguished ones. His research on inherited intelligence, indicating that intellect is born, not made, helped shape the British school system and was considered of such consequence that, in 1946, Burt became the first psychologist to be knighted. And yet, within a year of his death, his methods, data, and honesty were in serious question: A horrified psychology community had discovered that much of Burt's work rested on data that had been doctored and possibly made up.

Born in London in 1883, the frail, nearsighted intellectual turned to psychological studies at Oxford University's Jesus College, then studied at Christ's Hospital in London and, in 1908, moved to a teaching position at the University of Liverpool. In 1913 he joined the London educational system as a research psychologist, and there he began drawing together the research on which his views of inherited intelligence would rest.

He based some of his studies on comparisons of intelligence quotient (IQ) scores by sets of twins. In 1943, Burt reported results obtained from 156 pairs of nonidentical twins—twins who come from two fertilized eggs and thus share no more in common genetically than any other siblings—and 62 pairs of identical twins, whose genetic legacies are exactly the same. Fifteen of the identical pairs had been reared apart. The correlation of IQ scores between the nonidentical pairs was only 0.54, against a perfect correlation of

1.0. But identical pairs reared together showed the amazingly close correlation of 0.86, and even those reared apart scored high: 0.77.

His work had far-reaching effects. Partly because of Burt's results, the London school system adopted the so-called eleven-plus system, in which, at age eleven, children were assigned to one of three educational levels, depending on test scores. But it also reinforced such controversial theories—since generally rejected—as those of Arthur Jensen at the University of California, who claimed that the poor school performance of some racial minorities was a function of racially inherited deficiencies in intelligence.

Burt's next report came twelve years later, based on 83 pairs of identical twins reared together and 21 reared apart, along with 172 nonidentical pairs reared together. This paper also included data for 984 siblings, 131 of them reared apart, and 287 foster children. Much of this remarkable expansion, from 436 children to more than 1,800, Burt generously attributed to the efforts of his assistant, Miss J. Conway. Subsequent Burt papers bolstered the impression that he was working from a far larger, and more randomly assembled, sample of twins than anyone else in the field—and made his work the cornerstone of all theories of inherited intelligence. J. Conway contributed further papers, as did Margaret Howard, another valued colleague. In 1966, the eighty-three-year-old Burt published his final article on the subject, using an unprecedentedly large sample of fifty-three pairs of separately reared identical twins.

By the time Burt died in ◊

1971, however, his work had come under the scrutiny of Princeton University psychologist Leon Kamin. In several symposiums in 1972, and in his 1974 book, *The Science and Politics of IQ*, Kamin razed the empirical foundations of inherited intelligence—and Burt's reputation along with them.

Burt, he said, had never really described his methods or the popula-

tion that he tested. Instead, he had referred to methodological details in other publications that turned out to be either nonexistent or inaccessible. His reports crackled with internal contradictions. Most important, Kamin said, Burt's correlations simply could not be correct: Despite the greatly changing size and content of his sample, the IQ correlation figures in 1966 were iden-

tical to those he had presented more than twenty years earlier—virtually a statistical impossibility. But, for all that, Kamin only charged Burt with bad science. Worse was yet to come.

On October 24, 1976, London's *Sunday Times* published an article by the paper's medical correspondent, Oliver Gillie, alleging that Burt had faked crucial data, tailored results to theory—and invented at least two coworkers. If they had ever existed—and Gillie doubted that they had—J. Conway and Margaret Howard had not been in touch with Burt for years and certainly had not been around to gather his extensive data on twins.

In the ensuing controversy, many decided that Burt had simply been an outright fraud, and a bungling one at that; indeed, one of the chief arguments in his defense was that a man of his abilities could not have done such a poor job of deception. Others, more sympathetic, viewed the fraud as just the sloppy copy work of a frail old man. And no one could reconcile the great esteem in which Burt was held by his colleagues with the behavior that had come to light.

The most complete account of Burt's odyssey of deception is that of his official biographer, Leslie Spencer Hearnshaw, who worked from the late psychologist's papers, including his meticulously kept personal diaries. In his

1979 *Cyril Burt, Psychologist,* Hearnshaw depicted Burt as a man whose life was coming apart as early as the 1930s, when his marriage began to fail (his wife left him in 1952). German bombers handed Burt another shock: In 1941, an air raid destroyed almost all his research materials—presumably including his data on twins—which he had stored at London's University College. His health, always fragile, broke in 1941, when he was diagnosed as having Ménière's syndrome—an affliction of the inner ear that causes deafness, vertigo, and nausea. The ailment is now widely believed to be psychosomatic. His intellectual legacy at University College evaporated soon after his retirement. His editorship (since 1947) of the prestigious *Journal of Statistical Psychology* ended in 1963, when, coincidentally, the government was phasing out the eleven-plus system.

Having lost his home, data, position, influence, and health, Burt suffered a kind of psychic collapse into paranoia, according to Hearnshaw. Increasingly combative in his dealings with rivals, increasingly dogmatic and egocentric, and isolated by age and impaired hearing, Burt embarked on a single-handed campaign against a world he saw as hostile to him. Margaret Howard and J. Conway appear to have been two of perhaps twenty pseudonyms that Burt used to promote his ideas in his own journal. These phantoms also helped him spin an illusion, when he lacked both health and money, of important research in progress. The distinguished explorer of the human mind seemed to become lost within his own tortured psyche. □

The Stone Age in T-Shirts

The annals of deception are rich with tales of false clues to earlier epochs, usually in the shape of forged fossils or doctored rocks. Perhaps only once has an entire tribe of living, breathing people been offered to the public as a relic of the past: the primitive Tasaday (pronounced tah-SAH-die) of the Philippines, in 1972.

According to Manuel Elizalde, Jr., a playboy-bureaucrat in the since-deposed regime of President Ferdinand Marcos, the modern chapter of the Tasaday's timeless story began in 1971, when Elizalde, in charge of protecting indigenous minorities, visited the agrarian Blit Manubo tribe on the island of Mindanao. There, he reported later, a man named Dafal told him of a small, nearby tribe of surpassing antiquity. Its members lived in mountain caves, Dafal said, with only the most rudimentary Stone Age tools, scraping a meager living from the rain forest. They had no agriculture, no cloth, no weapons, not even domestic animals. Presumably, they had lived this way for centuries, an isolated handful of survivors from an age that ended everywhere else thousands of years earlier.

In 1972, Elizalde revealed the secret people to the world, using government helicopters to ferry a squad of journalists and social scientists into the Tasaday's wilderness domain. There, twenty-six Tasaday were found living as humans must have lived a hundred centuries ago. They squatted in caves wearing G-strings of leaves. They dined on grubs, roots, and wild fruit, especially wild yams scraped from the jungle soil. To a complex age that longed to return to a simpler life closer to nature, here were people who had never left—natural humans, living communally in a kind of Eden. One anthropologist called them "paleohippies."

The Tasaday were an immediate smash hit. *National Geographic* ran a cover story on their discovery, and NBC television handed Elizalde $50,000 to produce a documentary. Books were written, journal papers published, linguistic studies carried out. And then, as suddenly as they had appeared, the Tasaday were cut off from the intrigued outside world. The Marcos government made their mountain forests a 46,300-acre preserve in 1973. In 1974, martial law was imposed on the Philippines, and it endured until the regime was ousted in 1986.

That year, Swiss journalist Oswald Iten made his way back to the land of the Tasaday, hoping to get another close look at the planet's only extant Stone Agers. He found the caves empty and the two dozen Tasaday shuffled in among the villagers of the Blit Manubo and T'boli tribes. The erstwhile primitives now grew crops, slept on wooden beds in huts, and had given up their G-strings for T-shirts and shorts. According to Iten, some of the supposed Stone Agers confessed that they had been persuaded by Elizalde to pose as cave dwellers. The Tasaday, he declared, had been a grand hoax.

Most anthropologists agreed. For a human population to sustain itself, some argued, at least 400 individuals are required to keep reproduction clear of incest, a powerful taboo in all ◊

societies; a mere two dozen would have perished long before their "discovery" in 1971. Others noted that the seeming plenitude of the tropical rain forest actually offers so little for humans to eat that even the most primitive jungle tribes must augment their diet with cultivated foods. The stone tools were, one anthropologist remarked, "a joke." Perhaps most significant, the Tasaday seemed to have generated no garbage in their centuries of cave life.

Hardly anyone now credits that the Tasaday were isolated for thousands of years, but a small minority of scientists still maintains that they are nevertheless an old and long-isolated tribe. Stanford University linguist Carol Molony, for example, argues that their language is truly their own, albeit much like the languages of other neighboring tribes, and lacks the Spanish words that have percolated into other Philippine tongues. Besides, she points out, a

hoax would have required primitive people to act—and stay in character for weeks on end—in an invented language. "It's preposterous," said Molony, "to think they could have been trained for something like this."

In a sense, however, their authenticity has become irrelevant. Whether they were once real or just a living forgery, the Tasaday have discarded their old ways. Willing to visit, they show no inclination to live in the Stone Age. □

Supposed cave dwellers of the Philippines, billed as an extant Stone Age tribe called the Tasaday, appear to have been coached to perform for visiting journalists in 1972.

Creation from the Black Lagoon

As he explored a murky underwater cave in Puerto Rico's *Laguna Aguas Prietas*—loosely translated as the Black Lagoon—Alfredo Garcia Garamendi was suddenly attacked by . . . *something.* A champion swimmer and physical-education teacher, Garamendi said that he had been tried almost beyond his strength in the fierce contest that followed. "I shot it with my spear gun, but it kept coming," he told reporters in San Juan. "It wrapped its tail around my neck and began to choke me." Finally, the diver said, he had seized his knife and stabbed the animal until it went limp in death. When he dragged the body ashore, however, he recognized it immediately: a *Garadiavolo,* or devilfish, a bizarre creature that Garamendi had met before.

The underwater tussle occurred in August 1974 and yielded a carcass about three and a half feet long. Garamendi had seen a similar beast hopping along the beach some years earlier, and he had captured one in 1970. He sent that specimen to the University of Puerto Rico's Department of Marine Sciences, which thought the specimen might be a chimera, a rare relative of the skate. Then, after the school returned the animal, Garamendi ◊

This *Garadiavolo,* or devilfish, is really the modified belly of a guitarfish.

declared, two men "from a very well known intelligence agency" came to his home and said: "We want the monkey in the jar." He had not seen it since.

More careful the second time around, Garamendi set up a small laboratory next to his living room and put the creature, as preserved by taxidermists, into a tank of water. There it could be viewed by the press and interested public, and studied. Garamendi has speculated as to the origins of Los Garadiavolos. "The creatures are not of this earth," he theorizes. "But I do not believe they come from another planet, but from another dimension." Nevertheless, his own illustration shows them being dropped into the sea from flying saucers. "They were put here for a purpose," he explains to journalists. "Perhaps for the same reason we might send monkeys and other animals to an alien planet, to see how they survive in the strange environment."

In fact, his Garadiavolos were almost certainly put here for the same reason that similar beasts have been since at least the sixteenth century: as a biological spoof. The first one no doubt fol-

lowed the discovery that some ancient fish—shark relatives, such as skates and rays, that have cartilage instead of bones—seem marked with a devilish human face on their undersides. The prominent eyes above the fish's mouth are in fact the "nostrils" through which water is exhaled. Called Jenny Hanivers (perhaps as a corruption of *Anvers*, French for Antwerp, where they were said to be available centuries ago), these creations are made by modifying the animal so that it seems to have legs as well as a face. Jenny Hanivers are seen in texts going back to 1531, and representations of the deadly mythical reptile called the basilisk are apparently distorted skates or rays. As for Garamendi's Garadiavolo, it appears to have been a guitarfish, a slim-waisted relative of the ray.

Still, the fake creatures sometimes generate mysteries of their own. Garamendi's second specimen, for example, vanished as mysteriously as it had appeared. Following an explosion in his laboratory, only a few ashes remained in the Garadiavolo pool. A parapsychologist explained that Garamendi's wife had wrought the damage with her psychic powers. The creature "was beginning to change our lives," said Garamendi. "She destroyed it with her mind." □

The Garadiavolo "tail" was cut from the front of the rebuilt fish, whose eyes are on the back of its body.

Nessie's Name's Sake

Sir Peter Scott was a naturalist who for years promoted and defended the existence of Scotland's Loch Ness monster against all skeptics. In 1975, he proposed that the elusive beast be given a better name than just Nessie, its nickname, to protect it under British conservation laws, which require that protected species have a proper scientific name. Together with veteran Nessie searcher Robert Rines, whose underwater photographs suggested a large, finned creature of some kind in the depths of the lake, Scott devised a scientific sobriquet for the celebrated sea serpent.

In the December 11, 1975, issue of *Nature*, the pair offered *Nessiteras rhombopteryx: Nessiteras* for the name of the lake and the Greek word *teras*, meaning "marvel" or, perhaps, "monster"; *rhombopteryx* from the Greek *rhombo*, "diamond-shaped," and *pteryx*, "fin." The English translation: "Loch Ness monster with diamond-shaped fin."

Two days later, skeptical London newspapers translated it quite differently. *Nessiteras rhombopteryx*, they pointed out, was also an anagram. Sir Peter, who ardently believed in the existence of unknown Loch Ness creatures until his death in 1989, had inadvertently concocted a name that, with its letters rearranged, read: "monster hoax by Sir Peter S." □

Far-Flung Fossils

Although the geology of the Himalaya Mountains is on the grand scale, the lofty range has always seemed straightforward and simple to geologists. The mountains, the highest on earth, are believed to be the thousand-mile-long wrinkles created where the northward-creeping Indian subcontinent has shoved under the higher ground of the Tibetan Plateau. The history of this slow-motion collision is recorded in the rock composing those wrinkles, which in turn can be dated by the fossil remains of extinct animals: A particular species that lived at a certain time can be used to date a rock layer to within a million years on the four-billion-year geologic clock. Until about twenty years ago, the fossils and stones for this region told the same story. But then, this clear picture was suddenly rendered murky by a rash of fossil finds—finds that, some scientists believe, may have come not from India, Nepal, and Bhutan but from well-known fossil-bearing strata in Oklahoma, New York, and Morocco.

According to Australian paleontologist John Talent, the record of Himalayan geology has been so generously salted with spurious fossils that, as he wrote in the journal *Nature* in April 1989, scientific conclusions drawn from it are now in doubt—along with many years' labor by scores of geologists around the world.

The first sign of trouble came in 1971, while Talent was visiting colleagues in Kashmir. They had discovered that published descriptions of Himalayan fossils did not square with what they were finding on the ground. But it was not until

a 1986 visit to Paris that the scope of the problem became clear. There, like any good geologist, Talent stopped by the famous *Mineraux Fossiles* rock shop on the rue St. Louis. All fossils bear the unique mineral imprint of the place where they were found; some are replaced with iron minerals and distinctively weathered. He bought a few samples, including spiral-shelled fossils called ammonoids, quarried from a famous site near Erfoud, Morocco. Only then did he realize that identical ammonoids had been attributed to the Himalayas by a famous German expert and his Indian coauthor.

As Talent explored the Himalayan fossil record, he found other, similar anomalies. Conodonts—toothlike fossils, apparently from the jawless mouths of ancient fish—reportedly discovered in northeast India and Nepal turned out to have the environmental stamp of conodonts previously found at a well-known site in Amsdell Creek, New York. Fossils of a shrimplike crustacean called an ostracod, reportedly uncovered in Tibet, were identical to those dug out of the Haragan Formation in Oklahoma. Because each of these established sites has been extensively quarried, the fossils are available in most rock and fossil shops, and are part of many fossil collections. To find these same remains, with the same distinctive site markings, in the Himalayas was, Talent wrote, "paleobiogeographically enigmatic." Moreover, Talent and a legion of geologists have failed to corroborate the finds at twenty-three Himalayan sites, and another forty-nine sites have

been called into question. In some cases, the strata were so deformed that they held no fossils whatever.

The spurious relics, Talent noted, had entered scientific literature through the efforts of a single man: Vishwa Jit Gupta, an influential academic at India's University of Panjab, who in the last two decades has written, often with expert coauthors from other countries, more than 400 papers describing his fossil finds. He has denied Talent's charges of bad or fraudulent science. But many paleontologists, including some Indian colleagues of Gupta's, have crossed over to Talent's side in the conflict.

Perhaps the most damning accusation is that Gupta has not recorded who found which fossils where, and he has not identified the sites as narrowly as paleontology demands: One "site," for example, is a seventy-five-mile stretch of very rough mountain terrain, impossible to verify. And gulled scientists have begun to clamor: One reports having almost coauthored a Gupta paper on a new species of fossil fish that turned out to be common—and often given to visitors as gifts—in China.

Gupta, suspended by his university pending the outcome of an inquiry by Indian geologists, replies that he has been deliberately vague to protect his interests against the probings of competing geologists and to shield helpers who have gone into dangerous or forbidden areas to bring out fossils for him. The matter, he reportedly said, is just a minor disagreement among experts. But if it is not, most paleontologists lament, the last twenty years' geological record for the world's roughest ground is not worth a Moroccan ammonoid. □

Fossils *(above and upper left)* from sites in New York were reportedly "discovered" by one Indian geologist—and no one else—along the entire range of the Himalayas *(above)*.

April Is the Cruelest Month

The high seriousness of science begs to be mocked and is accommodated regularly on the first day of April—April Fool's Day.

That was the occasion, for example, for the *Scientific American* to remind readers, in an authoritative treatise by Martin Gardner, of sensational discoveries of 1974, incredibly overlooked at the time: "a special-purpose chess-playing computer" called MacHic because it played chess as though intoxicated; a logical flaw in one of Einstein's universal laws; the recovery of a page that had been missing from one of Leonardo da Vinci's notebooks, showing a flush toilet centuries before its time.

In its March 31, 1983, edition, the British journal *New Scientist* reported on an exciting development: the creation of hybrid cells obtained by crossing cells taken from plants and animals. Using a "heat-shock" process, researchers had fused cells of a tomato with those of a bull. "The resulting hybrid," the journal said, "grows like its tomato parent but develops a tough leathery skin." Its flowers, it turned out, were pollinated only by horse flies and ultimately developed "extraordinary clumps of discus-shaped bodies—microscopic examination shows that these bodies are a true hybrid of animal protein sandwiched between a thin envelope of tomato fruit."

Another kind of biological discovery was covered by National Public Radio's "All Things Considered" news program. A team of researchers in southern Wisconsin, it reported on April 1, 1979, had been exploring verbal communication between humans and Coho salmon—the Coho People, as they came to be called. The program featured interviews with two of the articulate, but shrill, salmon, Kathy and Larry.

For truly high-powered scientific reportage, however, one British newspaper—the *Guardian*—is in a class by itself. On April 1, 1981, for example, the publication announced a major breakthrough by British meteorologists. "After 13 years' work in top security, surrounded by guard dogs and living out of suitcases," it reported, "British scientists at Pershore have developed a machine to control the weather. Britain will gain the immediate benefit of long summers, with rainfall only at night, and the Continent will have whatever Pershore decides to send." □

Drawing in the style of Leonardo da Vinci, graphic artist Anthony Ravielli created this antiqued rendering of the Italian genius's valve flush toilet.

Live and Let Fib

Deception has always seemed a uniquely human skill, shunned by the presumably sweeter creatures of the natural world. But, at a symposium titled "Evolution of Deception," at the 1991 meeting of the American Association for the Advancement of Science, researchers noted that frauds and forgeries abound in nature: Indeed, deception is often a crucial step toward greater fitness for survival and is well rewarded in the evolutionary scheme.

Scientists find that virtually no form of life is free of fakery's taint. According to Washington University biologist Ursula Goodenough, even lowly bacteria spin illusions that foster their own survival. Some microorganisms evolve molecular camouflage to hide themselves from the patrolling killer cells of a host's immune system. Others adjust their chemical spots to blend with those of their host or coat themselves with the same protective substance used by host cells. Still others learn how to hide inside host cells, avoiding the immune-system death squads. A protozoan that causes a type of sleeping sickness baffles the immune system with false flags: As soon as one chemical tag is recognized and a response is mobilized, the intruder runs up another, different flag, and then another, causing the immune process to exhaust itself with repetition—to no effect.

While the simplest creatures seem adept in deception, the complexity of natural ruses appears to increase with intelligence. Ant-devouring beetles gain entry to anthills by covering themselves with the dried-out cadavers of ants, murdered for the purpose. Male scorpionflies, which offer prospective mates a tasty bug as a nuptial gift, are duped by female impersonators in need of a dead-bug offering themselves. Male fireflies are lured into ambush and eaten by comrades flickering their lights seductively. The bigamous pied flycatcher often maintains not one, but two, territories, widely separated from each other, each with an unsuspecting female in the nest. House cats bristle to make themselves seem larger. Monkeys, chimpanzees, and other primates use misdirection and other subtle

Carrying sleeping sickness for their host, protozoans called *Trypanosoma gambiensi* jam immune systems with false chemical signals.

forms of falsehood to have their way with their fellows.

While no longer able to claim deception as uniquely its own, humanity retains the championship for deception, using art and artifice to create worlds that are not real. Evidence of this, according to Washington University anthropologist Robert W. Sussman, is that only in the human realm does fraud achieve its highest and most complicated form: the deception of oneself. □

ACKNOWLEDGMENTS

The editors wish to thank these individuals and institutions for their valuable assistance in the preparation of this volume:

Florian Berberich, Militärgeschichtliches Forochungsamt, Freiburg; Gerhard Bosinski, Museum für die Archäologie des Eiszeitalters, Schloss Monrepos, Neuwied, Germany; Jeremy Campbell, *Evening Standard*, Washington, D.C.; Charles H. Carlson, Jr., Williamsport Bills Bowman Field, Williamsport, Pennsylvania; Patricia Chemin, Musée La Devinierè, Seuilly, France; D. Doughan, Fawcett Library, London; Sylvie Dubois, Département des Peintures, Musée du Louvre, Paris; Reinhold Dusella, Musikwissenschaftliches Seminar, Universität, Bonn; Michel Fluery, Paris; Louis G. Helverson, The Free Library of Philadelphia, Philadelphia, Pennsylvania; Leon Kamin, Psychology Department, Northeastern University, Boston, Massachusetts; René Rizq Khawan, Suresnes, France; Antonio Latanza, Museo Nazionale degli Strumenti Musicali, Rome; Gordon Leigh, Royal Air Force Museum, London; Rebecca Lintz, Colorado Historical Society, Denver, Colorado; Marie Montembault, Département des Antiquités Grecques et Romaines, Musée du Louvre, Paris; Roderick Conway Morris, Venice; Alain Pasquier, Département des Antiquités Grecques et Romaines, Musée du Louvre, Paris; Robert S. Pelton, The Barnum Museum, Bridgeport, Connecticut; Dan Rattiner, *Dan's Papers*, Bridgehampton, New York; Christopher Rawlings, British Library, London; Frank Spencer, Bayside, New York; John Talent, Macquarie University, Sydney, Australia; Marie-Hélène Tesnières, Département des Manuscrits, Bibliothèque Nationale, Paris; Peter Wollkopf, Rosgarten Museum, Constance, Germany.

BIBLIOGRAPHY

Books

Abel, Alan. *The Confessions of a Hoaxer*. New York: Macmillan, 1970.

Attiqur Rahman, M. *Reflections on the Principles of Surprise and Deception*. Lahore, Pakistan: Wajidalis, 1981.

Bain, David Haward. *Sitting in Darkness: Americans in the Philippines*. Boston: Houghton Mifflin, 1984.

Barham, R. H. Dalton. *The Life and Remains of Theodore Edward Hook* (Vol. 1). London: Richard Bentley, 1849.

Barnum, P. T. *The Humbugs of the World*. Detroit: Singing Tree Press, 1970.

Bell, Quentin. *Virginia Stephen, 1882-1912* (Vol. 1 of *Virginia Woolf: A Biography*). London: Hogarth Press, 1972.

Beringer, Johann Bartholomew Adam. *The Lying Stones of Dr. Johann Bartholomew Adam Beringer: Being his Lithographiæ Wirceburgensis*. Translated by Melvin E. Jahn and Daniel J. Woolf. Berkeley: University of California Press, 1963.

Bismarck, Otto von. *Reflections and Reminiscences*. Edited by Theodore S. Hamerow. New York: Harper & Row, Harper Torchbooks, 1968.

Bloodworth, Dennis, and Ching Ping Bloodworth. *The Chinese Machiavelli: 3,000 Years of Chinese Statecraft*. New York: Farrar, Straus & Giroux, 1976.

Broad, William, and Nicholas Wade. *Betrayers of the Truth*. New York: Simon & Schuster, 1982.

Brown, Charles Henry. *The Correspondents' War*. New York: Charles Scribner's Sons, 1967.

Carell, Paul. *The Foxes of the Desert*. Translated by Mervyn Savill. New York: E. P. Dutton, 1961.

Chandler, David G. *The Campaigns of Napoleon*. New York: Macmillan, 1966.

Charlesworth, Hector. *More Candid Chronicles*. Toronto: Macmillan, 1928.

Clark, Kenneth. *Leonardo Da Vinci*. London: Penguin Books, 1988.

Crichton, Robert. *The Great Impostor*. New York: Random House, 1959.

Cruickshank, Charles. *Deception in World War II*. Oxford: Oxford University Press, 1979.

Däniken, Erich von:

According to the Evidence: My Proof of Man's Extraterrestrial Origins. Translated by Michael Heron. London: Souvenir Press, 1977.

The Gold of the Gods. Translated by Michael Heron. New York: G. P. Putnam's Sons, 1973.

Davis, Natalie Zemon. *The Return of Martin Guerre*. Cambridge, Mass.: Harvard University Press, 1983.

De Guingand, Francis. *Operation Victory*. London: Hodder & Stoughton, 1947.

Delderfield, R. F. *Napoleon's Marshals*. Philadelphia: Chilton Books, 1966.

Denton, Kit. *Gallipoli Illustrated*. Adelaide, Australia: Rigby, 1981.

Dickson, Lovat. *Wilderness Man: The Strange Story of Grey Owl*. New York: Atheneum, 1973.

Domela, Harry. *A Sham Prince: The Life and Adventures of Harry Domela*. London: Hutchinson, 1928.

Doyle, Arthur Conan. *The Coming of the Fairies*. New York: George H. Doran, 1921.

Earle, Alice Morse. *Colonial Dames and Good Wives*. New York: Houghton Mifflin, 1845.

Edmonds, S. Emma E. *Nurse and Spy in the Union Army*. Hartford, Conn.: W. S. Williams, 1865.

Farrer, J. A. *Literary Forgeries*. New York: Longmans, Green, 1907.

Fay, Stephen, Lewis Chester, and Magnus Linklater. *Hoax: The Inside Story of the Howard Hughes-Clifford Irving Affair*. New York: Viking Press, 1972.

Fedler, Fred. *Media Hoaxes*. Ames: Iowa State University Press, 1989.

Franco, Barbara. *The Cardiff Giant: A Hundred Year Old Hoax*. Cooperstown, N.Y.: The New York State Historical Association, 1969.

Gardner, Martin. *Science: Good, Bad and Bogus*. Buffalo, N.Y.: Prometheus Books, 1981.

Garrett, Richard. *Hoaxes and Swindles*. London: Severn House, 1972.

Gary, Romain. *King Solomon*. Translated by Barbara Wright. New York: Harper & Row, 1983.

Gentry, Curt. *The Vulnerable Americans*. Garden City, N.Y.: Doubleday, 1966.

Great Hoaxers and Conmen. London: Angus & Robertson, 1974.

Hamblin, Dora Jane. *Pots and Robbers*. New York: Simon & Schuster, 1970.

Hamilton, Charles. *Great Forgers and Famous Fakes*. New York: Crown, 1980.

Harris, Neil. *Humbug: The Art of P. T. Barnum*. Boston: Little, Brown, 1973.

Hart, B. H. Liddell (Ed.). *The Rommel Papers*. Translated by Paul Findlay. Norwalk, Conn.: Easton Press, 1988.

Hearnshaw, L. S. *Cyril Burt, Psychologist*. Ithaca, N.Y.: Cornell University Press, 1979.

Herodotus. *The History*. Translated by David Grene. Chicago: University of Chicago Press, 1987.

Hill, C. W. *The Spook and the Commandant*. London: William Kimber, 1975.

Ingram, John H. *Claimants to Royalty*. London: David Bogue, 1882.

Jones, E. H. *The Road to En-Dor*. London: The Bodley Head, 1922.

Jones, Mark (Ed.). *Fake? The Art of Deception*. London: British Museum Publications, 1990.

Khawam, Rene R. (Trans.). *The Subtle Ruse: The Book of Arabic Wisdom and Guile*. London: East-West Publications, 1980.

Klein, Alexander. *Grand Deception*. Philadelphia: J. B. Lippincott, 1955.

Klein, Alexander (Ed.). *The Double Dealers*. New York: J. B. Lippincott, 1958.

Kohn, Alexander. *False Prophets*. Oxford: Basil Blackwell, 1986.

Kohn, George C. *Dictionary of Wars*. New York: Facts On File, 1986.

Larsen, Egon. *The Deceivers: Lives of the Great Impostors*. London: John Baker, 1966.

Lattimore, Richmond (Trans.). *The Odyssey of Homer*. New York: Harper & Row, 1967.

Lefebvre, Georges. *Napoleon* (Vol. 1). Translated by Henry F. Stockhold. New York: Columbia University Press, 1969.

Licks, H. E. *Recreations in Mathematics.* New York: D. Van Nostrand, 1941 (reprint of 1917 edition).

Liddle, Peter. *Men of Gallipoli.* Newton Abbot, Devon, England: David & Charles, 1976.

Lindsey, Robert. *A Gathering of Saints.* New York: Simon & Schuster, 1988.

Loe, Nancy E. *William Randolph Hearst.* Philadelphia: ARA Services, 1988.

Lord, John. *Duty, Honor, Empire: The Life and Times of Colonel Richard Meinertzhagen.* New York: Random House, 1970.

Lundberg, Ferdinand. *Imperial Hearst.* Westport, Conn.: Greenwood Press, 1970.

MacDougall, Curtis D. *Hoaxes.* New York: Macmillan, 1941.

McKelway, St. Clair. *The Big Little Man from Brooklyn.* Boston: Houghton Mifflin, 1969.

Mannix, William Francis. *Memoirs of Li Hung Chang.* Boston: Houghton Mifflin, 1923.

Maslen, Geoffrey. *The Most Amazing Story a Man Ever Lived to Tell.* London: Angus & Robertson, 1977.

Mehling, Harold. *The Scandalous Scamps.* New York: Henry Holt, 1959.

Meinertzhagen, Richard. *Army Diary, 1899-1926.* Edinburgh: Oliver & Boyd, 1960.

Mencken, H. L. *The Bathtub Hoax and Other Blasts & Bravos.* Edited by Robert McHugh. New York: Alfred A Knopf, 1958.

Meyerstein, E. H. W. *A Life of Thomas Chatterton.* London: Ingpen & Grant, 1930.

Montagu, Ewen. *The Man Who Never Was.* Philadelphia: J. B. Lippincott, 1954.

Moorehead, Alan. *Gallipoli.* Norwalk, Conn.: Easton Press, 1988.

Moss, Norman. *The Pleasures of Deception.* New York: Reader's Digest Press, 1977.

Mound, Andrew. *Heroic Hoaxes.* London: MacDonald, 1983.

Norman, Bruce. *Secret Warfare: The Battle of Codes and Ciphers.* Newton Abbot, Devon, England: David & Charles, 1973.

Norman, Frank, and Geraldine Norman. *The Fake's Progress.* London: Hutchinson, 1977.

O'Brien, Frank M. *The Story of the Sun: New York, 1833-1928.* New York: D. Appleton, 1928.

Ord-Hume, Arthur W. J. G. *Perpetual Motion: The History of an Obsession.* New York: St. Martin's Press, 1977.

Pardoe, Rosemary, and Darroll Pardoe. *The Female Pope.* New York: Aquarian Press, Crucible, 1988.

Pemberton, T. Edgar. *Lord Dundreary: A Memoir of Edward Askew Sothern.* New York: Knickerbocker Press, 1908.

Podell, Janet, and Steven Anzovin (Eds.). *The Annual Obituary 1982.* New York: St. Martin's Press, 1983.

Poole, Stanley B-R. *Royal Mysteries and Pretenders.* London: Blandford Press, 1969.

Potter, Jeremy. *Pretenders to the English Throne.* Totowa, N.J.: Barnes & Noble Books, 1987.

Pritchard, James B. *Archaeology and the Old Testament.* Princeton, N.J.: Princeton University Press, 1958.

Pritchard, James B. (Ed.). *Ancient Near Eastern Texts: Relating to the Old Testament.* Princeton, N.J.: Princeton University Press, 1950.

Rieth, Adolf. *Archaeological Fakes.* Translated by Diana Imber. London: Barrie & Jenkins, 1967.

Ripin, Edward M. *The Instrument Catalogs of Leopoldo Franciolini* (No. 9). Edited by George R. Hill. Hackensack, N.J.: Joseph Boonin, 1974.

Rose, June. *The Perfect Gentleman.* London: Hutchinson, 1977.

Scoundrels & Scalawags. Pleasantville, N.Y.: Reader's Digest Association, 1968.

Silverberg, Robert. *Scientists and Scoundrels.* New York: Thomas Y. Crowell, 1965.

Silverstein, Herma, and Caroline Arnold. *Hoaxes That Made Headlines.* New York: Simon & Schuster, Julian Messner, 1986.

Smith, H. Allen. *The Compleat Practical Joker.* New York: William Morrow, 1980.

Snyder, Louis L., and Ida Mae Brown. *Bismarck and German Unification.* New York: Franklin Watts, 1966.

Sox, David. *Unmasking the Forger: The Dossena Deception.* New York: Universe Books, 1987.

Sparrow, Gerald. *The Great Impostors.* London: John Long, 1962.

Spencer, Frank. *Piltdown: A Scientific Forgery.* London: Natural History Museum Publications; Oxford: Oxford University Press, 1990.

Stoker, Bram. *Famous Impostors.* New York: Sturgis & Walton, 1910.

Story, Ronald. *Guardians of the Universe?* New York: St. Martin's Press, 1980.

Stümpke, Harald. *The Snouters: Form and Life of the Rhinogrades.* Translated by Leigh Chadwick. Garden City, N.Y.: Natural History Press, 1967.

Sun Tzu. *The Art of War.* Translated by Samuel B. Griffith. London: Oxford University Press, 1963.

Taylor, A. J. P. *Bismarck: The Man and the Statesman.* London: Hamish Hamilton, 1955.

Thompson, J. W., and S. K. Padover. *Secret Diplomacy: A Record of Espionage and Double-Dealing, 1500-1815.* London: Jarrolds, 1937.

Vambery, Arminius. *The Story of Hungary* (The Story of the Nations series). New York: G. P. Putnam's Sons, 1886.

Varga, Domokos. *Hungary in Greatness and Decline: The 14th and 15th Centuries.* Translated by Martha Szacsvay Lipták. Stone Mountain, Ga.: Hungarian Cultural Foundation, 1982.

Virgil. *The Aeneid.* Translated by Robert Fitzgerald. New York: Random House, 1983.

Wace, Alan J. B., and Frank H. Stubbings (Eds.). *A Companion to Homer.* London: Macmillan, 1962.

Wade, Carlson. *Great Hoaxes and Famous Imposters.* Middle Village, N.Y.: Jonathan David, 1976.

Wheelwright, Julie. *Amazons and Military Maids.* London: Pandora, 1989.

Williams, Neville. *Knaves and Fools.* New York: Macmillan, 1960.

Woodruff, Douglas. *The Tichborne Claimant: A*

Victorian Mystery. London: Hollis & Carter, 1957.

Yadin, Yigael. *The Art of Warfare in Biblical Lands* (Vol. 1). New York: McGraw-Hill, 1963.

Periodicals

"Alan Abel, Satirist, Created Campaign to Clothe Animals." *New York Times,* January 2, 1980.

Anderson, Ian. "Tasaday: Stone Age Survivors or a Modern Hoax?" *New Scientist,* October 23, 1986.

"Art Gallery, Officers Convicted in Dali Case." *National Law Journal,* May 21, 1990.

Begley, Sharon, Phyllis Malamud, and Mary Hager. "A Case of Fraud at Harvard." *Newsweek,* February 8, 1982.

"The Big Fix." *Time,* October 19, 1959.

Black, Kent. "The Artist of the Hoax." *Town and Country,* January 1991.

"Bogus Prince Enters Films." *New York Times,* July 23, 1927.

Bompard, Paul. " 'Madonna with Cat' Fooled Art Critics." *London Times,* October 9, 1990.

Bower, Bruce. "The Strange Case of the Tasaday." *Science News,* May 6, 1989.

"Brains v. Dollars on TV." *Time,* February 11, 1957.

"Brian G. Hughes, Famous Joker, Dies." *New York Times,* December 9, 1924.

Brower, Kenneth. "Grey Owl." *Atlantic Monthly,* January 1990.

"Cairo Fakes Pictures and Foils Libyan Death Plot." *New York Times,* November 18, 1984.

" 'Cannibalistic' Outer Baldonia Invites Soviet Critic to 'Orgy.' " *Washington Star,* December 12, 1953.

Catterall, Lee. "Surreal Haze in the Courts for Dali Fans." *National Law Journal,* May 9, 1988.

Checkland, Sarah Jane. "Works of Great Faker Come to Auction." *London Times,* March 30, 1990.

"Chemical Analysis Foils Hitler Diaries Hoax." *Chemical and Engineering News,* May 16, 1983.

" 'Classics' His Own, Kreisler Reveals." *Musical America,* February 25, 1935.

Collins, Glenn. "A Showplace for a Showman." *New York Times,* June 6, 1987.

Cousins, Norman. "Decline and Fall of Congressman Day." *Saturday Review,* May 8, 1971.

Croffut, W. A. "Lord Gordon-Gordon." *Putnam's Magazine,* January 1910.

Crowe, Michael J. "New Light on the Moon Hoax." *Sky & Telescope,* November 1981.

Culliton, Barbara J.:

"Coping with Fraud: The Darsee Case." *Science,* April 1, 1983.

"Emory Reports on Darsee's Fraud." *Science,* May 27, 1983.

"Da Vinci Discoveries." *Time,* September 11, 1939.

Decker, Andrew. "Unlimited Editions." *ARTnews,* Summer 1988.

"Divorce Plot Laid to 'Prince Mike.' " *New York Times,* February 26, 1935.

Dodson, James. "The Myth Who Was the Man." *Yankee Magazine,* September 1989.

"Egyptians Say Libyan 'Death Squad' Hoped to Steal a U.S.-Made F-16 Jet." *New York Times,* November 19, 1984.

Esterlow, Milton. "Art Forger Determined to Make a Genuine Name as a Painter." *New York Times,* February 16, 1968.

Eyre, Lincoln. "Spurious Prince Is Tried." *New York Times,* July 19, 1927.

Friedrich, Otto. "German History, More or Less as Germans See It." *Smithsonian,* March 1991.

"Gallery Director Fired in Modigliani Scandal." *International Herald Tribune,* October 31, 1984.

Garvey, Jack. "Ferdinand Demara, Jr." *American History,* October 1985.

Gelineau, George. "Great Impostor's Last Wish Unfulfilled." *Lawrence Eagle-Tribune,* June 9, 1982.

Grossman, John. "Joe Bones, Phony." *Health,* October 1986.

Hall, Carla. "Vanilli: The Proof Is in the Pud-

ding." *Washington Post,* November 21, 1990.

Harrington, Richard. "Pop Duo Milli Vanilli Didn't Sing Hit Album." *Washington Post,* November 16, 1990.

"Heads and Tales." *Time,* September 24, 1984.

Hines, William. " 'Immoral' Outer Baldonia Riles Reds." *Washington Star,* January 25, 1953.

"Hitler's Forged Diaries." *Time,* May 16, 1983.

"Hitler's Secret Diaries." *Newsweek,* May 2, 1983.

"Hoax Muddies New York Lotto Same as Media Bites Baited Hook." *Sports Form,* March 10, 1990.

Johnston, Alva. "The Downfall of Prince Mike." *Saturday Evening Post,* March 20, 1943.

Jonas, Jack. "Inside Story of Outer Baldonia." *Washington Star,* April 11, 1956.

"The Keely Motor Deception." *Scientific American,* October 11, 1884.

"The Keely Motor Deception Again." *Scientific American,* June 10, 1876.

Kendall, Ena. "A Room of My Own." *London Observer,* December 12, 1984.

"A Lament for Charlie and U.S. Morals, Too." *Life,* November 16, 1959.

"Last Frontier." *New Yorker,* February 5, 1990.

"Law Permits Romanoff to Become U.S. Citizen." *New York Times,* May 17, 1958.

Lebelson, Harry, and Bette Rush. "Garadiavolo: The Devil Monster Hoax." *Sea Frontiers,* May-June 1985.

Lewis, Flora. "The Technique of Terror." *New York Times,* December 28, 1984.

Ley, Willy. "Fantastic Hoaxes." *Fantastic Adventures,* January 1940.

"Libya Says Its Squads Killed Ex-Prime Minister." *New York Times,* November 17, 1984.

Lindsey, Robert:

"Dealer in Mormon Fraud Called a Master Forger." *New York Times,* February 11, 1987.

"Mormon Admits 2 Bomb Murders; Rejects Appeal to Atone by Death." *New York Times,* January 24, 1987.

"Sotheby's Says Boone Letter Is a Fake." *New York Times,* August 14, 1987.

Lottman, Herbert R. "Romain Gary's Double Life: 'Literary Hoax of the Century.' " *Publishers Weekly,* July 24, 1981.

Lyons, Richard D. "The Origin of a Fabulous Species." *New York Times,* May 17, 1967.

McCoy, Bob. "Portolio." *San Juan Star,* September 28, 1974.

Magnuson, Ed. "Fakes That Have Skewed History." *Time,* May 16, 1983.

"Michael Romanoff, the 'Prince' and Restaurant Owner, Dead." *New York Times,* September 2, 1971.

" 'Michael Romanoff' Back as Stowaway." *New York Times,* April 26, 1932.

"Milli Vanilli to Return Grammy." *Washington Post,* November 19, 1990.

"Mr. Keely's Motor." *Scientific American,* December 22, 1888.

"Mr. Potato Dead." *Sports Illustrated,* September 14, 1987.

Morgan, Roger. "The Man Who Almost Is." *After the Battle,* 1986, no. 54.

"The Mormon Mystery." *Newsweek,* October 28, 1985.

Natanson, Ann. "Trouble." *People Weekly,* October 8, 1984.

"New Leonardo Work Believed Found in Italy; Said to Be Long-Sought 'Madonna with Cat.' " *New York Times,* August 31, 1939.

"A Notable American Family and a Question of TV Ethics." *Life,* October 26, 1959.

"Notorious Crook Is Back in Custody." *New York Times,* June 30, 1953.

"Notorious Impostor Shot Dead Defending Motel in Hold-Up." *New York Times,* August 28, 1960.

"Obituary Disclosed as Hoax." *New York Times,* January 4, 1980.

"One Week in the Life of Moammar Qaddafi." *The Economist,* November 24, 1984.

Peers, Alexandra. "Bogus Brushstroke: Is It Really a Matisse or a Forgery?" *Wall Street Journal,* May 22, 1989.

" 'Prince Mike' Jailed at Height of Career." *New York Times,* December 4, 1934.

" 'Prince Mike' Seized Near Fifth Av. Shop; Trapped by His Taste for Costly Tobacco." *New York Times,* December 29, 1932.

"Prince Mike's Story for Film." *New York Times,* December 30, 1932.

Radolf, Andrew. "Hoaxer Strikes Again." *Editor & Publisher,* January 13, 1990.

Rattiner, Dan. "Little-Known Winter Holidays." *Dan's Papers,* October 5, 1990.

"Reich Police Arrest Pretended Prince." *New York Times,* January 8, 1927.

Ripin, Edwin M. "A Suspicious Spinet." *Metropolitan Museum of Art Bulletin,* February-March 1972.

Schriftgiesser, Karl. "Art Fake Is Exposed." *Evening Transcript,* January 27, 1931.

Shirey, David L. "Faking It." *Newsweek,* August 26, 1968.

"Skeptical Agents Hunt 'Prince' Here." *New York Times,* December 24, 1932.

"Spurious Prince Is Tried." *New York Times,* July 17, 1927.

"A 'Stray Dog' Springs a Trap for Kaddafi." *Newsweek,* November 26, 1984.

Stümpke, Harald. "The Snouters." *Natural History,* April 1967.

"A Teacher's Big Take." *Life,* February 11, 1957.

"There Sits a State Terrorist." *New York Times,* November 20, 1984.

Verdi, Bob. "Sports Person of the Year: This Spud's for You." *Chicago Tribune,* December 20, 1987.

Westfall, Richard. "Newton and the Fudge Factor." *Science,* February 23, 1973.

Whitaker, Alma. "International Art Hoax Bared by Los Angeles Author." *Los Angeles Times,* August 14, 1927.

Whitman, Alden. "Career on a Truism." *New York Times,* September 3, 1971.

Wingerson, Lois. "William Summerlin: Was He Right All Along?" *New Scientist,* February 26, 1981.

Wulf, Steve (Ed.). "Two Potato." *Sports Illustrated,* April 11, 1988.

Other Sources

"The Story of a Modern Robinson Crusoe." Pamphlet. London: *The Daily Chronicle,* 1893.

"Thirty 'Masterpieces' by Elmyr de Hory." Auction catalog. London: W & FC Bonham & Sons, 1990.

Tyson, Gerald P. " 'Feast of Shells': The Context of James Macpherson's Ossianic Poetry." Unpublished doctoral dissertation, Brandeis University, Department of English and American Literature, May 1969.

"Violins and Other Stringed Instruments Bearing Famous Labels." Information Sheet. Washington, D.C.: Library of Congress, Music Division, n.d.

INDEX

Numerals in italics indicate an illustration of the subject mentioned.

Time-Life Books is a division of Time Life Inc., a wholly owned subsidiary of
THE TIME INC. BOOK COMPANY

TIME-LIFE BOOKS

Managing Editor: Thomas H. Flaherty
Director of Editorial Resources:
Elise D. Ritter-Clough
Director of Photography and Research:
John Conrad Weiser
Editorial Board: Dale M. Brown, Roberta Conlan, Laura Foreman, Lee Hassig, Jim Hicks, Blaine Marshall, Rita Thievon Mullin, Henry Woodhead

PUBLISHER: Joseph J. Ward

Associate Publisher: Ann M. Mirabito
Editorial Director: Russell B. Adams, Jr.
Marketing Director: Anne C. Everhart
Director of Design: Louis Klein
Production Manager: Prudence G. Harris
Supervisor of Quality Control: James King

Editorial Operations
Production: Celia Beattie
Library: Louise D. Forstall
Computer Composition: Deborah G. Tait (Manager), Monika D. Thayer, Janet Barnes Syring, Lillian Daniels

**Library of Congress
Cataloging-in-Publication Data**
Hoaxes and deceptions / by the editors of Time-Life Books.
p. cm. (Library of curious and unusual facts).
Includes bibliographical references (p.).
ISBN 0-8094-7715-7 (trade)
ISBN 0-8094-7716-5 (lsb)
1. Impostors and imposture—Miscellanea.
2. Deception.
I. Time-Life Books. II. Series.
CT9980.H63 1991
001.9'5—dc20   91-13463 CIP

LIBRARY OF CURIOUS AND UNUSUAL FACTS

SERIES EDITOR: Laura Foreman
Series Administrator: Roxie France-Nuriddin
Art Director: Cynthia Richardson
Picture Editor: Catherine M. Chase

Editorial Staff for *Hoaxes and Deceptions*
Text Editors: Carl A. Posey (principal), Sarah Brash
Associate Editor/Research: Barbara Sause
Assistant Art Director: Alan Pitts
Senior Copy Coordinators: Jarelle S. Stein (principal), Anthony K. Pordes
Picture Coordinator: Jennifer Iker
Editorial Assistant: Terry Ann Paredes

Special Contributors: George Constable, Barbara Holland, Leslie Marshall, George Russell (text); Judith N. Cohart, Catherine B. Hackett, Maureen McHugh, Kathryn B. Pfeifer (research); Louise Wile (index)

Correspondents: Elisabeth Kraemer-Singh (Bonn), Christine Hinze (London), Christina Lieberman (New York), Maria Vincenza Aloisi (Paris), Ann Natanson (Rome).
Valuable assistance was also provided by Pavle Svabic (Belgrade); Angelika Lemmer (Bonn); Judy Aspinall (London); Elizabeth Brown, Katheryn White (New York); Leonora Dodsworth, Ann Wise (Rome); Dick Berry, Mieko Ikeda (Tokyo); Traudl Lessing (Vienna).

The Consultants:
William R. Corliss, the general consultant for the series, is a physicist-turned-writer who has spent the last twenty-five years compiling collections of anomalies in the fields of geophysics, geology, archaeology, astronomy, biology, and psychology. He has written about science and technology for NASA, the National Science Foundation, and the Energy Research and Development Administration (among others). Mr. Corliss is also the author of more than thirty books on scientific mysteries, including *Mysterious Universe, The Unfathomed Mind,* and *Handbook of Unusual Natural Phenomena.*

Stanley Goldberg is an independent scholar who has taught at Antioch College, the University of Zambia, and Hampshire College. He specializes in the history of science and is currently working on a biography of Leslie R. Groves and the Manhattan Project.

Marcello Truzzi, a professor of sociology at Eastern Michigan University, is director of the Center for Scientific Anomalies Research (CSAR) and editor of its journal, *Zetetic Scholar.*

Bart Whaley is a military-deception consultant in San Diego, California, and author of *Stratagem, Code Word Barbarossa,* and *The Man Who Was Erdnase.*

Other Publications:

THE NEW FACE OF WAR
HOW THINGS WORK
WINGS OF WAR
CREATIVE EVERYDAY COOKING
COLLECTOR'S LIBRARY OF THE UNKNOWN
CLASSICS OF WORLD WAR II
AMERICAN COUNTRY
VOYAGE THROUGH THE UNIVERSE
THE THIRD REICH
THE TIME-LIFE GARDENER'S GUIDE
MYSTERIES OF THE UNKNOWN
TIME FRAME
FIX IT YOURSELF
FITNESS, HEALTH & NUTRITION
SUCCESSFUL PARENTING
HEALTHY HOME COOKING
UNDERSTANDING COMPUTERS
LIBRARY OF NATIONS
THE ENCHANTED WORLD
THE KODAK LIBRARY OF CREATIVE PHOTOGRAPHY
GREAT MEALS IN MINUTES
THE CIVIL WAR
PLANET EARTH
COLLECTOR'S LIBRARY OF THE CIVIL WAR
THE EPIC OF FLIGHT
THE GOOD COOK
WORLD WAR II
HOME REPAIR AND IMPROVEMENT
THE OLD WEST

For information on and a full description of any of the Time-Life Books series listed above, please call 1-800-621-7026 or write:
Reader Information
Time-Life Customer Service
P.O. Box C-32068
Richmond, Virginia 23261-2068

This volume is one in a series that explores astounding but surprisingly true events in history, science, nature, and human conduct. Other books in the series include:

Feats and Wisdom of the Ancients
Mysteries of the Human Body
Forces of Nature
Vanishings
Amazing Animals
Inventive Genius
Lost Treasure
The Mystifying Mind
A World of Luck